In 1966 Howard Hughes—forced to sell Trans World Airlines—arrived in Las Vegas and soon got with a burning desire to buy out and expand a local airline known as Air West. This report tells how he set about achieving that goal. It is based on *The Hughes Papers*—depositions, written court testimony, exhibits, memoranda—one of the largest collections of Hughes material ever assembled. Stored in hundreds of filing cabinets in California, it has been gathered together to shed light on the Air West takeover and Hughes' final years.

Howard Hughes' final years—
based on an examination of

The Hughes Papers

by Elaine Davenport
and Paul Eddy

with Mark Hurwitz

BALLANTINE BOOKS • NEW YORK

To Mark Moyle,
a better writer,
in partial payment of the debt we owe

ISBN 0-345-25572-0-195

Manufactured in the United States of America

First Edition: December 1976

CONTENTS

AUTHORS' NOTE

Separating the facts from the mythology is the principal difficulty facing anybody who writes about Howard Hughes, and in the past many nonsensical tales about him have appeared.

For that reason, this book relies almost entirely on the *sworn* testimony of those who were part of Howard Hughes' world. Specifically, we have used testimony, exhibits and evidence from the myriad of lawsuits that Hughes' years in Las Vegas inspired. Of course, testimony given on oath is not necessarily true, and so, as an added safeguard, we have narrated only those events for which it seems to us there is a preponderance of evidence.

For background material and to fill in the gaps, we drew a limited amount of information from previous books, including *Howard Hughes,* a biography by John Keats, *Howard Hughes in Las Vegas,* by Omar Garrison, and *Bashful Billionaire,* by Albert Gerber. We also consulted *Just About Everybody vs. Howard Hughes,* by David Tinnin, for the story of the TWA lawsuit, *Hoax,* by Stephen Fay, Lewis Chester, and Magnus Linklater, for the story of the Clifford Irving affair, and *Jimmy the Greek,* by Himself, for obvious reasons. *Nightmare,* J. Anthony Lukas' magnificent study of the underside of the Nixon years, provided invaluable background on the Hughes-Nixon connection.

We owe personal thanks to Georgetta Moliterno, Laurie Zimmerman and Diane Condon in New York and Pat Beaver in California, whose efforts were indispensable to this project. Finally, our gratitude goes to Robert Ducas, our agent and friend, who encouraged and hurried us on our way.

November 1976

CAST OF CHARACTERS

The reader is invited to use this list of the main characters of our story both as a preview of that to come and, later, as a reference for a name forgotten.

NADINE HENLEY	in charge of 7000 Romaine Street and queen of Hughes' empire
ROBERT HENRY	another Air West dissident
PATRICK HILLINGS	ex-Congressman with useful connections
JAMES HOFFA	former boss of the Teamsters union who saved Hughes from eviction
RAYMOND HOLLIDAY	the top man in the Tool Company's executive hierarchy
JOHN HOLMES	still another of the "Mormon Mafia"
JACK HOOPER	former Los Angeles cop who took care of Hughes' personal security
HOWARD HUGHES	The Man himself
HUBERT HUMPHREY	would-be President who denied getting $50,000 for his efforts to ban the bomb
LAWRENCE HYLAND	left alone to run Hughes Aircraft
CLIFFORD IRVING	hoaxer
LYNDON JOHNSON	the President Hughes wanted to bribe with $1,000,000
GORDON JUDD	a Hughes employee who testified he witnessed the delivery of a briefcase to Hubert Humphrey's limousine
KIRK KERKORIAN	rugged entrepreneur who challenged Hughes' bid to buy Las Vegas
RUBY KOLOD	Moe Dalitz's partner
PAUL LAXALT	Nevada's governor, now senator, who laid out the welcome mat
COLIN McKINLAY	the reporter who discovered Hughes' secret
WARREN MAGNUSON	powerful senator from Washington State
ROBERT MAHEU	Hughes' alter ego but eventually his most bitter adversary

1: A CHRISTMAS TALE

Keep Christmas in your own way, and let
me keep it in mine!

—*A Christmas Carol*,
Charles Dickens

Imagine, if you will, that you are a partner in a
business which is modest in size and very new. Since
the beginning your business has been in trouble. On
the very first day, for instance, the most important
single piece of equipment you had broke down and
your unsatisfied customers were furious. Since then
conditions have, if anything, got worse. Some of your
partners do not get along at all well and there are
fights among them over how to do almost everything.
You just cannot seem to get the business ticking over
properly and you are losing money. Indeed, you are
being forced to eat into your capital to pay the bills.
Your friendly bank is now distinctly less friendly.

Suddenly you discover that The Richest Man in the
World wants to buy you out. At least, you think he
does. The trouble with The Richest Man in the World
is that he talks to almost nobody; he lives in a penthouse on top of a hotel with the shades drawn so no
one can see in and he does not go out. So, you cannot
talk to him about his offer, only to the man who seems
to represent him, and he is a rather strange character.
On the face of it he is charming and amiable enough,
but his background is very mysterious and there are
stories that he used to work for the CIA. Perhaps he
still does.

Anyway, this man who represents The Man does
business in a peculiar fashion. He did not come to all
the partners with his offer openly. Instead, he secretly

1

negotiated with the partner the rest of you had elected chairman. The first you knew that anything was in the wind was when you learned through the grapevine that, without even consulting you, the chairman had agreed to sell out.

That makes you very angry. It also gives you pause for thought. You know that The Richest Man in the World does not go in much for charity. If he wants your business, it must be because, despite all the problems, he believes—as you do—that it has enormous potential. If only you could get over the teething troubles, and if only the newspapers would stop giving you bad publicity . . . Just a moment! It suddenly occurs to you that most of the bad publicity you have been getting has been coming out of the town where The Man lives. Might that be more than a coincidence? And might some of your other troubles have been Man-made?

You talk to some of the other partners and find that they too are unhappy about the deal—and suspicious. The question is, can you do anything to stop it? You hire a lawyer and he says you should fight. So you and some of your partners say no to the deal, and there are enough of you to prevent it from going through.

But, will The Richest Man in the World take no for an answer . . . ?

Howard Hughes wanted to buy an airline. He said he would pay around $90 million for it—in cash, of course. Twelve of the directors of the airline wanted Howard Hughes to buy it because it had been flying through troubled skies since the very first day it took off. The trouble was, there were twenty-four directors and the other twelve did not want to sell—at least, not to Howard Hughes.

Air West was not a major airline. Indeed, outside of the West Coast of the United States—where it operated, somewhat erratically—few people had even heard of it. But the airline fitted very nicely into Hughes' plans to build an empire, a new one, based around a kingdom that he was rapidly establishing amid the glitter and glamour of Las Vegas. Hughes, driven on by his legendary fascination for airplanes and the aviation business, came to want Air West very badly.

2

For five months he directed negotiations from the penthouse suite on the ninth floor of the Desert Inn Hotel in Las Vegas. He left the actual bargaining to two of his high-priced consultants—Robert Maheu, a former FBI agent and sometime front man for the CIA, and Chester Davis, a New York lawyer of awesome reputation—but he counseled them through every intricate step. Under his guidance they managed to secure the "best efforts" of Air West's chairman, Nick Bez, who, in turn, gathered the support of half of the board of directors.

But no amount of wheeling and dealing by Bez or Maheu or Davis could overcome the implacable opposition of the remaining twelve directors. And by Christmas 1968, time was running out. Hughes' offer for Air West was due to expire at midnight on the last day of that year.

December 25, 1968

Working for Howard Hughes meant working long hours, and for Bob Maheu, Christmas Day was no exception. He briefly joined in his family's Christmas celebrations and then retired to consult with his boss about the pressing problem of Air West. That is not to say that Maheu *met with* Hughes: He *never* did that. Maheu sat in the study of his house on the Desert Inn golf course and Hughes sat in his room of the Desert Inn penthouse, half a mile apart, and they wrote to each other. Security guards carried their letters to and fro.

Maheu's special concern on Christmas Day was over a meeting of Air West's stockholders, to be held in two days, when they would be asked to approve or reject Hughes' takeover bid. The problem, as Maheu saw it, was that "even if the stockholders [give] us an overwhelming vote of confidence," the "opposition" would not surrender. The twelve opposing directors had a lawyer named Martin who had "guaranteed that he could tie up the situation in litigation for two to three years—or else he did not deserve to be an attorney." Maheu did not regard Mr. Martin very kindly: "I say, Howard, that bums like this should not be attorneys in

3

the first place and I think we can make Martin to appear like a horse's ass. . . ." Maheu did not say how, except to suggest that "we should take the lead and lead from strength."

December 26, 1968

Maheu was right about the strategy the opposition was planning—not surprisingly, because he was having the twelve directors spied on, and their conversations listened to. The directors—known as "the dissidents" —received a welcome legal opinion from an eminent New York law firm that they should continue "to act in accordance with their own best judgment" regardless of the outcome of the stockholders' vote.

December 27, 1968

The day of the stockholders' meeting called for ten-thirty A.M. at the Thunderbird Hotel, Millbrae, California, had arrived. The morning edition of the Las Vegas *Sun* predicted the result:

> Local observers feel industrialist billionaire Howard Hughes today will win his $94 million bid to buy beleaguered Air West.
> The special stockholders' meeting has been called . . . amid threats of delaying tactics by Air West officials who oppose the sale to Hughes. Directors who favor the transaction can be expected to be equally vocal, led by Nick Bez, chairman of the board and principal stockholder in the airline . . .
> Bez has personally urged all stockholders to approve the Hughes offer . . .
> In this town, where you can get people to quote odds on just about everything, the odds today favor Howard Hughes in his multi-million-dollar battle for Air West.

The *Sun* was right—and wrong. As Maheu reported to Hughes, in a message dictated over the telephone to the Desert Inn penthouse, at eleven forty-five P.M. auditors from Wells Fargo Bank finally declared that fifty-

4

two percent of the stockholders of Air West had voted in favor of the takeover. In theory, that was sufficient to give Hughes victory, but the battle was far from over.

December 28, 1968

Air West's board of directors met to formally consider Hughes' offer to buy the airline's 3,792,988 shares of stock for about twenty-two dollars a share. The session was private, but someone took rough notes: "Mr. Grace [David Grace, one of the leading dissidents] spoke of a provision of the Hughes offer . . . [which] would give Hughes an opportunity to renegotiate the price he would pay at a time when he would have a stranglehold on the company. The chairman [Bez] conceded that such would, in his opinion, be the case but stated, 'He wants it so much he will pay the twenty-two dollars anyway.' Mr. Grace stated that this was a great deal to be asked to swallow and he could not swallow it. . . ." Neither could the *majority* of the board. One of the directors who had previously supported the takeover switched his vote, giving the dissidents a thirteen-to-eleven victory.

United Press International, the wire agency, circulated the news:

> The directors of Air West refused today to sell the regional airline to billionaire Howard Hughes for $95 million despite approval of the sale by the company's stockholders. . . .
> "The Hughes offer is dead at this point," said Gordon Kent, an assistant to the vice-chairman of the board. . . .
> Nick Bez, Air West board chairman and a proponent of the Hughes takeover, was asked after the vote what he would do next. "I don't know," he replied.

Bez might have thought the fight had been lost, but others did not. Howard Hughes would only repeat that his offer would expire in three days.

December 30, 1968

James Moyle, like every other dissident director, received a telegram:

> I have been notified and I feel I should inform you that legal action was filed today in Chancery Court, Newcastle County, Delaware, against you and twelve other directors who voted against authorizing Hughes' contract. . . .

The lawsuit had been filed, apparently, by dissatisfied stockholders who wanted the court to force the dissidents to approve the sale to Hughes. Failing that, they wanted damages. The Delaware court immediately ordered the confiscation of the Air West stock owned personally by Moyle and his colleagues, pending the outcome of the case.

December 31, 1968

Moyle, like every other dissident director, received another telegram:

> I, my wife, children and grandchildren—all holders of Air West stock or bonds—implore you to accept Hughes offer before it is too late. Otherwise, we will naturally join other stockholders in seeking damages. [Signed] George Crockett.

Not unnaturally, Moyle was becoming increasingly disturbed in the face of this gathering storm. Of course, he had no way of knowing that the storm was being carefully orchestrated.

George Crockett was a Las Vegas businessman and a longtime friend of Howard Hughes. In between sending telegrams to dissident directors, he was busily selling his Air West stock and bonds for whatever price the market would pay. Some years later, while giving testimony that would be used in evidence before a federal grand jury, Crockett was asked to explain the circumstances surrounding his activities on December 31, 1968:

Q. *Did you have any conversation in Las Vegas with Mr. Maheu?*

A. Yes . . . He called me on the telephone and asked if I would sell—or told me that if I would sell all of my stock at whatever price it would bring, that he would compensate me for the difference between that and the twenty-two dollars that they offered. I called my broker . . . and told them to sell.

Q. *Did he specify a date on which you should sell your stock?*

A. Immediately.

Q. *Was there any other part of that conversation?*

A. Only that he would see that I was compensated for the difference between what I got for it and the price of twenty-two dollars.

Q. *Did he tell you why he told you to sell?*

A. No.

Q. *Did you know why?*

A. Well, I could naturally assume that he was trying to put pressure to sell by forcing the price down.

Q. *You assumed that at the time he called you?*

A. Yes . . .

Q. *Is there a reason why you didn't ask him why he was asking you to sell your stock?*

A. No. I didn't ask him. The reason I didn't ask him is that I just assumed that he wanted to create a panic among the board of directors to influence them to change their minds.

Q. *What made you assume that, sir? Was there any indication prior to that time that Mr. Maheu had that in mind? . . . How did it occur to you?*

A. Just the fact that if people threw the stock in the market it would possibly scare this board of directors into thinking that they had made a bad decision in going against the wishes of the stockholders. . . .

Q. *You indicated that Mr. Maheu sent a wire to the directors?*

A. He asked me to send a wire over my name.

Q. *When?*

A. About the same time he asked me to sell the stock. . . .

Q. *As I understand, sir, Mr. Maheu indicated to you*

7

> *that he would personally pay you the difference in the price that you sold your Air West stock . . . and $22 a share. Is that correct?*
>
> A. The figures, I believe, are 12,000 shares, and he said that he would see I got paid the difference.
>
> *Q. Did, in fact, Mr. Maheu pay you that difference?*
>
> A. I was paid several months later. . . .

Crockett was not the only outsider who allegedly took part in the plot against the dissidents. David Charnay, the president of a Hollywood film production company called Four Star International, had originally approached Bob Maheu with the proposition that Four Star and the Hughes empire cooperate in making a television documentary on the life and times of Howard Hughes. There was about as much chance of that happening as there was of Las Vegas outlawing gambling, for no man abhorred personal publicity more than Hughes. Still, in Hollywood, dreams die hard, and on December 31, 1968, Charnay went to Maheu's house in Las Vegas to discuss the movie business.

Also there was James Simons, who worked for the fledgling Hughes Television Network, which made and sold (mainly sports) programs for independent TV stations. Simons held some hope that his network and Four Star might be able to undertake a few joint ventures, but he found Maheu—effectively his boss—in no mood to discuss movies. Later, like George Crockett, Simons gave testimony about what happened:

> *Q. What did he [Maheu] say? Did he say he was trying to resolve some problems?*
>
> A. Yes. The gist of the conversation was that the Air West directors had voted whether or not to accept the Hughes offer and there was a stalemate, so to speak. . . . He said unless this thing is resolved by midnight tonight Mr. Hughes is going to withdraw his offer and he said we have been in touch with various Air West people and one name I do remember is Mr. Bez. And there were efforts to talk to some of the directors to get them to change their vote in favor of the Hughes acquisition. . . .
>
> *Q. Now going back to what happened after Mr. Maheu*

The best in paperbacks *and* hardcovers.

paperback
booksmith
Dedicated to the fine art of browsing.

paperback
booksmith
Dedicated to the fine art of browsing.

made this statement that it would be beneficial to get the price of Air West stock down . . . what did Mr. Charnay do if you know?

A. I can't relate to you precisely moment by moment what was done or what was said, but in the course of the next 15 to 20 minutes Mr. Charnay—as a result of a conversation with Mr. Maheu—started to make phone calls. . . . From what happened I made an assumption that Mr. Charnay was trying to ingratiate himself with Mr. Maheu and that he was willing to participate in contacting his broker . . . to accomplish a lower price—market price— for Air West stock. It seemed to me that Charnay had made the determination that if he could, through his broker, borrow and sell short stock, it would depress the price. . . .

Selling "short stock" means selling stock you do not yet own, which can be a risky business. The idea is to sell stock which, you hope, will fall in value. For example, you contract to sell one thousand shares of stock in Corporation A at ten dollars a share. At this point you do not actually own any shares in Corporation A, but because there is a delay before you must deliver the share certificates, that hardly matters. You then wait for the share price to fall to, say, nine dollars, at which point you buy one thousand shares. You subsequently deliver the shares to whomever you previously sold them to—and collect a profit of a thousand dollars. Of course, if the share price should go up instead of down after you have sold it, you are in trouble. But, according to Simons' testimony, Charnay had nothing to fear on that score:

Q. *Now did there come a time when you heard Mr. Charnay ordering his broker to purchase Air West stock?*

A. I can't remember that. I can remember Mr. Charnay saying something about—on more than one occasion—about having to cover the shorts and that it could be costly to him.

Q. *What did Mr. Maheu say to that?*

A. He would make him well.

Q. *And by that what did he mean?*

9

A. In the terms of the jargon that I understand, that means he would make up the losses to him in some way. . . .

Apparently, the scheme worked perfectly. Simons was still at Maheu's house—where Chester Davis, the swashbuckling New York lawyer, had also been during part of the day—when some exciting news arrived:

Q. *Was there a discussion that the activity of Mr. Charnay had succeeded? Do you recall any discussion where it was stated that certain directors had changed their minds?*

A. I remember that happened. I can't tell you what time of the day it occurred, but I would say it was somewhere prior to 3 o'clock in the afternoon and I can't tell you whether it was Maheu calling Nick Bez or Nick Bez calling Maheu, advising that there was a change in the vote, and they had just polled a couple more directors and there were sufficient votes now for the acceptance of Mr. Hughes' offer.

Q. *And what did Mr. Maheu say if you recall?*

A. Well, it was like—no, I can't say the precise words —but it was like accomplished. We have been victorious. We have won. We done it.

Q. *Did he tell Mr. Davis that?*

A. Well, I think Mr. Davis was on another phone and he looked over at Bob and he said, Bob, what is your input? And Bob said, well I've got Nick on the line—something to that extent—and we've got enough votes to win it. Chester said great.

At five P.M. the wire services sent out the news: "Billionaire recluse Howard Hughes today succeeded in his $95 million bid to take over the regional airline, Air West. The surprise development was announced by airline chairman Nick Bez just hours before Hughes' offer was due to expire at midnight tonight. . . ."

Wasting no time, Maheu and Chester Davis took a private jet to Seattle, Washington, where Bez lived, to get his signature on the contract.

10

January 1, 1969

In the very early hours of New Year's Day, Maheu dictated a message to the Desert Inn penthouse:

> Howard, it is not necessary at all that you talk to him [Bez] either tonight or tomorrow, but this guy would be the proudest man in the world if you would just say hello to him this evening.
>
> If you will recall, at the beginning of the negotiations he was so proud at the fact that you, Howard Hughes, were interested in the acquisition of any entity for which he was so responsible. . . .
>
> Howard, I have seen evidence of hero worshipism before but never the likes of which this man holds you in his esteem. And as much as I would like to claim the credit for the consummation of this deal, it would never have been possible without the full dedication of this great human being who may have 60 or 90 more days to go, but by prompting on our part, has convinced the world that it could be 60 or 90 years.
>
> Howard, will you please reconsider and just say goodnight to this great guy.

As Howard Hughes knew, Nick Bez was suffering from terminal cancer of the liver. He got his phone call. Thirty-five days later he died.

Hughes also got what he wanted, although Maheu's enthusiasm proved to be premature: As we shall see, it was not until April 1970 that the airline deal was finally consummated.

The losers were most of the thirteen thousand stockholders who, when Air West eventually became Hughes Airwest, got nothing like the twenty-two dollars a share they thought they had been promised.

The reason for that, according to charges brought by the Securities and Exchange Commission—and criminal charges brought by the U.S. Department of Justice —is that Hughes, Maheu, and Chester Davis, among others, conspired to defraud the stockholders of roughly $40 million. It is alleged that with the help of slanted

11

publicity, questionable legal tactics, and friendly politicians they set out deliberately to destroy public confidence in Air West, that they made false promises, that they manipulated stock, that they intimidated their opponents, and that they paid what amounted to bribes.

All of those charges are vehemently denied, and the litigation—both criminal and civil—which has resulted from the Air West acquisition will take years to resolve. Indeed, because of the death of Hughes in April 1976, it is possible that a definitive resolution will never be achieved.

What the Air West affair has already done, however, is provide an opportunity for a closer examination than has, perhaps, ever before been possible of the world of Howard Hughes. Throughout his bizarre career, and especially toward the end of his life, Hughes regarded his own privacy as sacrosanct. He also preferred, so far as it was possible, to conduct his business in secret, and to a remarkable extent he was successful: Sooner or later the public usually got to know what Howard Hughes had bought or sold, but rarely did we learn how the deal had been done and, even more rarely, why. Of course, some of those who worked for Hughes, the men who actually did the deals, were aware of the details, but discretion—or secretiveness—was a quality Hughes looked for in his aides. And he seems, almost always, to have found it.

The attempts by the SEC and the Justice Department to prove that Hughes and some of his aides were guilty of fraud changed some of the ground rules. True, the SEC investigators were no more successful in their attempts to interrogate Hughes than scores of other investigators, lawyers, and journalists had been over the years. But Hughes' aides, particularly those alleged to have been coconspirators, could not so easily escape questioning.

And, as it happened, when the SEC investigation began, one of those men, Robert Maheu, was in no mood to be discreet. In December 1970, and in somewhat spectacular fashion, Maheu was fired—or, as he puts it, "the umbilical cord between Howard Hughes and me was very abruptly severed and I was not even given the courtesy by the Hughes executives to tie a knot in that portion of the cord left with me, but rather [they] kind of left me on a lonesome island, I guess hoping that I would bleed to death." Maheu talked. Subsequently, he also talked to the Watergate Committee of the U.S. Senate, the Internal Revenue Service, two federal grand juries, and—in an attempt to win $17 million in damages from Hughes—to a Los Angeles jury which was asked to decide if Maheu had been libeled.

Maheu also produced thousands of documents evincing his contentions of what had happened during the four years that he was an integral part of "the unbelievable world" of Howard Hughes. To support or rebut those contentions, or to defend themselves against charges, other people who shared that world have also talked and produced documents. Our story is taken from all this material, which includes notes written—on yellow, ruled, legal-size paper—by Hughes himself. It provides intriguing insights into the ambitions and frustrations of both Hughes and of some of the men (and one woman) who now control his empire.

When Hughes arrived in Las Vegas on November 27, 1966, he had visionary plans to turn the somewhat shoddy gambling town into a mecca of recreation. He also saw *his* Las Vegas as "a center of scientific research and space-age industry" with a new airport, the first in the world designed specifically to accommodate supersonic planes.

Four years later, almost to the day, Hughes left Las Vegas for good, as arid and as insular as he had found it. For the most part his plans had come to nothing, and he left behind him disillusioned and angry men. The squabbles and lawsuits that his stay in Las Vegas inspired were to pursue him, and keep him exiled from the United States, for the rest of his life.

When the story is told through the eyes of the men who lived in Howard Hughes' "unbelievable world"— and in the words of The Man himself—it is not too difficult to understand how and why that happened.

2: THE MAN

I've been around the world
Had my pick of any girl
You'd think I'd be happy
But I'm not
Ev'rybody knows my name
But it's just a crazy game
Oh, it's lonely at the top

—It's Lonely at the Top,
   Randy Newman

Howard Hughes' arrival in Las Vegas, and particularly the manner of it, was supposed to be a secret.
Shortly before five A.M. on Sunday, November 27, a
three-car train hired from the Union Pacific Railroad
Company stopped at a crossing in the Nevada desert
five miles north of the city. Waiting there were a
small truck, two cars, and a Ford station wagon that
could, if necessary, serve as an ambulance. The rendezvous point had been chosen by Union Pacific's
chief security officer as somewhere spectators would
be unlikely to be, especially so early in the morning.
   The transfer of passengers, a dozen or so, and bag-
gage from the train to the vehicles went smoothly, and
within ten minutes the motorcade left the unlighted
junction and headed for Las Vegas. Just short of the
city limits it turned into Las Vegas Boulevard South
and came to a halt outside the main entrance of the
Desert Inn Hotel and Casino. The early-morning gamblers, intent on other things, took no notice of the
new arrivals who walked through the lobby to one of
the elevators for a ride to the ninth floor. There, some
special preparations had been made. In Hughes' quarters—a living room, office, bedroom, bathroom, and
dressing room, looking out over the hotel's golf course

14

and swimming pool—an air purifier had been installed, along with a closed-circuit television system which allowed The Man to keep an eye on the happenings on the rest of the ninth floor, where his aides would live. In addition, the office had been supplied with an oversize desk, complete with an amplified telephone system to allow Hughes, nearly deaf, to carry on more or less normal phone conversations. But very few people were aware of these modifications to the ninth floor. Since about a week before Hughes' arrival, it had been out-of-bounds even to most of the hotel staff, and the elevators could no longer be persuaded to go beyond the eighth floor without the use of a special key. The emergency exit, leading to the fire escape, had been locked from the inside and continually, if discreetly, guarded.

Las Vegas being the kind of town it is, nobody might have known that it now contained the richest man in the world until he was ready to announce it—but for one remarkable coincidence.

Hughes' train, which had brought him 2,500 miles from Boston, Massachusetts, had been chartered to go all the way to Los Angeles, California—a device intended to conceal from the crew the fact that the anonymous passengers intended to go only as far as Las Vegas. The engineer was not told about the unscheduled stop in the desert until the very last moment, and then—unaware that all of his passengers had departed—he was instructed to continue on to Los Angeles. It was an ingenious ruse, because when the media, the bane of Hughes' life, eventually discovered that The Man had left Boston it would be assumed that he, like the train, had gone to Los Angeles: The resulting wild-goose chase around southern California would leave Hughes in peace, at least for a while.

It was, therefore, sheer bad luck that while the decoy train was traveling west to Los Angeles, a regularly scheduled train pulling behind it a private car used occasionally by the Las Vegas Press Club, should be traveling east. In that car among a group of reporters returning from a football game and a night on the town was Colin McKinlay, associate editor of the Las Vegas *Review-Journal*. He noted the obviously special

15

train going in the opposite direction and asked the Union Pacific official accompanying the press group about its purpose. In the way of officials, the man said he was not at liberty to disclose any information about that particular train, which, if McKinlay will forgive the simile, was akin to dangling a red rag before an angry bull. Back in Las Vegas, McKinlay made it his business to solve the mystery of the train, and through some enterprising detective work, he succeeded. (More people within Union Pacific than had been intended knew about the special charter, because in Ogden, Utah, just north of Salt Lake City, the locomotive pulling the three cars had broken down. Faced with a two-hour delay, Hughes' aides had demanded and, at a cost of an extra $17,000, got a replacement locomotive, which, in Ogden, was a noteworthy event.)

The resulting story which McKinlay wrote appeared in only the first edition of the *Review-Journal* before Hughes succeeded in having it "killed," but that was sufficient to infuriate Hughes. One of his main reasons for moving from Boston to Las Vegas had been to escape what he regarded as harassment from reporters. Hughes' first reaction to McKinlay's scoop was to say he was going to leave town. On second thought, he decided that the one to leave town should be the owner of the offending newspaper: He told his aides he wanted the owner "out of town, out of Nevada, by the weekend."

Donald W. Reynolds, who, besides the *Review-Journal*, owned a chain of newspapers as well as television and radio stations throughout the state, was not likely to be easily moved, so Hughes' aides decided to recruit some expert help. Herman "Hank" Greenspun was the owner and publisher of the rival daily newspaper in Las Vegas, the *Sun*, and therefore knew Reynolds well. In addition, he had what might be called a vested interest in the situation because he had been partially instrumental in persuading Hughes to move to Las Vegas, by extolling the tax advantages which Nevada offered to its residents. Naturally enough, then, it was Greenspun whom Hughes' aides approached, asking for help to buy Reynolds out, "before the end of the week, no matter what the price."

16

It did occur to Greenspun that if he succeeded in this mission he might find himself in an invidious position. His fond hope was that Hughes would eventually invest in businesses which, incidentally, the Las Vegas *Sun* relied heavily upon for advertising revenue. If Hughes controlled the rival newspaper, might not the *Sun* lose advertising? Even worse, might there not come a day when Hughes would be upset by the *Sun*'s editorial policy—which Greenspun jealously guarded—and, through ownership of the *Review-Journal,* attempt some form of retribution? Hughes' aides said absolutely not. Indeed, they were prepared to guarantee that Hughes' business empire would spend a minimum of $500,000 on advertising in the *Sun's* columns, regardless of the newspaper's future editorial policy. Suitably assured, Greenspun set out to persuade his rival publisher to leave town.

As it happened, Donald Reynolds had already temporarily obliged by leaving Las Vegas for a hunting trip to Texas. Greenspun tracked him down and, stressing the urgency, persuaded Reynolds to fly to Washington, D.C., for a private meeting. There, in the Madison Hotel, Greenspun frankly explained his mission and his belief that, in the circumstances, Reynolds could virtually name his own price. He suggested that Hughes might even pay as much as $21 million for the *Review-Journal* and the rest of the Reynolds chain, which would have been more than generous. The rival publishers discussed the details until five A.M. the next day when Greenspun was able to telephone Las Vegas and report that the deal was all but set.

It therefore came as something of a shock when, later that day, Reynolds met with Hughes' Washington lawyer and announced, "Well, you fellows seem pretty anxious—the price is $31 million."

At the Desert Inn, Hughes, "went through the ceiling" (which was probably what Reynolds had intended), called off the negotiations, and muttered darkly that he would find some other way to deal with the *Review-Journal.*

For Greenspun the whole business was, naturally, rather embarrassing. Under his instructions, the Las Vegas *Sun* had initially suppressed the news of Hughes' arrival, and then, after the brief appearance of Mc-Kinlay's scoop, roundly attacked the *Review-Journal* for intruding on Hughes' privacy.

In an editorial headlined "WELCOME TO NEVADA, HOWARD HUGHES," Greenspun announced that Hughes was "the world's greatest industrialist" and "a legend in his own time," who because of his "many contributions to the nation's progress, security and welfare of all mankind" was entitled to complete privacy. Hughes had thought of settling in Las Vegas once before, in the mid-1950s, but "continued snooping and harassment forced him out of our community" and into a life of seclusion. "We don't," said Greenspun, "want that to happen again."

He reckoned that at times Hughes must feel, "like Gulliver surrounded by Lilliputians intent on his destruction, or a stag held at bay by a pack of wolves." If the pack did not desist, the stag might flee once again and, therefore, "local newsmen who pry into his affairs and local newspapers who bandy his health and private life around on their front pages are doing the state of Nevada a great disservice."

Not surprisingly, Hughes was delighted with Greenspun's editorial, and one of his aides, Roy Crawford, was dispatched to purchase one dozen extra copies of the *Sun*. It was, however, a little rough on the *Review-Journal,* which had done no more than report a matter of legitimate local interest: After all, it was not every day that the richest man in the world came to town. It also has to be said that Greenspun's attitude was severely at odds with his reputation as a crusading and courageous publisher, normally a staunch advocate of freedom of the press.

But then, the circumstances were rather exceptional. Greenspun, and not a few other leading figures in Las Vegas, saw Howard Hughes' residency—if only he could be persuaded to stay—as an event of supreme importance to the future of their city. It was not a matter of what he might contribute so much as what he might drive away—the very last vestiges of the ghost that haunted the place, the ghost of Benjamin "Bugsy" Siegel.

If Siegel—Ben to his friends, Bugsy only behind his back—could see Las Vegas today he would be proud. When he arrived there just thirty years ago, it was little more than a couple of gas stations providing travelers across the Nevada desert with the means to keep on moving. Now, thanks largely to his vision, Las Vegas is a metropolis of some 125,000 people. Indisputably, it has become the gambling capital of the world, but it is also a thriving community: It has 143 churches, 93 schools, 159 Boy Scout troops, and so on and so on. Siegel would have especially liked that. He believed in maintaining a respectable front.

On the other hand, Las Vegas is not at all proud of Siegel. Although he founded modern-day Las Vegas as surely as Peter Stuyvesant founded New York City, there will never be a monument erected to Bugsy's memory.

The son of Russian immigrants, Siegel grew up and took his education from the teeming streets of New York's Lower East Side at the beginning of this century. By the age of fourteen he was a full-fledged hoodlum. His lack of Latin blood prevented his total acceptance by the dons—the bosses—of organized crime, but he became at least an associate member of the Family—the *Unione Siciliano,* aptly nicknamed by the newspapers Murder Incorporated. Even in such violent company, Siegel's propensity for violence was regarded as remarkable; his associates thought he was "nuts."

During his gangland career, Siegel was arrested for just about every crime in the book, ranging from rape to murder, but never convicted. The closest he came to meeting justice was in 1941 when he was arrested for the murder, two years earlier, of a fellow hoodlum, Harry "Big Greenie" Greenberg.* Siegel was held in a

* Greenberg had been an "enforcer" for Murder Inc. Wanted by the FBI, he had fled to Canada in the early 1930s where, injudiciously, he had written to some former associates asking five thousand dollars in return for his silence. A "contract" was put out on Greenberg, but he proved too elusive until November 22, 1939, when Siegel and two others caught up with him outside 1804 Vista Del Mar, Los Angeles. They shot him, several times, in the face.

19

Los Angeles jail pending trial, but had to be released after the star witness against him "fell" from a hotel window while in the protective custody of the New York police.

That narrow escape persuaded Bugsy that it was time to adopt what might today be called a lower profile. World War II gave organized crime syndicates the opportunity to diversify into legitimate businesses and Siegel looked around for some likely investments. He settled on Nevada because in 1931, in a desperate attempt to survive the Depression, the state had legalized gambling. He ignored Reno, in northern Nevada, which already boasted several large casinos, preferring instead to go where there was no competition: Las Vegas, or, more specifically, a small parcel of land just outside the city limits named Las Vegas Boulevard South, but known then and now as the Strip. In 1943 Bugsy persuaded his associates to invest $1 million to build in this middle of nowhere a hotel-casino to be called the Fabulous Flamingo.

Unfortunately, the war with its resulting shortages of materials and labor made the construction of the hotel a much longer and more expensive job than anyone could have expected. At least, that was Bugsy's story when, in 1946, he was obliged to explain to his colleagues why costs had risen to $6 million, and yet the Flamingo had still not opened its doors.

What might be called the board of directors of the *Unione Siciliano* was not altogether convinced. The Family had learned from sources, very good sources, that Bugsy's girl friend, an occasional actress named Virginia Hill, had been making regular trips to Zurich, where she had deposited something over $300,000 in a numbered Swiss bank account. Normally, even the suspicion of embezzlement would have been enough to get Bugsy prematurely and permanently retired, but the Family was reluctant to order his death because, at last, the Flamingo was about to open. As it happened, the board, under the chairmanship of Charles "Lucky" Luciano, was meeting at the Hotel Nacional in Havana, Cuba. It was of the unanimous opinion that Bugsy should be "hit" unless the opening of the Flamingo was sufficiently successful to earn him a reprieve. The board adjourned, pending the outcome of the grand opening.

It was a disaster. Bugsy had arranged some spectacular entertainment—Xavier Cugat and his band, comedian Jimmy Durante, and actor George Raft—but he set opening night for December 26, 1946, and almost nobody wanted to spend the Christmas holidays in this unknown sandtrap. When the bad news reached Havana at three A.M. on December 27, Siegel's death sentence was confirmed.

In the nature of these things, it was thought advisable that the contract be postponed until Siegel was off guard. Officially, therefore, his colleagues commiserated with Bugsy and agreed that the Flamingo should be thrown into bankruptcy to avoid paying the debts that were due. Through a series of complex transactions, the Mob then rebought the hotel and Bugsy planned the reopening for May 1947. This time the celebrations were much more modest, but more successful. Bugsy's belief that people from all over the United States would be willing to travel to Las Vegas to lose their money amid luxurious surroundings was beginning to be vindicated.

Siegel was, therefore, very pleased with himself—and careless about his personal safety. On June 20, 1947, after his customary visit to the Flamingo's barber shop, he flew to Los Angeles and let himself into Virginia Hill's house on North Linden Drive in Beverly Hills. At ten-thirty P.M. that night, while he sat in an overstuffed sofa, a fusillade of shots was fired through the window from a .30-.30 carbine, a weapon of awesome power at short range. Three shots missed, but Siegel was hit five times, and his head was ripped apart. Meanwhile, in Las Vegas, a trio of men from "head office" walked in the Flamingo's front door and announced that they were taking charge.

Siegel's character and the manner of his assassination should not be allowed to disguise the fact that he was right about the potential of Las Vegas. The Flamingo was quickly followed by more hotel-casinos on the Strip, which succeeded in drawing thousands, and eventually hundreds of thousands, of visitors every year.

Not all of the Flamingo's rivals, by any account,

were Mob-controlled, a fact which suited the gangsters because it made them less visible, and therefore less vulnerable. (Again, Bugsy had pointed the way by inviting legitimate—and unsuspecting—businessmen to be partners in the Flamingo.) Nevertheless, Mob influence upon this burgeoning city was considerable. That disturbed not only the law-enforcement agencies but some of Las Vegas's new citizens, such as Hank Greenspun, who had traveled west—in Greenspun's case, from Brooklyn, New York—to grab a share of this new bonanza.

Greenspun had arrived in town as one of the publicists for Bugsy's Fabulous Flamingo. Like many others, he soon realized that behind the glitter and the bright lights of the Strip lay a sinister and potentially violent influence; unlike most, he decided to do something about it.

In 1953 Greenspun founded, on little more than a wing and a prayer, the Las Vegas *Sun,* as a rival daily newspaper to the established *Review-Journal.* He soon began to create waves by campaigning vigorously against the evil he perceived, which was, under the circumstances, a courageous thing to do.

Although Greenspun's campaign enjoyed some successes, its main effect was to drive the gangsters deeper underground: Their interests became better disguised, and new, untainted managers were installed to, apparently, run the show, while real control remained in dubious hands. Even by the mid-1960s Las Vegas was still, for Greenspun's liking, far too much of a Mob town.

The idea that Howard Hughes, with his vast financial resources, might be able to finally break the Mob connection by buying up "dubious" casinos occurred to Greenspun in the summer of 1966. In July, Hughes had moved from Los Angeles to Boston, primarily to undergo medical tests (he suffered from anemia) at the Peter Bent Brigham Hospital. His stay there had been made intolerable by the zeal with which Boston reporters had attempted to penetrate Hughes' security. He was, therefore, open to suggestions as to where he might find a more hospitable climate.

Greenspun and Hughes had been vaguely acquainted

back in the days when Greenspun was founding his newspaper, and Hughes, then far less reclusive, could sometimes be seen along the Strip. Invariably dressed in a rumpled suit and canvas shoes, Hughes would gamble—usually at the craps table—but only cautiously and with small amounts of money. He obviously enjoyed the anonymity, based on indifference, which Las Vegas afforded visitors. And being prone to irregular sleeping habits, he also found it convenient that most things stayed open twenty-four hours a day. Indeed, for a while, it had looked as though Hughes might make Las Vegas his home: He bought a 22,000-acre parcel of land just outside the city and encouraged talk that he might build an aircraft factory there. Neither the plant nor anything else materialized and his visits to the city abruptly ceased. According to one of his closest friends of that period, Las Vegas businessman George Crockett, Hughes abandoned his plans because he was apprehensive about what kind of welcome he might receive—from that young, crusading publisher, Hank Greenspun.

But ten years or so later, Greenspun, anxious to finish the job of cleaning up the town, sent a message to Boston, via an East Coast lawyer, saying that Hughes would be very welcome in Las Vegas. He pointed out that Nevada levied neither personal nor corporate income tax, or gift or inheritance tax, upon its residents and that tax on real estate was limited by the state's constitution. He added a personal pledge that if Hughes should move to Las Vegas his lust for privacy would be honored.

In those circumstances, it was understandable that Greenspun should have been so put out when Colin McKinlay and the *Review-Journal* placed his scheme in jeopardy by treating Hughes' arrival as nothing more than a good story.

What was remarkable was that Greenspun, or anybody else, should have looked upon Hughes as some kind of white knight, willing to gallantly rescue cities in distress. As even a cursory examination of Hughes' life would have confirmed, any kind of savior he was not.

Howard Robard Hughes, born in Houston, Texas, on Christmas Eve, 1905, grew up with certain advantages—those which only very large sums of money can provide. The source of the revenue was a drilling bit, which, in the search for oil, could cut through rock more effectively than anything else on the market. Howard's father, "Big" Howard, invented the bit, patented it in every corner of the globe to prevent others from copying the design, and then refused to sell a single working example. Oil companies could only *lease* the Hughes bit, at $30,000 a time. As Big Howard pointed out, that did not give him a monopoly in the oil-drilling business: as an alternative prospectors could always use a pick and shovel.

Young Howard—known, to his chagrin, as "Sonny," —therefore enjoyed a financially secure childhood, but in emotional terms he was not so lucky. An only child, he was introverted and painfully shy. In strident contrast, his parents were wildly extrovert and much given to lavish parties staged for the benefit of Houston's society. (His mother, by all accounts a very beautiful woman, was a descendant of the Huguenots and the granddaughter of a Confederate general. She behaved appropriately.)

It was Big Howard's desire that his son follow in his footsteps and attend Harvard University. To prepare him for the ways of the East Coast, Sonny was packed off to a boarding school in Newton, Massachusetts. There, young Howard lived an awfully lonely life, prevented from making friends by his shyness, which was made more acute by both a stammer and slight deafness. He did well in mathematics and his conduct was excellent, but in every other way he was a very mediocre student.

It was only when he was at home, working alone in his father's workshop behind the house, that young Howard seemed truly happy. He was by nature a tinkerer and able to amuse himself for hours by playing with bits and pieces of anything. By the age of thirteen, for example, he had built himself a usable ham radio set. And when his normally indulgent father refused to buy him a motorcycle, he made one, utilizing a bicycle, a battery, and a starter motor taken from one of Big Howard's cars.

Despite young Howard's disinterest in academic subjects, his parents remained insistent that he should be given, in his father's words, "as good an education as possible." But before they could see to that, both of them died. First, Mrs. Hughes succumbed while undergoing a major operation. Two years later, Big Howard, who had spent the interim in the company of as many Hollywood actresses as his money could buy, dropped dead in his office.

Young Howard, now eighteen years old and in many respects woefully unprepared for life, became overnight the owner of seventy-five percent of the stock of the Hughes Tool Company. On paper, his inheritance was worth around $500,000. In fact, because of the drilling bit and its 166 marvelous cutting edges, it was worth millions, which would keep on flowing until the patents on the bit ran out, or man stopped searching for oil.

There was only one snag. In spite of the fact that Big Howard's motto had been "Never do business with partners," he had saddled his son with three of them by bequeathing one-quarter of the Tool Company to young Howard's grandparents and an uncle. And to make matters worse, because Texas law insisted that no one under twenty-one could sign contracts, he could not even run the business he overwhelmingly owned.

Ignoring the pleas from his relatives that he complete his formal education, young Howard went on a trip to Europe to learn about life. There, he discovered an impressive fact that Harvard would not have been anxious to teach him: As John Keats, one of Hughes' biographers later put it, "Money talked—not age, nor courtesy, nor precedent, nor wisdom, nor social condition, nor reputation. Just money. Given sufficient money anyone could get whatever one wanted, no matter if one was only eighteen years old." *

Back in Houston, young Howard applied the lesson well. He spent large sums of money employing the

* *Howard Hughes—A Biography*, published in the U.S. by Random House, 1966.

expertise of lawyers who soon found the loophole in Texas law which would allow their young client to gain control of his own company. All he had to do was convince a judge to declare him a "legally responsible adult." Suitably coached by his lawyers, young Howard went before Judge Montieth—an old friend of the family—and did just that. Now in command of the Tool Company, but not yet the total owner, he began the process of persuading his relatives to sell him their stock. They held out for a while, but when it came to persistence they were no match for Big Howard's son, and they eventually surrendered. Still not nineteen years old, Sonny became the total master of one of the most potentially profitable companies in the world.

Hughes was a fraction under six feet four inches tall, but in Houston he could never be "Big" Howard. Similarly, the Tool Company would, in local eyes, always remain the father's business, no matter how well the son ran it. The reason quite simply was that Big Howard was a legend in Texas and in Texas legends die hard.

Not surprisingly, therefore, Hughes found himself suffocating under his father's shadow. He also found running the Tool Company very boring. In truth, there was a great deal more to it than counting the profits, and under young Howard's guidance the company expanded and increased its prosperity at an impressive rate. But the job provided Hughes with no real challenge and certainly no opportunity to prove himself, which, above all, was what he needed to do. Even when it came to figures, the only field in which Hughes had academically excelled, he soon found his own wizardry far surpassed by that of Noah Dietrich, a brilliant young accountant he had hired. Finally, and perhaps inevitably, young Howard decided to abandon Texas, leaving the Tool Company in Dietrich's capable hands, while he found new endeavors in which to invest the surplus profits.

Like many others before and since, Hughes' search for an identity took him to Hollywood, California. There, appropriately, he played a series of real-life roles, each one of which was extraordinary.

Hughes' first attempt at making a movie was a disaster, but really, that was Big Howard's fault. He had said "after I'm gone" that he would like his son to take care of an old friend, an actor named Ralph Graves. Graves wanted to direct and act in a film based on the story of a Bowery bum who adopted a baby, and Hughes agreed to put up the money. The resulting *Swell Hogan,* made at double its original budget of $40,000, was so bad as to be unshowable and it was never released. Hughes was on the point of giving up the movie business when his relatives arrived on the scene to persuade young Howard to return to Houston. That gave him the incentive to continue, and by spending money on the best talent available, he more than made up for his flop by producing three very credible films: *Everybody's Acting, Two Arabian Knights,* and *The Racket.* None of them was a masterpiece, but all made money and *Two Arabian Knights,* a slapstick account of two U.S. infantrymen imprisoned during World War I, won the 1927 Academy Award for comedy.

With those successes behind him, Hughes, still only twenty-two, decided he would both produce *and* direct his next picture, the now lengendary *Hell's Angels.* The plot, concerning two young British pilots who, when not winning the war against the Germans, competed for the attention of an English society girl, was terrible. But the point of the movie was that it provided the opportunity for several aerial battle scenes, and Hughes spent the then astronomical sum of $2 million recording on film flying sequences which, even by today's standards, are remarkable. Unfortunately, *Hell's Angels* was still not complete when the first sound picture, Al Jolson's *The Jazz Singer,* was released, revolutionizing the film industry. Almost overnight silent movies became obsolete, and all the advice that Hughes received was to the effect that he should scrap *Hell's Angels* and write it off as a tax loss. Instead, and to the horror of his Hollywood peers, Hughes proceeded to spend another $2 million adding a sound track to his film, which involved reshooting most of the scenes. It also involved finding a new leading lady, because the original star, a Norwegian actress, could not produce the accent of an English socialite. To confirm his apparent insanity, Hughes rejected all established actresses and chose instead an unknown named Jean Harlow.

The eventual release of *Hell's Angels* coincided with the onset of the Great Depression. Nevertheless (or perhaps because of the overwhelming need for escape), it smashed box-office records wherever it played and earned, eventually, some $8 million—double its investment. It made Jean Harlow a superstar and Howard Hughes a household name.

There were more Hughes movies—among others, *Scarface* (the glamorized story of Al Capone), *The Front Page* (a satirical comedy about muckraking journalists), and, much later, *The Outlaw**— but for their producer they were anticlimactic. After *Hell's Angels,* Hughes felt no further need to prove himself to Hollywood. And anyway, he was by then much too busy pursuing a far greater passion.

---

* Released in 1943, *The Outlaw* was an appallingly bad movie, yet it earned a great deal of money for which the credit must go to the anatomy of Jane Russell and some very clever publicity. During the shooting of the film, a western, Hughes was heard to complain, "We're not getting enough production out of Jane's breasts." As no one else could come up with a remedy, Hughes sat down and designed a cantilever bra, which, like a cantilever bridge, provided support for its load at one end only. Jane's breasts, accordingly, received very ample production indeed, and as a result, the film was banned in several states. A Baltimore judge, upholding the decision of the state of Maryland to ban the film, said, "Miss Russell's breasts hung over the picture like a summer thunderstorm spread out over a landscape. They were everywhere. They were there when she first came into the picture. They were there when she went out." Inevitably, in states where the film was not banned, people flocked to see what all the fuss was about, and in Los Angeles, for example, one million customers enjoyed the benefits provided by the cantilever bra. In all, *The Outlaw* grossed $5 million—double its cost—before Hughes, without explaining why, withdrew it from distribution.

Hughes had fallen in love with flying when he was still at school in Newton, Massachusetts. Big Howard had come to town to take his son to the Harvard-Yale boat race, promising the boy anything he wanted if Harvard won. It did, and Sonny chose as his reward a flight on a flying boat that was moored on the river near the scene of the race. That brief ride was the beginning of Hughes' most passionate affair.

Back in Houston that summer, young Howard secretly took lessons from a barnstorming pilot. And after his mother's death (when his father was lavishing upon him an allowance of five thousand dollars a month) he took three complete flying courses, starting from scratch each time, never telling his instructors he had flown before.

During his movie career, he would frequently disappear from the set to take a joy flight or, more commonly, to don mechanic's overalls at Burbank Airport, where he would tinker, with considerable basic expertise, on aircraft engines. And in 1932 he disappeared completely for two months to assume the false identity of Charles Howard, a guise under which he obtained a job as a copilot with American Airlines.

In 1934, with little apparent planning, he formed the Hughes Aircraft Company, calling as always on the Tool Company to provide the necessary funds. The only objective of the little concern (it employed eighteen people and rented a hangar at Glendale Airport, near Los Angeles) was to build the fastest plane in the world, and in under eighteen months it did just that. The H-1 (H for Hughes, of course) was a single-seat, single-engine monoplane which, in September 1935, with Hughes at the controls, flew at 352.39 miles per hour to establish a new world speed record.

Two years later Hughes flew the H-1 from the West Coast to the East Coast of the United States in the record-breaking time of seven hours, twenty-eight minutes.

And then, in 1938, Hughes and a crew of four flew a Lockheed Lodestar around the world in the time of ninety-one hours, fourteen minutes, and twenty-one seconds, for yet another record. The day after they landed, Hughes and his crew were honored with a ticker-tape parade through the streets of New York, which, according to the city's sanitation department, produced 1,800 tons of trash—200 tons more than Charles Lindbergh had attracted following his solo flight across the Atlantic.

Nowhere was the flight more celebrated than in Texas, where a banquet was given in his honor, babies were named after him, and the governor made him an honorary Texas colonel. It was generally agreed, at least in Houston, that young Howard had overcome that most deadening of handicaps—great wealth in youth. But neither the records nor the praise meant very much to Hughes. His shyness prohibited him from enjoying the celebrations, and anyway, he was never satisfied with his achievements. Unlike movies, aviation was an unconquerable challenge: Meeting it would almost cost Hughes his reputation, his fortune, and his life.

The Patriotic Man

The Hughes Aircraft Company did its bit in helping to win World War II. Hughes designed an ammunition holder for the machine guns fitted to U.S. bombers which allowed five hundred rounds to be loaded at a time. It also, in cooperation with the Tool Company, produced landing-gear struts, aircraft wings, fuselages and seats for other aircraft manufacturers, and artillery shells and cannon barrels.

The trouble was, Hughes had not produced any aircraft, yet he had received $60 million from the U.S. government to do just that.

One plane which the company was supposed to have developed and supplied for the war effort was a photo-reconnaissance aircraft code named the XF-11. By the end of the war, even the prototype had not emerged from Hughes Aircraft's new plant at Culver City, near Los Angeles, and the contract was cancelled. However, Hughes spent his own money to complete development, and in July 1946 the XF-11 finally flew—for the first and last time. Typically, Hughes was at the controls for the maiden flight. Moments after takeoff, the plane went out of control and plunged toward Beverly Hills, where it sliced through two houses and rammed into a third. Barely conscious, Hughes managed to drag himself from the shattered cockpit only seconds before the wreckage burst into flames. He was taken to the hospital suffering from a fractured skull, nine broken ribs, a broken shoulder, a broken nose, and a collapsed lung.

The doctors had expected Hughes to die before the day was out. He did not, of course, but it took him nine months to recover from his injuries and he emerged from his ordeal looking twenty years older. (He now sported a mustache to cover scars on his upper lip resulting from the crash.)

It might, under the circumstances, have been appropriate to set aside any questions about the wartime role of the Hughes Aircraft Company, but there were politicians in Washington, D.C., who had no intention of doing so. In 1947, Owen Brewster, a Republican senator from Maine who was chairman of the Senate's Investigating Committee, decided to investigate wartime defense contracts. It soon became clear that his main target was Howard Hughes, and he did not, it seemed, lack ammunition. While the XF-11 contract had been, literally, disastrous, there had been another Hughes project, also funded by the taxpayers, which had been farcical.

In 1942 Hughes had been given $18 million to develop a giant flying boat, and produce three working examples, each of which, Hughes promised, would be capable of carrying seven hundred fully armed troops. The three monster boats, 220 feet long and 100 feet high, with a wingspan of 340 feet, were supposed to be delivered by the end of 1944. By the time the war was over, not one had materialized.

Much of the Brewster hearings, which began in July 1947, concerned the way in which Hughes had won his wartime contracts, a subject which we will deal with later. But inevitably, some of the sessions dissolved into arguments over whether Hughes' wooden monster could even fly.

One prototype model, rather than three, had been almost completed, but Senator Brewster dismissed it as a "flying lumberyard" that would never get off the ground.

"If the flying boat fails to fly," said Hughes, "I will probably exile myself from this country. I have put the sweat of my life into this thing, and $7.2 million of my own money. My reputation is wrapped up in it. I have stated that if it fails to fly, I will leave this country. And I mean it." The hearings were adjourned, formally to allow time for "further inquiries" into the defense-contract issue, but actually to see who was right.

Hughes ordered work to proceed on the giant boat —officially called the Hercules, but known by almost everybody as the Spruce Goose—around the clock. Finally, on November 1, 1947, before a considerable audience of journalists, the Spruce Goose was ready for a trial run across the harbor of Long Beach, California. The boat was not supposed to take off on this first run, but with Hughes at the controls it did: The eight engines lifted the two hundred tons of wood seventy feet above the water. It flew for just over a mile and then landed safely. It never took off again, but in terms of the contest with Brewster, that did not matter. Although it is difficult now to perceive the logic, the Spruce Goose's brief flight somehow confirmed in the public eye Hughes' patriotism. He had in effect been accused by Brewster of profiteering; the flight cleared him of the charge.

Actually, of course, it did nothing of the sort, but only diverted attention from the unanswered questions as to why Hughes had failed to deliver the planes he had promised and been paid for.

The Man Under Fire

Big Howard's advice about the undesirability of partners was good. Every time Hughes ignored it, he got into big trouble.

Strictly speaking, Hughes Aircraft was entirely Hughes' private concern, but it relied almost entirely on U.S. government contracts, which, as Hughes discovered, is almost the same as having partners. After the Spruce Goose fiasco, he virtually ignored the company, which began recruiting a team of first-rate scientists and engineers who could produce sophisticated electronic equipment. All went well until the early 1950s when Hughes suddenly resurrected his interest in the company—and began interfering. Almost to a man, the scientists rebelled, demanding the freedom to get on with their work. Hughes denounced them all as "Communistic," and almost to a man, they quit. So, too, did General Harold L. George, who managed the Culver City plant. Hughes told him, "You are proposing to take from me the rights to manage my own property. I'll burn the plant down first." To which the general replied, "You are accomplishing the same result without matches."

The net result of this fracas was the arrival in California of Air Force Secretary Harold Talbott, who told Hughes, "You have made a hell of a mess of a great property, and by God, as long as I am Secretary of the Air Force, you are not going to get another dollar of new business." Hughes was obliged to virtually surrender effective control of his company.

His dispute with his partners in Trans World Airlines (TWA) was not so easily resolved. He had bought 78.2 percent of TWA's stock, for about $80 million, in the late 1930s and had interfered in its management whenever he saw fit. Undoubtedly, Hughes contributed a good deal to TWA's expansion into one of the world's biggest international airlines, and personally encouraged many innovations, including in-flight movies. But on the debit side, his interference sometimes had disastrous results. In the mid-1950s, for example, when jet aircraft were being introduced, Hughes delayed the decision as to which planes to buy for so long that TWA fell far behind its competitors. When Hughes did finally get around to choosing the jets he wanted, he ordered too many, saddling the airline with $375 million worth of debts which it could not pay. His partners eventually forced him to give up control of the airline—and, alleging gross mismanagement, sued him for $150 million.

These kinds of disputes led *Fortune* magazine to

describe Hughes as "The Spook of American Capitalism." The magazine had no time for his erratic management methods, describing him thus: "Suspicious and withdrawn, elusive to the point of being almost invisible, he is loath to give anything up, loath to admit error . . . There is one other aspect of his character about which his former associates are agreed: he abhors making a decision."

That judgment may seem a little harsh, but there is a surfeit of evidence to support it. For yet another example, consider what happened in 1948 when Hughes bought a majority stockholding in the RKO Picture Corporation. In five years under Hughes' control, RKO lost $20 million, the payroll dropped from two thousand to under five hundred, and film production ground to a halt—not least because Hughes, in support of the McCarthy witch-hunt, closed down the studios for three months while the staff was investigated and the so-called Communist sympathizers routed.

Appalled by the whole mess, Hughes' partners in RKO filed $30 million worth of lawsuits against him. Among other things, they claimed that he was driving the studio bankrupt by putting actresses on the payroll "solely for the purpose of furthering his personal interest."

The Ladies' Man

Before he left Houston to shake off the shadow of Big Howard, Hughes had married Ella Rice. A dark-haired beauty from a socially prominent Texas family —which had given the Rice Institute its name—Ella was totally unsuited to Hollywood life, and after four years she left. The couple were divorced at a cost to Hughes of $1,250,000.

Hollywood was well stocked with potential substitutes for Ella who found Hughes very attractive: He was good-looking, a successful filmmaker, and a daredevil aviator to boot. However, Hughes preferred to believe that his only attraction was his wealth. "Aside from my money," he asked a friend, "who'd want to marry me?" With that attitude firmly fixed in his mind,

Hughes proceeded to buy companionship, rather than court it.

Because he was still painfully shy, the talent scouts he employed to seek new starlets had a dual role. Any lady who took Hughes' fancy would be invited to dinner—by the talent scout. Hughes would arrive after dinner had begun, and having been spared the embarrassment of the preliminaries, would take the evening from there.

It should be said that he did not lack in either courtesy or consideration. For instance, on the evening of July 11, 1936, he was with a young actress when his car struck and killed a pedestrian named Gabe Meyer on Third Street in Los Angeles. The girl could, presumably, have testified that Hughes was not to blame for the accident, but he insisted that she leave the scene and gave her the cab fare home. Hughes would not reveal the identity of his witness even when he was arrested by the police, fingerprinted, and booked on suspicion of negligent homicide. (He was absolved from blame at the subsequent inquest.)

Hughes was often an exciting companion. On the strength of his whim, a date that began in Los Angeles might finish at the best restaurant in New York, or in a plane flown by Hughes simply to get a better view of the sunrise.

Over the years Hughes conducted a great many routime relationships with a whole cast of very beautiful women—including Olivia de Havilland, Billie Dove, Ginger Rogers, Katharine Hepburn, Loretta Young, Lana Turner, Ava Gardner, and Mitzi Gaynor—but any appearance in their company would inevitably send the gossip columnists rushing to their typewriters, and Hughes grew heartily sick of the rumors.

He did eventually find some measure of happiness through his second and last marriage in May 1957 to the actress Jean Peters,* but it came too late. By then

* Miss Peters was under contract to Twentieth Century-Fox from 1947 to 1955, and in that time made nineteen movies, including *It Happens Every Spring, Viva Zapata, Apache, Blueprint for Murder,* and *Three Coins in the Fountain.* Using false names—G. A. Johnson and Marian Evans—she and Hughes were married secretly in a motel room in Tonopah, Nevada.

he was well on his way to becoming a total recluse, cutting himself off from even his friends. In the long run, the strain on the marriage proved to be too great.

The Invisible Man

In 1956 Hughes circulated a memorandum to all the executives (except Noah Dietrich) in his empire, forbidding them from telephoning him. Henceforth, he said, all communications intended for him should be sent to what had been the headquarters of his film company, Hughes Productions, located at 7000 Romaine Street in North Hollywood. Within its gray stucco walls, Hughes established what he liked to call the Communications Center, ruled over by his personal secretary, Nadine Henley, and manned twenty-four hours a day by her very carefully chosen assistants. For the next four years, Miss Henley was one of only a handful of people who knew how to contact Hughes.

Part of the reason for this withdrawal was undoubtedly Hughes' embarrassment at his increasing deafness. Another factor was his conviction, which fell little short of paranoia, that he was being continually spied on by undefined enemies who would stop at nothing to discover the secrets of his empire. To increase his protection against these "enemies," Hughes arranged for twenty Chevrolet cars to be based at 7000 Romaine Street along with twenty incorruptible drivers who were on constant call. When he needed transportation, Hughes would choose one of the vehicles at random, believing that anybody would be hard-pressed to follow or bug twenty vehicles and subvert twenty drivers.

In the early 1960s, Hughes came to believe that even these extraordinary measures were not enough. To remove himself one step further from the world, Hughes took five of the male staff from the Communications Center and appointed them his personal aides, to live with him and provide for his needs twenty-four hours a day. Four of them were Mormons—members of a religion with a strict moral code—and the fifth was married to a Mormon. From then on, Nadine Henley's

Communications Center dealt with the aides, and only rarely with Hughes personally.

With very occasional exceptions, nobody saw or spoke to Hughes except for the aides and his wife. Until 1966 he lived in total seclusion either in a rented mansion in Bel Air in Hollywood or on a ranch near San Diego, California. The major parts of his empire, the Tool Company and the Aircraft Company, were left to run themselves. So long as they kept on laying the golden eggs, their executives might not hear a word from their sole stockholder for years on end.

This, then, was The Man on whom the hopes of a respectable future for Las Vegas rested.

It is true that by the time he arrived in Las Vegas, Hughes was $546,549,771 richer than he had been: In May 1965, while the TWA lawsuit dragged on, he had sold his entire holding in the airline. It is also true that he needed to reinvest a hunk of that money before the Internal Revenue Service claimed a significant share of it in tax. Naturally enough, Hank Greenspun hoped that Hughes would spend some of it buying out the Mob.

But as Hughes had demonstrated time and time again in his career, he was a poor administrator, capable of ruining even those businesses he knew something about. What effect might he have on Las Vegas' precious gambling industry, about which he knew nothing?

There was one more factor which sober minds might have considered. Because of Hughes' now total reclusiveness, the success of any business ventures he mounted in Las Vegas depended to a large extent on the caliber of the men he employed to help him.

When they arrived, they turned out to be a very unlikely crew.

3: THE RISE OF
ROBERT MAHEU

Nothing recedes like success.
—Walter Winchell

In June of 1959 Robert Maheu learned, he says, that he was to become Howard Hughes' alter ego. More realistically, what Hughes had selected was a front man. Even so, it was, on the face of it, a profound piece of miscasting.

Nothing in Maheu's background would seem to have fitted him for the role, and in character, experience, temperament, and philosophy he shared little common ground with Hughes. If either needed proof of the disparity between them it was available during the very telephone call in which Hughes revealed his plans for Maheu's future.

Hughes was in the Bahamas. Maheu, then spending perhaps half his time as a consultant for Hughes, was in Los Angeles but planning to return immediately to his home in Virginia, where Yvette Maheu was about to give birth to their fourth child.

Hughes "told me not to go. He told me I could send someone else to hold her hand, that I could hire people to take care of all her needs. He told me that he had seen women walking in parks with a big basket on their head who would stop just long enough to have a baby and then walk away with the baby in the basket. . . ."

That kind of dispute, with each man adopting a position beyond the other's comprehension, was to recur frequently. Eventually, as was bound to happen, their association and quixotic friendship ended disastrously for both men.

And yet, over a period of eleven years, Maheu did increasingly become in the public eye the ringmaster of Howard Hughes' circus, the holder of The Man's writ. Exactly how he achieved that position is open to considerable dispute, which we shall come to. What is certain is that after Hughes moved to Las Vegas, Maheu emerged from obscurity to a position as the public embodiment of Hughes—who remained in obstinate hiding. There were people physically closer to Hughes—the five male secretaries—and people with more fiscal power—Raymond Holliday, Bill Gay, and Nadine Henley—than Maheu. But they were shadowy figures in the background. The man in the limelight was a rather large, amiable, slightly ominous former spook.

In 1968 a writer named Ovid Demaris went to Las Vegas (with tongue in cheek) in search of Howard Hughes. He did not get to Hughes, of course, but he did get an appointment with Maheu. On the day of the meeting an assistant of Maheu's telephoned Demaris and said: "I hope you understand the kind of man you're going to meet today. This is a great American. Some day he'll be written up as one of the great-greats. He's done things no other businessman in America could have done. Just one success after another. . . . Success is his habit."

That was, as Demaris discovered when he followed Maheu through the casino of the Frontier Hotel, an intoxicating precept. "It is like being sucked up in the drag of Boston Blackie: eyes pop, heads snap, shoulders brace, toothpicks vanish, heels click—my clout has jumped a thousand points. 'Aren't you the gentleman who was with Mr. Maheu this morning, sir? Step right this way, sir. Will ringside be satisfactory, sir?' "

The trappings of success were there, too—a salary of more than half a million dollars a year, mock French Regency splendor in which to live, a state governor for a tennis partner, dinner with Presidents, a private jet and oceangoing yachts.

The success turned out to be as fragile as its foundation. When, in December 1970, Maheu was stripped of the Emperor's clothes, he was left hopelessly in debt with his business and personal affairs in chaos. But by then he had been "waltzed to the top of the mountain," as he would later say, and not many poor grocers' sons from Waterville, Maine, have flown quite that high.

Robert Maheu's arrival into Hughes' make-believe world was fortuitously timed, though Maheu did not at first know whom he was working for. In 1954 he was hired by a Washington law firm, Hogan and Hartson, to make discreet inquiries for an unnamed client. "It was a very insignificant assignment, of determining whether a certain individual was engaged in undercover work for the U.S. Government," said Maheu.

According to testimony Maheu later gave, the individual was a man who "was either courting or subsequently married" Jean Peters—the Hollywood actress Hughes had pursued on and off for eight years. (In February 1954 Miss Peters met Stuart Cramer III, an oil man from Charlotte, North Carolina. They were married in May but the marriage broke up within four months and ended in divorce in December 1956. Three months after that Miss Peters married Hughes.)

Exactly why Hughes was interested—or, indeed, if the individual concerned was Stuart Cramer—is not clear but Maheu has testified that "with the permission of the authorities in Washington" he was able to reveal that the man was "involved in a certain type of undercover work."

Hughes must surely have been impressed with Maheu's apparent ability to open secret doors in Washington so easily that his fee, including expenses, was only $164. And, perhaps, the impression that Maheu made was all the greater because the assignment concerned Hughes' emotional interests. In any event, more and more assignments followed until Maheu was spending about half of each year working for Hughes.

As it happened, Maheu's increasing role in Hughes' affairs coincided with the fall from grace of Noah Dietrich, the man who for thirty years had been primarily responsible for guiding the destiny of the Hughes Tool Company.

Throughout the years that Hughes was making movies, flying airplanes, and courting beautiful women, Dietrich was home in Houston, minding the store. His wizardry for figures and his strong business nerves were said by many to have been the primary reason why Hughes' $500,000 inheritance became a multi-billion-dollar fortune.

As Hughes retreated increasingly from public view, Dietrich, who was never bashful, stepped willingly into the spotlight. But during the mid-1950s the relationship between the two men cooled. Dietrich, whose salary was $500,000 a year, was irritated that he paid, on average, ten times more tax than Hughes, and in 1957 he became insistent that he should receive a bonus of stock options in the Tool Company. Hughes refused on the irrefutable grounds that it would dilute his (100 percent) holding. The two men parted company, not the best of friends.

It was this vacuum that Maheu eventually stepped in to fill, and it is understandable that Hughes should have been attracted by a man who bore not the slightest resemblance to Dietrich.

Noah's best friends described him as rough-and-ready, crude, uninhibited, irreverent, brusque, rude, and impatient. Maheu, a devout Catholic and a dedicated family man, was charming, considerate, reserved, patient, and given to only occasional lapses of profanity.

More important, Dietrich was, in the field of business finance, little short of a genius, and as such he held the respect and loyalty of many of the executives in the Hughes empire. His acrimonious departure caused considerable disruption within the Tool Company which Hughes found both infuriating and painful.

Maheu could never pose such a threat. He knew practically nothing about Hughes' business affairs and his abilities in the field of finance were uninspiring. Maheu graduated from Holy Cross College in Worcester, Massachusetts, with a degree in economics. But when, in 1940, he applied to join the FBI and took the accounting examination—then an entry requirement—he flunked it. As his accountant was to testify later, even when it came to handling his own financial affairs, Maheu was a "walking calamity."

After the Dietrich experience, Hughes must have

seen Maheu as the ideal candidate to become his alter ego. And then, as we have already said, there was the added attraction that Maheu seemed to have friends in high and mysterious places. Whether that reputation was deserved or not is, like so many other facets of Robert Maheu's career, open to debate.

Robert Aime Maheu was born October 30, 1917. His grandparents were French-Canadians and the Maheus were proud of their heritage. Young Robert grew up bilingual, a capacity that proved to be invaluable when he applied to join J. Edgar Hoover's FBI. Having failed the accounting examination and thus the FBI's entrance requirements, Maheu was allowed a second try only because of his knowledge of French.

At that time, with World War II raging in Europe and the imminence of America's involvement, the FBI was recruiting furiously and had cut its training program from sixteen to six weeks. Maheu, in his own words, became "the last trained agent ever to hit the field." Nevertheless, "I was very proud of being a heap big G-man with a badge and a gun and credentials."

He did not make an auspicious start. His first assignment, in Arizona, was to make inquiries about a suspect, and Maheu called at the house of a neighbor. "An old man answered the door. I showed him my credentials. I was the first FBI agent in the flesh that he'd ever seen and before I had a chance to ask him any questions he went to get a file of the correspondence that he'd had with J. Edgar Hoover. He was so pleased to finally meet 'one of the super guys with whom Mr. Hoover has been able to surround himself.' It took two hours to go through that dissertation. Then I asked him a couple of questions about his neighbor. He didn't know him."

The nice old gentleman followed Maheu out of the house—to discover that the super G-man had locked himself out of his car. "He almost started crying," said Maheu.

In Seattle, Washington, Maheu opened a resident FBI bureau and got married. (He had known Yvette since he was eleven.) And then, in 1942, he was summoned to Washington, D.C., and told that he was going into the counterespionage business.

Maheu's mission was the stuff of which spy thrillers are made. In the invasion of France, the Germans had captured a distinguished aviator named Dieudonne Coste who, in 1930, had made the first nonstop flight from Paris to New York. (Charles Lindbergh's legendary flight three years earlier was in the opposite direction.)

Because of that exploit Coste was something of a celebrity in America, and the Germans planned to send him there as a spy. The plot, according to testimony Maheu has given, called for Coste to get caught. He would then, in contrition, offer to become a double agent for the Americans and feed false information to Germany. Actually, of course, he would, unbeknownst to the Americans, also collect genuine intelligence and feed that back as well. The inducement offered to Coste by the Third Reich was the promise that his family in occupied France would suffer if he failed to cooperate.

The plan went wrong before Coste even got to America. Through a tip-off from British Intelligence he was captured in Spain by U.S. agents and he willingly revealed the details of the scheme. He also offered to go through with the plot—or rather, to appear to go through with it in the hope of convincing the Germans that they really were getting high-grade intelligence.

The problem from the FBI's point of view was deciding whether Coste was truly a friend or an enemy. What if the plot was even more devious than it seemed? Coste's capture in Spain, his confession, and his offer could all have been part of the original conspiracy.

There was a further complication. According to Coste, the Germans had arranged for another Frenchman—this one a committed Nazi—to join him secretly in America. While Coste was pretending to help the Americans by feeding false intelligence, the second Frenchman would be sending genuine material via a radio transmitter hidden somewhere on Long Island. Obviously, even if Coste really was on the side of the angels, the American counterplot was not going to work unless the radio operator could be duped.

Maheu, with his linguistic talent, was given the job of keeping an eye on one Frenchman and fooling the other. Once again he made an inauspicious start.

To play his role of traitor, Maheu had to be stripped of any link with the FBI, and in Miami, Florida, a whole new identity was created for him under the name of Robert A. Marchand. (In the spy business it is, apparently, reckoned there is less chance of a slip-up if an undercover agent keeps his own first name and initials.) Forty-five minutes after Robert Maheu became Robert Marchand he bumped into one of Robert Maheu's best friends.

"It is the life of living a lie, which is a very difficult one," Maheu says. "I began the assignment with a hairline just a little bit above my eyebrows and I ended it with a bald pate."

The mission was, however, a success. Coste turned out to be a friend, not a foe, and for two years the radio operator and the Germans were successfully deceived.

Maheu's reward was promotion. In 1944, at the end of his undercover assignment, he became senior assistant to Hoover's deputy, E. J. Connally, and was made responsible for the administrative division of the FBI's New York bureau.

There is no doubt that Maheu's prospects were considerable. By all accounts the young agent, still not thirty, had impressed Hoover with both his zeal and his loyalty. (In return, Maheu remained a votary of Hoover's long after he left the FBI, and remembered to send the Director a birthday telegram each year. One of them read: "Happy Birthday. Those of us who truly comprehend the insidious forces which you have consistently and are continuing to combat, thank the Good Lord that he has blessed you with so many years of physical and mental health. We pray that He may continue to do so.") Maheu's future seemed to hold a logical sequence of ever more important and high-paying jobs within the FBI.

But in 1945 personal tragedy intervened. Yvette Maheu contracted tuberculosis, still at that time a potentially lethal disease. It was imperative that she leave New York, and Hoover created an FBI bureau in Waterville to enable the Maheus to breathe the comparatively unsullied air of Maine.

After the suspense of espionage and the excitement of New York, Maheu found Maine very boring. His only quarries were draft dodgers and car thieves who had crossed state lines. In those McCarthyan days, Waterville didn't boast a single Communist. In 1947 Maheu resigned.

Much later, when Maheu had risen to the heights where he required spokesmen, they would tell how Hoover had tears in his eyes when the two men said good-bye. That does not sit too well with the Hoover legend, but it is true that the Director did not forget his young protégé.

Two years after leaving the FBI, Maheu found himself—for the first but not the last time—in serious financial difficulties. In an attempt to "encourage commerce between the United States and Canada," he had acquired from a Montreal company the U.S. rights to a new process for canning pure cream. He founded a company called Dairy Dream Farms, Incorporated, kept seventy percent of the stock for himself, and persuaded a manufacturer in Wisconsin to supply the American market.

Yvette Maheu had "miraculously recovered," business was booming, and the family moved to New Rochelle in New York State. "It looked like the world was our oyster," said Maheu.

The bubble burst when the Montreal company discovered that the canned cream had a limited shelf life, after which the cream could become contaminated and potentially poisonous. The cost of retrieving cans from supermarkets and warehouses all over the United States was ruinous.

To his credit, Maheu refused to declare bankruptcy and negotiated with the company's creditors to pay them off in monthly installments. It was Hoover who provided the means by getting Maheu a job as Director of Compliance and Security for the Small Defense Plants Administration, in Washington, D.C.

When that agency evolved into the Small Business

Administration, Maheu became special assistant to the administrator. His job was to establish security criteria, to check on the backgrounds of prospective employees, and to study the companies the SBA was loaning money to. "If there was suspicion that the loans we made were not going for the stated purpose," said Maheu, "we would investigate the violation and recommend prosecution."

Maheu, again, did his job well and was highly thought of. But the debt of nearly $100,000 that he had incurred in the Dairy Dream Farms fiasco preyed on his mind. He had been paying some of his creditors as little as five dollars a month, just to indicate an intent to repay, and "my wife and I would sit down at night and figure out that by the time we were 67 or 68 years old, we'd have everyone repaid."

That prospect was so daunting that Maheu decided to gamble. In 1955 he gave up the security of his relatively well-paid job, took the $1,800 owed to him from the SBA's retirement fund, and set up his own company, Robert A. Maheu Associates.

The title was, perhaps, a little pretentious for what was really a one-man operation, but Maheu had a plan for acquiring "associates" around the world.

The Society of Former Special Agents of the FBI, with headquarters at the Statler Hilton Hotel in New York, is primarily a means for allowing ex-FBI agents to keep in touch with one another. Once a year the society holds a convention where it passes resolutions supporting law enforcement—or deploring the lack of it—and it is, according to Maheu, the greatest organization in the world, save only the U.S. Marine Corps.

On a more practical level, the society publishes a directory of its members, and Maheu's scheme was to farm out the assignments he received to these former agents. His fee was fifty dollars a day, which he would share with the agent in the field.

To begin with, Maheu Associates also shared an office, one secretary, and a telephone with Carmine Bellino, an accounting-fraud specialist (later renowned as the senior fiscal investigator for Senator Sam Ervin's Watergate Committee).

46

Exactly what business Maheu Associates was in is difficult to say. The circular Maheu mailed to potential clients when he founded the company said it would be an investigative agency, but it soon began to dabble in public relations and management consultancy as well.

It also, in a minor way, became a front for the Central Intelligence Agency. Maheu had not long been established in Bellino's office when the CIA offered to subsidize grander accommodations. In return Maheu was to be available for special undisclosed assignments which the CIA might ask him to perform from time to time.

When he accepted the offer, Maheu imagined, he says, that the assignments would be fairly innocuous, such as helping disguise the identity of CIA agents by placing them on the Maheu Associates payroll. In time he would need to think in much more sinister terms.

Fulgencio Batista, Cuba's dictator since 1952, fled to the Dominican Republic on January 1, 1959, leaving Fidel Castro to run the largest and westernmost island in the West Indies. The sudden change in government deprived the U.S. of a friendly, even malleable, neighbor, and organized crime of some very lucrative interests.

Castro proved to be very unfriendly. He confiscated U.S. investments in banks and industry and seized large American-owned landholdings, turning them first into collective farms and then into Soviet-style state farms. He also seized Havana's casinos, from which organized-crime interests had skimmed—or stolen—countless millions of dollars.

On January 3, 1961, the U.S. severed diplomatic relations with Cuba, and Castro retaliated by declaring his alliance with the Soviet Union. With the cold war assuming this new and appalling dimension, the CIA decided that Castro would have to go. It was perhaps natural, if a little unorthodox, that because of their coinciding interests, the CIA should turn to the Mob for help.

Obviously, this unlikely alliance needed to be negotiated with some delicacy, and the CIA looked for

for a suitable intermediary who, should things go wrong, could not easily be linked with a U.S. government agency. Robert A. Maheu Associates, still ensconced in its CIA-subsidized office, was called upon to fulfill its part of the contract.

Maheu entered into the plot enthusiastically. In fact, he spent so much time in Florida planning Castro's assassination that his major client, Howard Hughes, began to complain about Maheu's unavailability. Maheu sought and obtained permission from the CIA to reveal to Hughes what he was up to. Hughes, with his abiding fear of Communism, approved and gave Maheu his blessing to spend whatever time was necessary.

According to the plot, Castro was to die by sniper fire, explosion, or poison capsule. Thereafter, Cuban exiles, secretly financed and trained in Florida and Guatemala by the CIA, would invade the island and restore democracy. To preserve the illusion that this was an indigenous uprising, it was necessary that Castro die by a Cuban hand, and Maheu's job was to recruit hoodlums who—with some expertise in the art of murder—would, in turn, recruit and train a Cuban assassin. Maheu chose Salvatore "Sam" Giancana and John "Johnny" Roselli. They accepted the assignment, but, according to Roselli, they turned down Maheu's offer of a $100,000 fee, feeling that Castro's assassination was a patriotic duty.

Patriotism apart, Giancana and Roselli had good reason to be mad at the bearded revolutionary. Through the 1930s and early 1940s, Giancana had risen to head the Chicago rackets with Roselli as his protégé. Three years after Bugsy Siegel's sudden and involuntary retirement, Roselli was sent to Las Vegas to supervise the Mob's gambling interests there and he was also made responsible for the casino operations in Havana.

(Siegel's murder had focused unwelcome attention on the connection between legalized gambling and organized crime, and part of Roselli's function in Las Vegas was to make the Mob's activities less visible. He was to some degree successful in creating a respectable front until December 1958 when one of his associates was suddenly "retired" in traditional underworld style. Gus Greenbaum, head of the Riviera Hotel, and his wife, Bess, were found at their home in Phoenix, Arizona, with their throats cut from ear to ear. The murders were unsolved, but they inspired renewed interest in the seamier side of Las Vegas and Roselli transferred his activities to Los Angeles.)

So far, no details of Giancana and Roselli's recruitment by Maheu for the anti-Castro plot have surfaced, although presumably Maheu's FBI friends were helpful in supplying a list of likely candidates. In any event, the bizarre scheme foundered. Roselli later claimed to have made several exploratory visits to Cuba in a high-speed launch provided by the CIA, but, says Maheu, the operation was "always subject to a 'go' signal which, to my knowledge never came."

When an invasion force of Cuban exiles landed at the Bay of Pigs on April 17, 1961, Castro was very much alive and furnished considerable resistance. Lacking air support, which President John Kennedy had refused to sanction, the invaders were routed.

At the time, of course, the involvement of the CIA and the underworld in the Cuba crisis was a closely held secret. Maheu returned to his business, and the affairs of Howard Hughes, and the gangsters returned to theirs. (Roselli moved back to Las Vegas, where, as we shall see, he helped Hughes acquire his first casino.)

The story only emerged in 1975 when the Senate Intelligence Committee began to inquire into the excesses of the CIA. Roselli was then under the threat of deportation following the discovery that his real name was Filippo Sacco and that his entry into the U.S. as a child had been illegal. To save himself, Roselli agreed to testify about the Castro plot. He also volunteered the startling information that he and Giancana had been amorously linked with Judith Campbell Exner at a time when she, in her own words, enjoyed a "close, personal" relationship with President Kennedy.

Giancana never had the opportunity to tell his side of the story. On June 19, 1975, a few days before he was due to testify to the Senate committee, Giancana went on a nighttime raid of the refrigerator in his suburban Chicago home. The next day police found his body in the kitchen, face-up, in a pool of blood, with a cluster of .22-caliber bullet wounds around his mouth.

The investigation into that murder and into the Castro plot were continuing when, on July 28, 1976, Johnny Roselli, then seventy, disappeared. He had been living "in retirement" at his sister's house in Plantation, Florida. He left to play a round of golf, and never returned. His car was found abandoned at Miami International Airport.

On August 8, 1976, Roselli's body was found, wrapped in chains, in a fifty-five-gallon oil drum floating in Biscayne Bay near Miami Beach. The old man had been stabbed in the lower abdomen and asphyxiated.

Bob Maheu enjoyed intrigue and the results were not always so dismal. When the Greek shipowner Stavros Niarchos plotted against Aristotle Onassis, Maheu was able to pull off a spectacular coup.

Onassis had signed a contract with the Saudi Arabian government which gave him exclusive rights to ship every drop of that country's oil. Niarchos did not want Onassis—his brother-in-law but also his archrival—killed; he simply told Maheu to find some way to sabotage the deal.

Having checked with the State Department—and, inevitably, the CIA—to make sure that "Niarchos' desires did not conflict with the best interests of the United States," Maheu began to educate himself about the oil business and Saudi Arabian politics. He learned that an American named Carl Twitchell was well versed in both subjects and, more important, was acquainted with Saudi Arabia's King Ibn Saud.

The king had great respect for Twitchell, who was obviously the man to go to Saudi Arabia and begin asking questions about the Onassis contract. After an investigation that dragged on for eighteen months, Maheu received what he was looking for: evidence that Onassis had paid a bribe of $1 million to someone in the Saudi cabinet.

Maheu flew to the Saudi capital of Riyadt to present the evidence to officials. Afterward he spent some anxious hours in his hotel room awaiting the reaction. He did not have an exit visa to enable him to leave the country, and neither did he have any idea of exactly who had gotten the million dollars. What would happen if Maheu's evidence fell into the hands that had taken the Onassis bribe?

He need not have worried. The evidence reached the king, who gave Maheu both an exit visa and instructions to break the story of the bribe in Europe as quickly as possible. The scandal reached epic proportions and Onassis' contract was eventually abrogated by an arbitration tribunal.

Back in Washington, D.C., Maheu met Niarchos at the Mayflower Hotel for a celebration dinner. Niarchos congratulated Maheu on his imagination and his creativity and, especially, on having the nerve to go to Saudi Arabia himself to present the bribery evidence.

But, said Niarchos, Maheu had made one terrible mistake. Before risking his neck, Maheu should have demanded a $500,000 bonus payable in advance. Maheu said well, it was not too late.

"Yes, it is too late," said Niarchos, according to Maheu's version of the conversation. "You have certain good things about you but you are a very poor businessman. You'll never learn your business lesson unless you do it my way, so I'm going to cut it to 10 per cent." To emphasize his point, Niarchos paid the shrunken bonus not at once, but at the rate of $1,500 a month "because this may teach you a lesson on how to charge clients in the future."

Maheu learned. His next major client, the United Steelworkers of America and the union's president, David McDonald, retained Maheu Associates for $7,500 per month, a sum Maheu considered "very substantial." Maheu did public relations work for the labor union and served as adviser to McDonald for nearly three years.

Howard Hughes was not—yet—paying Maheu that sort of money, but from about 1957 onward he was the most consistent client. Maheu was averaging twenty trips a year from Washington to Los Angeles and spending at least six months out of every twelve on Hughes projects.

51

The Maheu family began to spend their summers at a rented house in California, and, finally, in 1961 Maheu moved his home from Virginia to Los Angeles. Hughes told him to get rid of all his other clients. "He said that we would be together for the rest of our natural lives."

Exactly what Maheu was doing for Hughes between 1961 and November 1966, when the circus moved to Las Vegas, was not easy to determine, even for highly placed members of the Hughes empire. Month by month, Robert A. Maheu Associates submitted invoices for its services to the Hughes Tool Company, but they were written in code.

Among those who were intrigued by the mystery was the IRS. In 1963—and not for the last time—the tax men began to inquire into the nature of the relationship between Maheu and Hughes. Putting it bluntly, they suspected that Maheu was being used as a conduit for illegal political contributions.

On July 10 an IRS agent named Otho King went to Houston to interview Calvin Collier, the treasurer of the Hughes Tool Company. Immediately afterward Collier wrote an internal memorandum in which he recorded, as best he could, the substance of the interrogation.

What, asked King, were the services that Maheu provided? Collier replied that he could not be too specific because he had no definite information, but he could offer some suggestions.

"The company [Hughes Tool Company] has for years diligently strived to market its products only in the free world. Special efforts have been made and are currently being made to prohibit the shipping of any of the company's products behind the iron curtain or to communist-controlled countries." Maheu's job, apparently, was to "investigate the activities of foreign-based companies." Exactly who had been investigated and how could not be disclosed. "It goes without saying that this particular service by necessity be tightly controlled and kept very secret. . . ."

Maheu had also been called upon to investigate Hughes Tool Company executives—or, at least, that

52

is what Collier believed. He told the IRS agent: "Although I do not know for sure I am positive that I was thoroughly investigated by the Maheu organization and I believe such investigation began in 1957 and probably continued in 1959."

The 1957 date was critical, said Collier, because that was when Noah Dietrich "was creating tremendous problems for the company. It was obviously critical to determine without question those individuals who were loyal to Noah Dietrich and those who were loyal to the Hughes Tool Company."

And that assignment explained at least to Collier's satisfaction why Maheu's bills had to be submitted in code. As company treasurer, Collier approved or had access to all of the bills. "It would be impossible for the Maheu organization to investigate C.J. Collier if itemized detailed accounting statements were furnished to C.J. Collier."

What else did Maheu do for the Hughes Tool Company? As it happened, said Collier, he could show the agent an example of the Maheu men in action.

He took King to his office window and pointed out that on the roof of the brewery opposite there was a ladder propped up against a ventilation shaft. At that very spot for the past several weeks, said Collier, he had seen a man in workman's overalls keeping the Hughes building under surveillance through a pair of binoculars. The man came every night at five P.M. and stayed until dark. Sometimes he brought a bucket with him, but Collier had noted that he spent most of his time looking at the Hughes Tool Company plant through his field glasses.

Collier surmised that the man was one of Maheu's agents who was trying to catch an industrial spy. Recently someone had infiltrated the company and stolen a set of engineer's drawings for a new lubricant seal designed to increase the life of the famous Hughes drilling bit.

How did Collier know that the man with the binoculars was working for Maheu and was not an enemy agent? Collier replied that he had reported the daily surveillance to his superiors, but had received no reply. As the workman had continued to arrive every day. Collier assumed that it *had* to be Maheu's man.

Maheu was also a bug hunter. Collier said that Maheu sent experts to Houston to search for electronic eavesdropping equipment which might be helping others spy on Howard Hughes' affairs. He said a bug had been found in the Tool Company's boardroom. Maheu also sent his experts (usually former FBI, CIA, or IRS agents hired on a freelance basis) to Chester Davis' office in New York. They claimed to have found traces of a former bug in one of the attorney's phones.

Collier said he was sure, "although I have no way of knowing," that large numbers of Maheu men were helping Hughes fight the TWA litigation.

(He was right. Hughes was convinced that the lawsuits against him represented a conspiracy between the directors of TWA and the banks and insurance companies which had forced him to put his stock into a voting trust. In an attempt to prove that charge, Maheu's freelance agents spied on eighteen people and even obtained copies of their telephone bills.)

Collier emphasized to the agent that all of this information was highly confidential. "I again cautioned him as to the secrecy and the detriments that could fall upon the Hughes Tool Company if the services performed by the Maheu organization should become general knowledge."

King, for his part, appears to have been satisfied. In his memorandum, Collier concluded: "Apparently the payments to the Maheu organization are no longer open for discussion . . . unless the review section of the I.R.S. should direct to us additional inquiries."

It has to be said that not all of Maheu's assignments were as spooky as those described by Collier. Some of them were simply bizarre.

He was, for example, called upon to save Hughes' beloved Spruce Goose, which, since its maiden and only flight in 1947, had been stored in an atmosphere-controlled hangar at Long Beach harbor, California. The flying boat belonged to the U.S. government, and in the early 1960s the General Services Administration recommended that the wooden relic be sold for scrap. Maheu, called in by Hughes at the last moment, opened one of his secret doors in Washington, D.C., and got the decision postponed. Later he negotiated a a deal with the GSA which allowed the Hughes Tool Company to lease the plane from the government for "continued research." (The Spruce Goose remains undisturbed at Long Beach; the Summa Corporation pays the city of Los Angeles $100,000 a year for the storage space. In late 1976 the National Aeronautics and Space Administration and the U.S. Navy said they were interested in it for a "vehicle research project" and might try to fly it again.)

Maheu was also required to do a little dusting of Hughes' public image. The Man owned 17,000 acres of land in Arizona which he had bought for a song on the understanding that it would be used to provide factories and jobs. The land remained undeveloped and the natives became restless.

One night, just before midnight, Maheu got a telephone call from Hughes. Without explanation he was told to fly to Tucson, check into a motel, and wait for a telephone call from Hughes that would come at seven A.M. the next morning. There were no commercial flights from Los Angeles to Tucson at that time of night, so Maheu chartered a private plane.

The next morning the call came. Hughes said that he might be moving part of the Hughes Aircraft Company to Tucson at any moment. Maheu was to go out and buy or rent houses which were to be held in constant readiness for occupation by Hughes executives.

The plans of each house and a description of its location were submitted to Hughes for approval. For every one he liked, there were nine he rejected, but eventually Maheu won approval to buy or rent six houses. He also rented a cottage at the Arizona Inn in Tucson for $100 a day (where people speculated Hughes would stay) and 710,000 square feet of land at Tucson Airport, where, presumably, the new factory would be located. Off-duty Tucson policemen were hired to guard the empty properties round-the-clock.

Seven years later they were still empty. Then one day the houses were sold, the leases were canceled, and the entire project was abandoned.

If Maheu was bothered by the futility of it all, he could at least take consolation that his assignments were earning him somewhere in the region of $400,000 a year. The debts from the Dairy Dream Farms debacle had been paid off long ago, and the Maheus were able to live in some style in a $100,000 house in Pacific Palisades near Los Angeles. And because of Hughes' eccentricity, life was always unpredictable and exciting.

Things became very exciting indeed in July 1966 when Hughes moved to Boston. The logistics of that trip and the planning involved would have daunted a less resourceful operator; Maheu was in his element.

The major problem was created by Hughes' refusal to make the cross-country trip by private plane. He wanted to travel in two private Pullman cars hooked to an express train, the Super Chief, which runs between Los Angeles and Chicago. There, the cars were to be hooked onto another scheduled express for the remainder of the journey to Boston. All of that had to be accomplished in total secrecy.

Through friends of friends, Maheu negotiated with the presidents of three railroad companies. They took some persuading because an airline strike had created unusually heavy demands and the railroads already had problems enough coping with extra (and considerably less demanding) passengers. Eventually, however, a deal was made.

It was agreed that on the night of Sunday, July 17, 1966, the Super Chief would leave Los Angeles on schedule, pulling the two private cars. Ten minutes out of L.A. it would make an unscheduled stop near the sprawling suburb of Pomona, where, under the cover of darkness, one extra passenger would embark. Throughout the rest of the journey the privacy of the Pullman cars would be ensured, politely but firmly, by security guards under the command of a former Los Angeles policeman, Jack Hooper. (Hooper had begun doing "chores" for Maheu while he was still a sergeant of detectives for the West Los Angeles division of the LAPD. In 1961, at the age of forty-seven, he retired from the force and bought the Bel Air Security Patrol, a private police force that guards an exclusive housing estate in West Hollywood. Bel Air's residents included, periodically, Hughes and his wife, who rented a house there for $50,000 a year.)

One problem remained. As Maheu and his eldest son, Peter—who was then working full-time for Maheu Associates—sat down to review the arrangements, they realized that success depended on Hughes and the Super Chief arriving at Pomona at roughly the same time. If Hughes, a notorious procrastinator, should be late, the train would have to leave without him or the main track out of L.A. would be blocked. Peter Maheu was dispatched to surreptitiously locate the master switch to the signal system—just in case.

Hughes was late. In fact, when the Super Chief began its journey, he was still procrastinating at his house in Bel Air. Maheu says he telephoned and warned: "If you don't get off your ass it's going to leave without you." Hughes did make the rendezvous, just in time, but rail traffic around Los Angeles was snarled for hours.

Inevitably, the cross-country odyssey attracted considerable attention, and by the following Wednesday, when the Pullman cars arrived in Boston, reporters and cameramen were in pursuit of the mysterious passenger. Hughes was smuggled into the Ritz-Carlton Hotel, where the entire fifth floor had been reserved, and that gave the press people the clue they needed. The reservation had been made by Maheu Associates, which had also ordered special telephone lines to be installed. It did not take long for the reporters to make the connection.

Denied any access to Hughes, the media turned its attention to Maheu, who had remained in Los Angeles. It was his first exposure to national limelight and he basked in it, answering the endless questions about Hughes evasively, but with great charm.

But if Maheu enjoyed the experience, Hughes did not. The reporters laid siege to the Ritz-Carlton and even set off the hotel fire alarm in the hope that fire fighters could be persuaded to storm the fifth floor. After a few weeks—and when the medical tests at the Peter Bent Brigham Hospital had been completed— Hughes called Maheu and asked him to make arrangements for another move. This time, Hughes said, he wanted to go to North Lake Tahoe in Nevada.

Maheu had no sooner made the plans than Hughes called again. Tahoe was out, he said. Now it was the Bahamas he wanted to go to—or, perhaps, Montreal.

It took one more call to finally fix the destination. Hughes said he had now definitely made up his mind. The circus was going to the place it had, perhaps, always belonged—the very last frontier.

Maheu arrived in Las Vegas to prepare for Hughes' arrival in September 1966, calling himself Robert Murphy. In view of what had happened in Boston, the subterfuge was, no doubt, necessary. It also, no doubt, added spice to the assignment, and in later years Maheu enjoyed telling the story of how his cover was nearly blown when his youngest son, Billy, announced in a hotel lobby that if the false-name game was going to continue then somebody had better tell him how to spell Murphy.

Maheu's first task was to find somewhere for Hughes to live, and while Las Vegas must contain more hotel rooms, acre for acre, than most other cities, that promised to be no simple matter.

None of the major hotels in Las Vegas is really in the business of renting rooms. Each one prospers by providing accommodation—often subsidized, sometimes even free—for gamblers who will, hopefully, leave behind in the hotel's casino far more than the price of a room. In that scheme of things, Howard Hughes, the legendary hermit, held little attraction as a potential guest—the more so because what he wanted was not a room but an entire floor.

Maheu first tried the Dunes Hotel, but the management would only spare half a floor. Hughes wanted all or nothing.

Next Maheu tried Wilbur Clark's Desert Inn, a casino and nine-story hotel slap in the middle of the Las Vegas Strip—and discovered that he had a very influential connection. In residence at the Inn was his old mobster friend John Roselli.

The Desert Inn was Wilbur Clark's in name only. An amiable card dealer who had worked at private resorts in New York and California, Clark began developing the Desert Inn in the late 1940s, but ran out of money. He accepted help from a Cleveland group, giving up over eighty percent of the stock and any voice in management. It turned out that the group from Cleveland contained some exotic characters. Later, during a Senate investigation into organized crime, Clark was called to testify and was asked: "Before you got in bed with crooks to finish this proposition, didn't you look into these birds at all?"

"Not too much," said Clark. "No, sir."

When Maheu arrived in Las Vegas, John Roselli was not listed as an owner of the Desert Inn, he had no title, and he received no salary. He did, however, have some influence with one of the casino's more prominent owners, Ruby Kolod. Kolod was only too happy to oblige Maheu: Hughes could have the entire ninth floor, made up of seven penthouse suites, for an indefinite stay.

That decision did not go down well with one of Las Vegas' leading citizens. Moe "Barney" Dalitz was a former member of an organized crime syndicate, one of the original members of the Cleveland group that invested in the Desert Inn, and, more important, now the senior partner in the casino. (Dalitz grew up in Detroit but moved to Cleveland during Prohibition. Along with two other partners in the Desert Inn, Morris Kleinman and Samuel Tucker, he was indicted for smuggling liquor from Canada during Prohibition. The charges were eventually dropped, but when Dalitz was asked during a Senate investigation if he had made "a little nest egg" out of rumrunning, he replied, "Well, I didn't inherit any money, senator." Before moving to Las Vegas he operated illegal gambling clubs in Ohio and Kentucky.)

Dalitz was furious at the arrangement that Kolod had made with Maheu but it was too late to cancel it, and Hughes and his entourage moved into the Desert Inn during the early hours of Sunday, November 27.

Dalitz grew even angrier when Hughes showed no sign of moving out. The penthouse suites, each with its own bar and spacious living rooms, had been furnished luxuriously to attract high rollers, not hermits, and Dalitz believed the Hughes' occupation was costing his casino $3,000 a day. With the New Year holiday approaching and the really big high rollers heading for town, that figure would escalate. Just after Christmas, Dalitz summoned Maheu to his office and demanded that Hughes leave the hotel before the week was up.

Faced with that crisis, the ever resourceful Maheu turned to another of his very special contacts. Edward P. Morgan, senior partner of the law firm Welch and Morgan, is one of Washington, D.C.'s superlawyers. Like Maheu, he was a wartime special agent for the FBI and in 1947 was counsel for the joint congressional committee which investigated the Japanese attack on Pearl Harbor. In 1950, he was counsel to the Senate Foreign Relations Committee that investigated Senator Joseph McCarthy. Morgan and Maheu had met in the early 1950s in Washington when for a while they had offices in the same building, called the Farragut. They had been friends ever since, and Morgan had advised Maheu on several investments over the years.

Maheu knew that Morgan from time to time represented James Hoffa, former president of the International Brotherhood of Teamsters. Maheu also knew that the Desert Inn had a substantial loan from the Teamsters' pension fund. In due course Hoffa called Dalitz—they were both raised in the same part of Detroit—and asked, as a favor, that Hughes be allowed to stay over the New Year.

The tactic worked, but it made Dalitz even madder. He resented being pressured, no matter how gently, by Hoffa, and when the New Year began to grow older with no sign of movement from Hughes, Dalitz arbitrarily raised the rent of the ninth floor by $3,000 a day.

Still Hughes would not go. On February 13, Dalitz got the general counsel and executive vice-president of the Desert Inn to send Hughes, via Maheu, an eviction notice by registered mail. Hughes was to be out by February 20. "Our request must be considered as a legal demand upon which we may act without further notice," said the letter.

Maheu told Hughes in a memorandum that Dalitz was impossible to deal with. He "has become senile and his nose has been out of joint since we were able to maintain the 9th floor over the holiday weekend after he had stated to his friends that this was an impossible task." There were, said Maheu, only two alternatives: Either they should fight Dalitz in court or find a more friendly landlord who—with a loan from Hughes—could buy the Desert Inn.

As it happened, Dalitz was thinking along roughly the same lines. He was, obviously, having difficulty maintaining any semblance of harmony with his fellow owners, and especially with Kolod, and he was exasperated with the pressure from the Hughes forces. One day, over a steak in the restaurant of the Desert Inn, he told his troubles to Hank Greenspun, the owner and publisher of the Las Vegas *Sun*. "If ever a man was ready to sell something I am ready to sell this place," Dalitz said.

It was, on the face of it, curious that Dalitz should choose Greenspun's shoulder to cry on. Dalitz, who was also part owner of the Stardust Hotel, had tried at one time to purchase a large interest in another casino. Greenspun had campaigned vigorously in the *Sun* against what he saw as the threat of a gambling monopoly, and in citing Dalitz's former links with the underworld he had pulled no punches.

But the two men had remained civil to one another and now their interests coincided. If Dalitz sold the Desert Inn, his influence on Las Vegas gambling would obviously diminish. And Greenspun, as he had already shown, was anxious that Hughes should remain in Las Vegas.

Greenspun told Dalitz that he had a friend with something of a reputation for bringing sellers and buyers together. "You call him," said Dalitz.

It was, apparently, a pure coincidence that Greenspun's friend, who arrived in Las Vegas a couple of days later, should turn out to be none other than Washington superlawyer Ed Morgan. They had known each other since 1954, when Morgan had successfully defended Greenspun against a charge arising from an article Greenspun wrote in the *Sun*.

After establishing that Dalitz really was determined to sell the Desert Inn, Morgan began sounding out the other partners. He found that Ruby Kolod was not only of the same mind but that he had already asked Johnny Roselli to look around for a buyer. There was momentary confusion over who should handle the deal, but Roselli gracefully offered to drop out.

The most obvious potential buyer for the Desert Inn was, of course, Hughes, and Morgan approached Bob Maheu. "Why don't you ask your boss if he would like to buy it," said Morgan.

"Howard Hughes would never put his name on a gambling license," said Maheu. But Morgan did persuade him to at least broach the subject. Hughes said he was interested.

The asking price for the Desert Inn was $7.5 million plus the hotel's outstanding debts, which stood at around $7.25 million. Maheu handled the negotiations, but he went armed with a script supplied by Hughes: "You say this, and if they say this, you answer thusly, and if they say no, you answer thusly."

Most of the negotiations were taken up with haggling over the price. Hughes told Maheu to get a quarter of a million dollars knocked off the price. He succeeded and reported the good news to the penthouse. "I thought I'd done a reasonably good job and he said, 'Go back and try for another quarter.'" Maheu succeeded in getting a second reduction only to be told by Hughes to go back and try for a third. "Frankly it got to the point where I thought the trips would continue forever," said Maheu.

Finally, the two sides agreed on a price of $6.25 million for the hotel-casino, plus the debts, for a total of $13 million.

At least, Maheu thought it was agreed. He and his wife were celebrating by having a late dinner in the Gourmet Room of the Desert Inn when he was told that Hughes was trying to change the deal at the last minute. The owners, led by Dalitz, had met and decided to throw Hughes out of the penthouse bodily within thirty minutes.

Furious and humiliated, Maheu went through the casino and, using his special key, took the elevator to the ninth floor. He walked by the guard on duty and went into the suite opposite the one in which Hughes was staying. There, he wrote out his resignation, gave it to the male secretary on duty, and stormed out.

Within ten minutes, says Maheu, Hughes had called him by telephone, "begging of me not to pack my bags and leave Las Vegas." They both agreed to sleep on it and talked again, early the next morning, for about two hours. It must have been a touching conversation. Hughes said the Desert Inn deal would go through as planned and repeated that he wanted the two of them to be together for the rest of their natural lives; Maheu promised he would *never* leave.

The contract was signed on February 28, 1967. What Hughes got for his $13 million was a lease to operate the hotel-casino until the year 2022 at an annual rent of $1,115,000. (The land on which the Desert Inn stands is owned by another entity.)

He also got the Desert Inn's assets, which included the hotel furnishings, the gaming equipment in the casino, and $905,277 in markers—gamblers' IOUs. To everyone's embarrassment, the assets also included $18,000 worth of State of Israel bonds. In the belief that that fact, should it emerge, would not go down well with the Tool Company's numerous Arab customers, the bonds were quickly and quietly disposed of.

Hughes was to take control of his first casino at one minute past midnight on April 1, 1967, but that was subject to his being able to obtain a gaming license. For others, that has sometimes proved to be a troublesome, time-consuming business.

Technically, two gambling licenses are required to operate a casino in Nevada—one from the state and one from the county in which it is going to do business. The state body, the Nevada Gaming Commission, requires applicants to file a personal history, including a financial report. The commission's rules also say that applicants should be fingerprinted in the presence of a public official and photographed to enable the FBI to check criminal records. A body called the Gaming Control Board then investigates the applicant, usually at its leisure. If the board eventually recommends that the commission grant a license, the county authority often follows suit.

It could be said that Howard Hughes received preferential treatment. "Mr. Hughes' life and background are well known to this board and he is considered highly qualified," said the chairman of the state's gaming board, Alan Abner. No photograph was submitted, and an old set of fingerprints sufficed. There was, of course, never any question that Hughes, unlike other applicants, would be required to personally appear before the board.

The Nevada Commission issued Hughes his license in record time and the local authority, the Clark County Licensing Board, called a special meeting to do likewise. The licenses were issued despite the fact that none of the people in the Hughes empire had any experience in running a hotel or restaurants, let alone a casino. And—Hughes' experience in the movie industry aside—they knew nothing about entertainment, which in Las Vegas is thought to play an important part in attracting gamblers. (Just how important entertainment is can best be illustrated by the contracts which Hughes inherited when he bought the Desert Inn. Phil Harris and Andy Williams were signed up, each for $35,000 a week, the McGuire Sisters were getting $25,000, and Bob Newhart was booked for $15,000. Lesser names, such as trapeze artists Galla Shaw and Erik Badicton and His Educated Dogs were getting about $1,000 a week, and the violinist in the Monte Carlo Room made $650.)

There was a chance that Maheu would be able to find some honest help from among his former FBI friends, and the Tool Company's auditors, Haskins & Sells, could keep an eye on the books, but amateur casino operators are like sheep among wolves.

What Hughes needed was an experienced veteran to act as guide and teacher, and he got one. Moe Dalitz, no longer angry (or, presumably, senile) offered to do the job unpaid. "I felt that it was a good thing for Las Vegas when they moved in here and I was glad to be on their team, so to speak." He also said that he did not ask for a salary because he did not really need the money.

Everybody was happy. Bob Maheu had, at last, got a proper job to do. He also got a house—formerly Dalitz's—on the Desert Inn golf course to live in. Edward Morgan, the superlawyer, got a "finder's fee" of $150,000 from Dalitz for his part in fixing up the deal, and he gave $50,000 of that to Johnny Roselli, the former gangster, who had, so gracefully, dropped out of the negotiations. Morgan also gave $25,000 to Hank Greenspun, the newspaperman. Greenspun did not want it, at first. "I wanted to return it and he insisted I have the check. He said, 'No, you earned it—your telephone calls and your trips and all that; your expenses, if nothing else.'"

Through curious chance, almost by accident, Howard Hughes was now in the gambling business.

4: CASTLES IN THE AIR

"I just got a call from Howard Hughes."
"Are you sure it was him?"
"Must have been. When I answered the phone, no one was there."
                                        —Anonymous

It soon became clear that Howard Hughes regarded Las Vegas as more than just another place to hide. Frank Sinatra, who had been known to look upon the city patriarchally himself, made the point with some perception: "You're wondering why I don't have a drink in my hand," Sinatra told his audience at the Sands Hotel. "Howard Hughes bought it." Pretty soon afterward, Hughes bought the Sands, too, as well as a great deal more real estate. And, as might have been expected of anyone who had arrived in town with $500 million or so to play with, he began demanding a voice in its affairs. Sometimes he concerned himself with the gritty details of government such as the selection of street names and the choice of a new manager for the city's convention center. Sometimes he tried to interfere with more profound issues such as the integration of local schools.

But buying up large chunks of Las Vegas and meddling in its government were only the first steps down a road of much grander design. Viewed from the Desert Inn penthouse (figuratively speaking, because the view was always blocked by drawn shades), Las Vegas seemed far more than a desert oasis of rather spectacular vulgarity. To Hughes it had the potential of being the gateway to the western United States. He saw it, he said, as becoming "the most complete vacation and pleasure complex anywhere in the world" and, at the same time, "a center of scientific research and space-age industry" with a new airport, the first in the world designed to accommodate supersonic planes.

Of course, Hughes was not the first man to gaze down upon a city and entertain absurd notions about reshaping its destiny. What made Hughes' "master plan" so remarkable was that for a while at least, many people who should have known better professed to believe in it.

And so, during the first couple of years of Hughes' residence in Las Vegas a great deal of poppycock was written and spoken about what The Man was going to do. The governor of Nevada forecast "substantial industrial development," and the Las Vegas Chamber of Commerce talked about the "unseen hand of one of the world's greatest industrialists" steadying the city's economic outlook.

In the columns of the Las Vegas *Sun,* Hank Greenspun went so far as to compare Hughes, favorably, with Sir Isaac Newton. "Fortunately for our nation and the world," Greenspun wrote, "Las Vegas presently has a man [like Newton] who early in life acquired the ability to cultivate thought." With Howard Hughes in residence at the Desert Inn, "in preferred solitude, thinking and working," there was nothing to prevent Nevada's transformation from one of the least populous and prestigious states "to one of the greatest in the nation. . . . Through his efforts he's helped to make our nation secure from its enemies and its people secure from physical wants. He has now placed his thoughts and visions to transforming the last frontier to an active new frontier which holds forth great promise for our area. How fortunate Howard Hughes has found a home in southern Nevada and will now help find Nevada for all of us."

That kind of extravagant nonsense was encouraged by handwritten epistles which Hughes would occasionally send down from his "preferred solitude" to the local media. In September 1967, for example, he revealed the "vision" he had to grace Las Vegas with a supersonic transport (SST) airport "to serve entirely southern Nevada, California and Arizona."

The vision had been provoked by the news that Clark County's commissioners were considering spending some $20 million on expanding Las Vegas' exciting airport, known as McCarran Field. Hughes proposed that instead, an SST airport should be built further away from Las Vegas from which "passengers may be flown by regular jet aircraft to any normally located present-day airport. Also, from this same SST terminus they may be flown by new and thoroughly proven helicopters and other VTOL [vertical takeoff and landing aircraft] to the many landing terminals which may be closer to the passengers' ultimate destination—on top of buildings downtown, on top of hotels and in residential areas."

For those passengers heading for the attractions of Las Vegas, Hughes said: "It might be found that, at a comparatively small cost, a micro-meter-laid track down the present freeway could permit air-conditioned cars just as plush as the present airliners, which could transport all of the passengers arriving or accumulated at the airport, to a point at or near Las Vegas, suitable for transfer to taxi. It might be found that these trains could leave on the order of one every 10 minutes. And with accumulated trains waiting for large incoming aircraft the trip, from the best information available, should require 6½ minutes."

Read with any care, Hughes' statement did not even

hint that he was proposing to build an SST airport —indeed, he specifically said that the plan was "pure speculation"—but where Howard Hughes was concerned, Las Vegas was never short of people with the ability to read between the lines. The very fact that Hughes' statement had broken fourteen years of silence on his part was enough to confirm that something momentous was in the works. One by one the Clark County commissioners appeared on television to state their excitement at "this announcement" that Las Vegas was going to become "the world's largest air center."

There were some who saw this for the moonshine it was, asking if the supposed advantages of supersonic travel might not be somewhat nullified if those who had paid to be sped to the West Coast of the United States found themselves deposited in the southern Nevada desert hundreds of miles from almost anywhere. And as Vaughn Clayton, an official of the Federal Aviation Administration, was moved to point out, regional airports located far away from the population centers they were supposed to serve had, in the past, turned out to be white elephants. The existing airport was ideally located, Clayton said, and Las Vegas should hang on to it.

None of this eminently good sense succeeded in tempering the enthusiasm of the city fathers, especially when Hughes was provoked by the detractors into putting pen to paper again.

The second epistle, delivered like the first to the media by Bob Maheu, positively dripped with scorn. Hughes agreed that McCarran Field was the ideal site for an airport, but "There is only one trouble —somebody built a city on the same site.

"If you feel that Las Vegas will remain unchanged, without any further growth, and if enough land is purchased to extend the runways and to clear a path of obstructions extending fanwise out from each end of the runway (the cost of which would be astronomical); and then if you give up completely the possibility of Las Vegas becoming the southwest terminus for SST, then, in that event, McCarran would be able to offer the same service it has in the past.

"However, I do not believe Las Vegas will remain dormant without future growth. There is no reason in the world why this city should not, in a reasonable number of years, be as large as say, Houston, Texas* is today. If this sort of growth should take place, the present location of McCarran Field would be approximately comparable to having the airport for Los Angeles located on Wilshire Boulevard [one of L.A.'s main arteries]. . . . Also, if more and higher high-rise structures continue to be built in Las Vegas at the present rate, I wonder if some airline pilot coming in for a landing may not just be possibly reminded of a newsreel he saw the night before, showing the slalom event in a ski meet."

As for those who had suggested that supersonic aircraft, with their inevitable booms, might not be welcomed overland, Hughes had nothing but contempt: "I feel it is absurd to assume that Yankee ingenuity will not find a way to fly at SST rates of speed nonstop from here to London, Paris or Rome."

There was still no mention of anything very concrete, no indication that Hughes intended to put his money where his claims were by actually building a new airport. But, still reading between the lines, the city fathers took the second statement as confirmation that Hughes was intending to "make a dream become a reality." Of course, The Man himself was unavailable for further comment, but Robert Maheu was always available to those who mattered in Las Vegas and he came under some pressure from the Clark County commissioners to provide the details of exactly what Howard Hughes had in mind.

Hughes probably had nothing in mind, but with his newfound reputation as an oracle of sorts he could hardly say so. Instead, Maheu was instructed to take to the commissioners an offer that was loaded with promise: Hughes would arrange and pay for a feasibility study of the proposed airport; if the results were positive he would build the place and then give it to Las Vegas—as a swap for McCarran Field.

* At the latest count Las Vegas still had a little way to go, with a population of 125,000 compared with Houston's 1,232,000.

When news of this offer leaked out, as anything so exciting was bound to do, there were cynics who believed they had spotted the catch. Because of its proximity to Las Vegas, McCarran Field was potentially valuable land. Perhaps, the cynics said, all this talk about SSTs was merely a device to acquire some real estate in return for a piece of desert and an implausible scheme.

That piece of malicious speculation prompted Hughes to write to the newspapers yet again: "I only proposed to trade the new airport for the old because I did not think the county would want the expense or the capital investment of two airports. But in case anyone thinks I have secret information disclosing that someone left a package of diamonds behind in one of the lockers at McCarran airport or something along that line I will gladly give the county the option of buying the new airport at its cost instead of exchanging McCarran Field for it. And, in this event, the cost will contain no profit or fee of any kind, also no interest for the use of the funds involved."

Now here, at last, was an offer that could not easily be refused. Within two weeks the Board of Commissioners had signed an agreement with the Hughes Tool Company which said in part that the company "proposes to commence, as judiciously as practical, the design and construction of a true jet-age airport." Meanwhile the Tool Company would pay for a study to determine "whether or not it is feasible for Clark County to acquire the airport mentioned above." If the study came to a negative conclusion, "such a determination shall effect a termination of this contract and shall completely release Clark County from any obligation whatsoever."

Las Vegas sat back and waited with some eagerness for the feasibility study to begin. A year later it was still waiting and the Board of Commissioners felt obliged to go ahead with the $20 million redevelopment of McCarran Field. Board Chairman William Briare was at pains to make it clear that this did not mean Clark County had lost faith in Hughes or his "jet-age" airport. As Briare said in a telegram he sent to the Desert Inn penthouse, "Common sense dictates that such foolish action on our part would qualify us for the idiot award of the year, not only in the eyes of our local citizens, but also in the opinion of the entire nation." In retrospect it is easy to see that common sense would actually have dictated the opposite conclusion, but the aura that surrounded Howard Hughes was powerful magic in Las Vegas—which, after all, exists on the premise that something can be gained for nothing, although only the tourists are supposed to fall for that. And, in fairness, the Clark County commissioners were not the only ones to fall under Hughes' spell.

For those who could not quite bring themselves to believe in the airport, there was the promise of "industrial development." Since Bugsy Siegel began it all, Las Vegas had never really been happy with its role or its image, and it sought respectability as a harlot might seek marriage. Clean-cut, well-connected industry was the bridegroom it wanted.

To begin with, Hughes promised very little—only "some kind of small industrial effort in some part of Nevada with no agreed or committed time schedule" —and Maheu protested, "I have nothing to say about our plans for the future since we have no plans at this time." Few people cared to believe them, especially since all around was evidence to belie their words. In June 1967 Hughes purchased a 525-acre ranch 25 miles west of Las Vegas (from the former wife of German steel magnate Alfred Krupp, for $600,000) which abutted on 27,000 acres he had owned since the early 1950s; he also bought the site of the North Las Vegas Air Terminal, with options to acquire a further 1,000 acres nearby, and he acquired property on and near McCarran Field. According to no less an authority than Mr. A. M. Smith, president of the Bank of Nevada, "You just don't buy this much property without a plan."

And in January 1968 Mr. Smith, seemingly, was proved right. At a press conference at the Desert Inn hosted by Nevada's Governor Paul Laxalt, an electronics company named Solitron Devices Incorporated announced its plan to build a research and manufacturing plant on a parcel of land near McCarran Field that was owned by Hughes. Solitron's president, Benjamin Friedman, said at least one million dollars would be invested initially and the plant would be in full operation in six or seven months. He ventured to predict that within the next five years Hughes would attract another twenty or so companies to Las Vegas, providing jobs for more than five thousand people. Bob Maheu, in smiling attendance as Hughes' representative, did not contradict him.

The press conference was the last Las Vegas saw of Solitron, and it heard no more of the other twenty or so companies. Indeed, as things turned out, the only "development" Hughes brought to Las Vegas during his four-year stay was a new house he had built for Robert Maheu.

Nevertheless, Hughes did manage to become Nevada's biggest private employer—not by building or expanding anything, but by buying existing hotels and casinos. Eventually he owned six on or near the Strip and a seventh, Harold's Club, in Reno, in northern Nevada. That made him easily the largest casino operator in the state with a payroll of around eight thousand people.

Once again many of the good people of Las Vegas saw this as evidence of some grand scheme devised by Hughes to transform the little city. There were even those who believed that Hughes, under the influence of his Mormon aides, intended to buy every casino so as to close them all, and that his "master plan" was to create a second Salt Lake City, dedicated to sober ideal. They were wrong. In fact, judging by the evidence of the written instructions which Hughes sent primarily to Maheu, there was no real plan. Most of the investments Hughes made in Las Vegas—which amounted to a total of, perhaps, $350 million—seem to have been as whimsical and arbitrary as his purchase of the Desert Inn had been.

It also seems that the day-to-day running of Hughes' empire in Las Vegas relied little if at all on orthodox business practice. On the contrary, the impression left behind is of a group of children let loose in Disneyland, running breathlessly from one exciting attraction to the next.

For quite a while the Hughes empire did not even have a telephone number in Las Vegas. The only relevant listing in the local telephone directory said that Hughes Tool Company could be reached at 734-6661 or "if no ans. call 878-7949." By the time that directory had been printed a call to the first number would never produce an "ans." At 878-7949 a lady would explain with commendable patience that her husband did at one time work for the Tool Company, but no more.

Calling the Desert Inn and asking for Howard Hughes was equally unproductive. Those who did manage to talk themselves into being connected with the penthouse were answered by one of the five male secretaries—Howard Eckersley, Roy Crawford, George Francom, John Holmes, and Levar Myler—who, to strangers, could be staggeringly uncommunicative.

The only way to do business with the empire was to find Robert Maheu or one of his staff, and at least for the first eighteen months of the Las Vegas odyssey, that was no simple matter. Maheu had wanted to set up a small office in Las Vegas, and indeed, he had rented accommodation. But he had neglected to get Hughes' permission for the office, and much against his will, he was forced to vacate it. For a time, a hotel room at the Desert Inn served as the empire's headquarters; later the HQQ was a house on the Desert Inn golf course which the Maheu family took over from Moe Dalitz. But Maheu was rarely to be found at either of them.

The best way of catching him was to go at around seven o'clock every morning to the Desert Inn coffee shop, where Maheu and his small staff would plan the day's work and eat breakfast. They would then go their separate ways, returning twelve or perhaps fourteen hours later to report in, catch up on the day's gossip, and have a drink or two. For Maheu, the day was even longer, with reports to Hughes to write and more often than not, a business dinner. And at any time, but usually in the early hours of the morning, he could expect a call from the penthouse.

The lines of communication between the man who did most of the work and The Man who made most of the decisions were not as precise as they might have been. Maheu could call the penthouse at will, but he did not often succeed in getting straight through to Hughes. Rather, he would dictate over the telephone a message to whichever secretary was on duty (at least one was available twenty-four hours a day), which was a time-consuming process because none of them took shorthand, and then wait for a reply. When it came it might be delivered verbally by an aide, but more often Hughes himself would call—ten minutes, ten hours or even days later. Invariably, at the end of those conversations, according to Maheu, Hughes would say, "Bob, let me put my thoughts down on paper." Some time afterward, one of the security guards, stationed on the ninth floor of the Desert Inn to keep out intruders, would deliver to Maheu a sealed envelope containing a message, handwritten on sheets of ruled, yellow, legal-size paper.

Most of those messages concerned what Hughes might buy next. There was clearly a need to invest some of the $546 million he had received from the sale of his TWA stock before the tax men demanded a large share, but Hughes had no clear idea of what he wanted to own. So Maheu and his staff* ran around looking at almost everything—hotels and casinos, to be sure, but also disused silver mines, real estate, radio and TV stations, publishing companies, and the hundreds of propositions, ranging from the ridiculous to the sublime, which arrived with every day's mail.

It was hardly surprising that hotel-casinos should have been at the top of Hughes' shopping list, because his takeover of the Desert Inn had been made so miraculously painless by the gaming authorities. The

* As a matter of detail, Maheu remained an independent consultant to the Hughes Tool Company, but he worked full-time for Hughes and for all intents and purposes he ran what became known as the Hughes-Nevada Operations. The Tool Company paid Robert A. Maheu Associates a fee of $520,000 out of which Maheu paid the salaries of his son Peter and a small staff of assistants and secretaries. However, most of the people Maheu recruited to help him in Las Vegas were put on the payroll of the Tool Company, although they were universally regarded as "Maheu's men."

problem for Maheu and his men lay in deciding which one to buy next. They eventually settled for the best.

The Sands Hotel was considered to be the Tiffany's of the Strip. Opened in December 1952, it was luxuriously furnished to the point where it could afford to rent its 777 rooms for as much as $100 a day, and its casino attracted a good class of clientele —which, in Las Vegas terms, means people willing and able to gamble small fortunes. The Sands also offered very high-class entertainment, including as regular attractions the likes of Dean Martin and Frank Sinatra, both of whom at one time owned a piece of the action. Sinatra had been obliged to give up his shareholding in the hotel in 1963 when it was discovered that he had entertained Sam Giancana (an alleged participant in Maheu's anti-Castro plot), who was among eleven racketeers listed by the Nevada authorities as personae non gratae. But Sinatra had remained the Sands' most significant attraction, and business was good enough in July 1967 to persuade Hughes to pay just under $14.6 million for the hotel. (The money was divided among the Sands' seventeen stockholders, who got $20,563.38 for each of the 710 shares they held among them; Dean Martin's cut was $617,000.)

By all accounts, everybody thought it was a good deal for both sides—everybody, that is, except Frank Sinatra. As he was no longer among the shareholders, Sinatra had no say in the manner of its sale, but as one of its assets, he could remove himself and he proceeded, in some secrecy, to negotiate with a rival establishment, Caesar's Palace. It is not really clear why Sinatra was so unhappy at Hughes' takeover. It may have had something to do with the fact that twenty years before, the men were apparently rivals for the affections of the actress Lana Turner, but more likely Sinatra simply appreciated that his reign as the uncrowned king of the Sands was over. He never did like second billing.

In any event, the secret of Sinatra's negotiations with Caesar's Palace was not as well guarded as it might have been and Maheu's men found out. So when, in the early hours of September 19, 1967, Sinatra went into the Sands casino and, as was his custom, asked for gambling chips on credit, he was refused. Apparently he already owed the casino $200,000, and in view of his impending departure —coupled with the fact that gambling debts are not legally collectible in Nevada—that was thought by the new management to be enough.

Old Blue Eyes was not amused. He told the unfortunate messenger of the bad tidings, "I'm gonna break both your legs." He told everybody else, "I built this place from a sandpile and when I'm through that's what it's going to be again." Then he overturned a table onto the casino's manager, Carl Cohen. That last act was a mistake. Cohen was reputed to be a nice, easygoing, gray-haired fifty-five-year-old, but there was the additional fact that he weighed 250 pounds, a good proportion of which went into the punch he delivered to Sinatra's mouth, removing the caps from two of the singer's front teeth. Sinatra recovered sufficiently to hurl a chair at Cohen (it missed) and then stormed out of the Sands for good. When Hughes heard the news he said, reportedly, "Frank who?"

This unpleasantness aside, Hughes' takeover of the Sands was a success. Indeed, in the years to come, when other parts of the Hughes-Nevada empire fell upon lean times, the Sands continually made a healthy profit. The credit for that may have belonged in large part to the man Maheu found to run the operation, although at first sight he seemed to be spectacularly unqualified for the job.

Edward Nigro and Maheu had been friends since their college days at Holy Cross in Worcester, where Maheu (a boarder) had allowed Nigro (a day student) to share his room. While after college Maheu had joined the FBI to fight the enemy at home, Nigro had joined the U.S. Air Force to carry the fight overseas, and subsequently he had carved for himself a remarkable career. At the age of forty-eight he was a three-star general and had just been appointed deputy director of the Pentagon's planning department when he was invited by his old friend to join the Hughes empire. After what Nigro described as "six

76

days and nights without sleep, trying to determine the best course," he ended his twenty-seven-year career with the Air Force and headed for the bright lights of the Strip, saying, rather curiously, "I felt that I could come out here and still serve my country." Whether the country benefited or not, Nigro found that he "just loved" his new job. Perhaps his greatest talent was in recognizing that he knew nothing about running a casino, which he left to veterans like Carl Cohen, while he concentrated on "man management and building teamwork" among the staff.

One of his first jobs was to make it very clear that under the new management certain things were going to change. Prostitution was (and is) a major industry in Las Vegas, and even "quality" establishments like the Sands had not been out of bounds to the girls (and boys) who, for a price, would celebrate with a winner and console a loser. There had even been whispers that some members of the staff of the Sands had been known to supply introductions to the needy. Howard Hughes, no longer the swinger he once was, and surrounded by Mormons, wanted none of that in his hotels, and General Nigro, as he was known, issued the necessary orders. It is doubtful if prostitution was stamped out entirely at the Sands, but apparently the General made it a good deal tougher for a girl (or boy) to make a living out of The Man's clientele.

The Las Vegas Strip consists of three long blocks of hotels and casinos which, in the main, are of particularly undistinguished architecture. In the light of day, the overall impression is one of shoddiness. But at night the Strip undergoes an almost magical transformation, becoming brash and vulgar, to be sure, but also seductive and, at first sight, quite overwhelming.

The magic is achieved through electricity—thousands upon thousands of kilowatts of it—which nightly is burned to feed miles of fluorescent tubing and countless light bulbs. The tubes and the bulbs are employed, often with considerable ingenuity, to make up illuminated signs which advertise the Strip's rival attractions. They flash and sparkle with the intensity of elaborate fireworks, drawing people, like moths, to the source of the light.

These signs are very seriously regarded by their owners. For example, when Bugsy Siegel's old place, the Famingo, got a new sign in 1968, it was launched with all the ceremony—if not the dignity—of a battleship. Lifted ninety feet into the air on a motorized boom, the "beauteous wife" of the Flamingo's president poured champagne over the beak of a neon flamingo which, with the aid of six thousand bulbs, two miles of fluorescent tubing, and a solid-state computer, fluttered its pink feathers.

The owners of the Frontier, a new hotel-casino built on the site of the Last Frontier and exactly opposite the Desert Inn, did not go quite that far. But in the spring of 1967, to mark the opening of the new venture, they did erect an electronic sign of considerable proportions which stood on top of a pole more than one hundred feet tall. The sign made Howard Hughes very nervous, because he feared it might fall down onto his penthouse sanctuary.

Bob Maheu was dispatched to talk to the Frontier's owners with the aim of persuading them to take down the sign. He reported back to Hughes that the owners had said there was no cause for alarm: If it fell anywhere—which was highly improbable—the sign would fall on the Desert Inn parking lot, leaving the penthouse unscathed.

Actually, what the Frontier's owners had said was that Howard Hughes could "drop dead," but Maheu saw no reason to upset The Man, especially since he realized that the Frontier was ripe for a takeover.

Within months of its opening, the new hotel-casino was in serious financial trouble. Two of its owners, Warner Richardson and Maurice Friedman, had been indicted for their parts in a crooked card games fraud at a private club in Los Angeles—a well-publicized fact that frightened many customers away from the Frontier. By the autumn of 1967 business was so bad that a takeover was the only alternative to bankruptcy. The owners wanted $15.5 million for the hotel and the twenty-nine acres of land that surrounded it, but on September 22, 1967, they sold out to Hughes for just under $14 million.

Initially, the deal did not give Hughes any active participation in the Frontier's casino, for under the terms of the agreement he was required to lease the gambling facilities to an "operating company" for $1,200,000 a year. However, while the ink on that agreement was still wet, doubts emerged—abruptly—about the bona fides of some of those who were or might have been stockholders of the "operating company."

"Acting on information received," two deputies from the Clark County Sheriff's Department burst into a suite at the Frontier where one of the former major stockholders of the hotel was enjoying a drink with a group of visitors from Detroit, including Anthony J. Zerilli. Mr. Zerilli was a perfectly respectable businessman, but he possessed the unfortunate heritage that his father, Joe, had been the reputed boss of the Detroit Mafia. His son suffered guilt by association and the sheriff's men arrested him on a charge of vagrancy.

The charge was dropped the next day and Zerilli was released, but the raid was sufficient cause to bring murmurs from the Gaming Control Board about the need to investigate "hidden interests" in the Frontier's casino. Within a week, and reportedly for no more than $1 million, Hughes acquired the right to operate the casino. With unprecedented haste, and no formalities, the authorities gave Hughes the necessary licenses.

With the Nevada empire growing at such a rate, the Hughes Tool Company thought it necessary to create some kind of administrative setup. Haskins & Sells, the Tool Company's auditors, were prevailed upon to open a branch office in Las Vegas. The Tool Company also sent an accountant, Robert Morgan, and a lawyer, Richard Gray, from Houston, who, at the behest of Raymond Holliday, chief executive of the Tool Company, set up a modest headquarters toward downtown Las Vegas. Their job was to exercise fiscal control over what became known for convenience as the Hughes-Nevada Operations.

So far as Holliday was concerned, Hughes-Nevada was no more than a handy title to describe the growing number of properties which the Tool Company was acquiring at the whim of its sole stockholder. However, Bob Maheu saw things very differently. He owed no allegiance to the Tool Company, cared little for Holliday, and regarded Hughes-Nevada as an autonomous empire over which he intended to exert control.

To demonstrate his independence, at more or less the same time as Holliday was causing one HQ to be established in Las Vegas, Maheu was establishing another. At the rear of the Frontier Hotel a dozen or so bedrooms were remodeled into offices—each with its own private bathroom—and a corner suite was converted into an immodest office-cum-boardroom for Maheu. From there he ruled. He appointed himself—on Hughes' instructions, he says—chief executive officer of Hughes-Nevada and made General Nigro his deputy. Whatever theory might have said about Houston having control, there were very few people in Las Vegas who failed to regard Maheu as the boss.

It may seem strange that Holliday tolerated this situation. He was, after all, the most senior executive in the Hughes empire— and, at $120,000 a year, the best-paid—whereas Maheu was nothing more than a free-lance consultant. The reason why Holliday did not feel able to exert his authority is perhaps best demonstrated by a report* of a Hughes-Nevada staff meeting.

Present at what Maheu liked to call the "Table of Twelve" at the Frontier were the men charged with the responsibility of running different bits of the Nevada empire—such as the hotels, a television station, and the Krupp ranch—and the Tool Company men, Morgan and Gray. Most of the discussion concerned the pros and cons of sales taxes versus income taxes and the advertising merits of swizzle sticks, matchbooks, and napkins. Maheu did not contribute very

* The report comes from Ovid Demaris' splendid article on Las Vegas which we quoted earlier. Called "You and I Are Very Different from Howard Hughes," it was originally published in *Esquire* in March 1969.

much until the end of the meeting, when he said, "Mr. Hughes wanted me to express his appreciation for last month's effort. . . ."

That was a climax that Holliday could never have provided. Despite the eminence of his position, Holliday's only contact with the Desert Inn penthouse was through the aides: Howard Hughes rarely, if ever, called or wrote to *him*. Not surprisingly, then, Holliday treated Maheu with great circumspection.

It was an odd way to run a business, and difficult for Houston to impose any real control over the burgeoning empire. But that, apparently, was the way The Man wanted it.

After the Frontier deal, a joke went around Las Vegas that Hughes would next buy Caesar's Palace so that he could cancel Frank Sinatra's credit again. In fact, he and Maheu turned their attention to some of the Strip's less illustrious attractions.

First, for $3 million Hughes bought the Castaways, located next door to the Frontier, which offered its customers 230 cheap rooms, low-stake gambling, and splendidly bawdy revues. Next came the Silver Slipper Casino, which, Maheu learned "through confidential sources," a "group from Texas" was anxious to buy. Hughes preempted them by offering $5.36 million. (As we shall see later, the Silver Slipper was destined to make a unique contribution to Nevada's political affairs.)

And then, at the top of Hughes' shopping list, stood the Stardust. Like the Castaways and the Silver Slipper, it was a lower-class joint—or, to use Maheu's description, "the rooms were cheap and they encouraged conventions." There were, however, 1,500 bedrooms and a casino which, thanks to the conventions, did a mouthwatering amount of business. Hughes was prepared to pay what was, even by his standards, a great deal of money for the Stardust. As things turned out, he did not get it, but the negotiations are worth recording because they give some insight into the way Hughes did business. They also demonstrate that gambling is not the only way to make a quick buck in Las Vegas.

The Stardust was owned by the same people from whom Hughes had purchased the Desert Inn: Moe Dalitz and his partners, known corporately as Karat Inc., who had finally decided it was time to get out of the gambling business. That fact became public knowledge and local newspapers speculated that the place would sell for around $40 million. The figure was a little optimistic, but Dalitz—feeling, perhaps, that he had let the Desert Inn go too cheaply—used it as a bargaining lever. He told Maheu that he could not sell the Stardust for less than $40 million without appearing to be a fool.

Hughes saw the point immediately. In a note to Maheu, written on March 17, 1968, he said: "I think, in fact, the public would be very disappointed if the deal comes thru below that [and] I know that the public reaction to this deal concerns Moe more than the money." So, Hughes suggested, they should lie. He would pay around $35 million for the Stardust, but also "guarantee that *nobody,* but nobody, will learn the figure. We will announce the deal at 42-43 million, or any figure Moe prefers, in line with the publicity to date. . . . Please try to sell this to Moe. We can control the issuance of info. concerning the Stardust deal and if we peg it at 43,000,000, which would be better for all concerned, us as well, *nobody* will dispute it. Believe me, I know."

Outflanked on that front, Dalitz was reduced to orthodox bargaining, but once again he found Maheu more than a match. (As was the case during the Desert Inn negotiations, Maheu was continually coached by Hughes. For example, as the Stardust deal was about to be closed, Hughes wrote: "I hope you will make an effort to improve the terms before you accept. Moe expects us to haggle a little over the deal because he remembers the Desert Inn negotiation. I am sure he has a cushion built into his price for last-minute give and take with us.") They finally settled at $30,509,035, which, had it known, the public presumably would have found very disappointing. In addition, Hughes agreed to accept any liabilities the Stardust may have had up to a maximum of $3.5 million, but that still left him with a bargain.

As it happened, all was for naught, because the Justice Department in Washington, which guards against the formation of monopolies, reckoned that Hughes had already acquired enough of the gambling industry. While the Nevada gaming authorities were content to let Hughes buy the Stardust, the Justice Department let it be known that if he did, he might find himself in court, charged with an infraction of the antitrust laws. It was even hinted that if Hughes pressed the point, he might be forced to divest himself of some of his earlier acquisitions. In August 1968 a terse statement was issued: "The Stardust Hotel and the Hughes Tool Company have terminated any existing plans for purchase of the hotel."

It has to be said, however, that for some the abortive deal was not without its rewards. Dalitz and his partners pointed out to Maheu that in anticipation of the sale they had made certain capital expenditures to improve the Stardust, and that they felt some kind of compensation was called for. Eventually, to set things right, Hughes approved a loan to Dalitz of $3 million, at the extremely generous interest rate of three percent.

Dalitz was not the sole beneficiary. The Stardust deal had originally been "packaged" and presented to Maheu by the Washington lawyer, Ed Morgan, who had, of course, played a substantial role in the Desert Inn negotiations. According to Morgan, "I got hold of Bob Maheu and told him there was an indication that the Stardust was going to be sold. And I said, 'Here's the economics of it. Do what you like with it.'"

In return for his efforts, Morgan had expected to receive from Dalitz a "finder's fee" of $500,000. However, when the Justice Department intervened, and when Dalitz was obliged to seek another buyer, he made Morgan an alternative proposition: Instead of the half a million dollars, the lawyer could have an option to acquire ten percent of the Stardust. Morgan would not be required to actually put up any money unless he exercised the option. And if he did not want to exercise it, he could, when the time was right, sell the option—probably for a good deal more than $500,000.

It was an extremely generous proposal, and Morgan accepted. He then decided to share his good fortune with Bob Maheu by offering him a third of the option. Explaining his largesse, Morgan said, "My reason for it was a very simple one—he'd been very generous to me."

Maheu was reluctant, but not very. According to Morgan: "I think, probably, his problem was the possibility of conflict [which he] resolved in his own mind by realizing it wasn't a problem until such time as the option might be exercised." It never was, because Dalitz soon found another buyer for the Stardust, and he asked Morgan to cancel the stock option and revert to the idea of a finder's fee. Morgan—and Maheu—agreed, and on March 6, 1969, Morgan received a check from Karat Inc. for $500,000. "In due course," says Morgan, "I sent Bob Maheu aproximately a third —$150,000." Motivating Morgan was the desire to "do a substantial kindness to him. . . . You'll have to appreciate the kind of relationship that existed, so far as I was concerned, with Bob Maheu. It was not a matter of whether you needed to draw contracts, dot *i*'s and cross *t*'s. It was a gentleman's understanding which I honored."

The Morgan-Maheu relationship was not a one-way street. For his part, Maheu had shown Morgan a "substantial kindness" by recommending that the lawyer be retained by the Hughes Tool Company for $100,000 a year. The retainer was agreed upon in December 1968, and made effective from the beginning of that year.

It would be wrong to leave the impression that Howard Hughes conducted his invasion of the Las Vegas gaming industry entirely without rhyme or reason. Obviously, he had a plan of sorts, although it seems to have consisted of little more than a standing instruction to Maheu and his men to acquire anything they would lay their hands on. What the evidence firmly contradicts is the myth, widely believed at the time, that Hughes was much more than just an entrepreneur out to grab a sizable slice of the action. And, it has to be said, Hughes was not always too fussy about the ethics he employed.

In January 1968 Hughes put pen to paper to write to the media again, this time to announce that he was going to build "the most complete vacation and pleasure complex anywhere in the world."

The "New Sands," to be built alongside the existing one at a cost of $150 million, was going to be forty or fifty stories high and would contain four thousand bedrooms. It all sounded very exciting. "Any guest will simply have to make a supreme effort if he wants to be bored," Hughes wrote. "It is our hope that this hotel will be something completely unique and novel, like nothing anyone has ever seen before, a complete city within itself." One entire floor was going to be devoted to shops, open twenty-four hours a day, seven days a week. Another floor would be dedicated to recreation with, among other things, a bowling alley, an ice-rink, quiet rooms for chess and bridge, and facilities for Ping-Pong. There would also be a first-run movie theater fitted out with projection equipment "so modern it has not even been shown yet to the public in literature or trade publications." As a final touch, there would be an indoor electronic golf course "so skillfully designed that the shots feel just like those outdoors and the spin of the ball in a slice or a hook, is even measured electronically and indicated to the player."

The New Sands, like the SST airport and the promised industrial development, never materialized. It was, according to Maheu, "one big sham," invented partially to keep the natives from becoming restless but largely to fight off the competition.

The competition that consistently concerned Hughes the most was that provided by another entrepreneur every bit as rugged as himself, a man named Kirk Kerkorian. The son of an Armenian-American fruit seller, Kerkorian's origins were drastically different from Hughes', but in many respects their interests were similar.

Young Kirk had dropped out of high school and spent the Depression years hanging around Civilian Conservation Corps camps until he was able to make a few dollars by fixing and reselling old cars. The money he earned was enough to buy some flying lessons and, eventually, get a commercial pilot's license, and he spent World War II instructing U.S. Army pilots and ferrying planes to England for the Royal Air Force. After the war he specialized in fixing and reselling planes rather than cars until 1947, when he had acquired enough capital to begin a charter airline. Los Angeles Air Service became in time Trans International Airlines, which Kerkorian sold in 1967 for $90 million worth of stock in the Transamerica Corporation.

At roughly the same time as Hughes began investing in Las Vegas, so, too, did Kerkorian. For a while he became landlord of Caesar's Palace—the establishment Frank Sinatra abruptly transferred to from the Sands—and he outbid Hughes for Bugsy Siegel's old place, the Flamingo. But what disturbed Hughes most was Kerkorian's plan to build a new hotel-casino, called the International, which would be "the biggest and costliest gambling complex of its kind in Las Vegas."

The International was to be located on Paradise Road, which runs parallel to the Strip and which is, more importantly, the main thoroughfare for traffic coming to Las Vegas from McCarran Airport. Hughes wrote to Maheu: "I have invested 200,000,000 [dollars] in this Strip region and I simply cannot see K [Kerkorian] stand between the airport and our area. . . ."

Hughes therefore decided to announce the "New Sands." According to Maheu, he later admitted that he had never been serious about building it. "Hughes felt that if he made the announcement on the Sands . . . it would make it impossible for Kerkorian to gather the proper financing."

The ploy did not work, and Hughes was obliged to announce that he was "postponing" the New Sands. However, not all was yet lost. Another of Hughes' abiding concerns was to persuade the U.S. government to stop testing nuclear weapons in the Nevada desert. Maheu came up with the idea of pretending to blame the bomb for the postponement of the New Sands—in the hope that Kerkorian might have second thoughts about the International. Hughes was effusive:

"Bob, the more I think about your Kirkorian [sic] strategy, the more I like it! I think the idea of telling him we postponed the 4000 room Sands because of the tests is terrific. We could even say that in addition to the fear I have of actual damage to the high-rise structure, I simply did not want to pour that huge sum of money into the Las Vegas area and virtually put all of my eggs into one basket until I was assured that the tests really would be moved. . . .

"Now, I think you should tell K I at no time announced to anyone that our reason for cancelling the hotel was related to the bomb tests. . . . However, now with the resumption of testing (and at an even greater level) I feel it is my firm duty to tell K the whole story."

That ploy did not work, either, and construction work on the International went ahead. Still Hughes would not give up. At that time, he thought he was going to be allowed to acquire the Stardust, and he proposed to Maheu that it be used in a last-ditch effort to stop Kerkorian.

"Bob—Please clear the decks and fasten your belt etc., because I have a blockbuster. . . . Suppose we offer to K. that we will turn the S/dust over to him (on what ever kind of deal it takes) and we will buy from him his Int. Hotel property plus the bldg. [building] in progress at his cost, agreeing not to complete it."

The money for this bizarre exercise was going to come from the $200 million or so which Hughes no longer planned to spend on the SST airport he had promised. "What is beginning to seep thru to me," he told Maheu, "is that if we can take the Int. Hotel out for less than the cost of the airport, we are ahead." Hughes realized that stopping the International in mid-construction might cause something of a fuss— after all, the city fathers were looking to Hughes for development—and so, "we will probably have to persuade K to stop it gradually before he delivers it to us.

"I know one thing—I may not live to see that airport completed. I would [instead] like to spend that effort in removing the International in one way or another and then spend the rest of my life under just a little bit less tension."

Given Kerkorian's personality—he is an outgoing man who, as the *National Observer* once put it, lives in a house with wife and kids and talks to strangers—it seems unlikely that he would have accepted this strange deal. But in any event, the idea collapsed because Hughes was not allowed to acquire the Stardust. Work on the International continued and, located as it was next-door to the Las Vegas convention center, if threatened to do serious injury to the Strip's business. There was only one thing left for Hughes to do: If he could not beat Kerkorian, he would have to join him.

Slap opposite the site of the International stood Las Vegas' white elephant—the thirty-one-story Landmark Tower, which, as of September 1968, had been completed for two years but because of lawsuits and colossal financial problems, had never opened its doors. Hughes offered to buy the place, for around $17 million, and to pay all the Landmark's numerous creditors (who included the Teamsters Union) in full, which was generous, but also sound tactics. The Justice Department remained opposed to Hughes' acquiring any more casinos, but found it difficult to counter the argument that, in the case of the Landmark, Hughes should be seen as an angel of mercy. In Washington, D.C., Nevada Senator Howard Cannon, stressed the needs of "the unemployed and the small businessmen" who would benefit if the hotel opened. Hughes was the only angel in sight, and, said Cannon, blocking the sale would be completely contrary to "the purpose of the antitrust division, whose responsibility is to protect small business."

Actually, it was not quite true that Hughes was the only potential provider of salvation. Maheu discovered "from a thoroughly reliable and confidential source" that a fast-food chain called Denny's was contemplating making an offer for the Landmark "which will top ours by well over $1 million." As Maheu pointed out to Hughes, "Needless to say if such an offer were made our posture vis-a-vis justice [department] as to the failing business doctrine would go out of the window." Fortunately, however, Maheu's source was in a position "to tell Denny's management to 'lay off' without our being identified in any way whatsoever."

Hughes got the Landmark and Maheu announced that it would open, with something of a bang, on July 1, 1969. Kirk Kerkorian announced that the International would open, also with something of a bang, on July 2. Those who were there generally agree that the contest ended in a draw.

It took a while, but in time most people in Las Vegas lost their illusions about Hughes, and none more so than Hank Greenspun, the publisher of the Las Vegas *Sun*. Greenspun would probably now be the first to admit that he went overboard in his welcome for Hughes, but at one time he sincerely believed that Hughes would be able to drive the Mob out of Las Vegas—a crusade to which Greenspun has devoted much of his career as a newspaperman.

It also has to be said that Greenspun was temporarily blinded by his early exposure to Hughes' great wealth. Besides running the *Sun*, Greenspun had, since 1955, owned KLAS-TV, the Las Vegas affiliate of the Columbia Broadcasting System (CBS). Says Greenspun: "Right after Mr. Hughes appeared in Las Vegas, I began getting calls that he'd like the station to stay open a little longer, because he liked to watch television between midnight and six o'clock in the morning, and we used to go off the air at one o'clock. The first conversations were could we keep the station open a little longer? And I said it would be uneconomical for us to do so. Then I think I prolonged it for another hour or so, just to please the man. Then they wanted to know if we'd put on Westerns or whether we'd put on airplane pictures. And I said we can't afford those type of pictures. So this went on for months and months, you know. I would get calls from Maheu and I would get calls from [Richard] Gray. And I'd get calls from Hughes' aides to actually change the format of the television station so that Hughes could watch it all night long. Finally, I'd say, in exasperation, I'd say, Why doesn't he buy the damned thing and run it the way he pleases?"

He did, without quibble, for $3.65 million.

Not unnaturally, Greenspun was interested in doing more deals with Hughes, and he began negotiations through Maheu to sell him the Paradise Valley Country Club and Golf Course in Las Vegas, which the publisher owned, along with 3,600 acres of land surrounding it. The two sides settled on a price of $7 million, but there was an obstacle in the way of the sale in that, to refinance his newspaper, Greenspun had taken out a mortgage on the property; obviously it would have to be paid off before the title to the land could be transferred to Hughes.

The problem was solved through a $4 million loan which Hughes made to Greenspun on fairly generous terms, enabling him to pay off the mortgage. All was now set: Hughes would buy the Paradise Valley club and the land and Greenspun would use part of the proceeds to pay back the loan. An agreement was signed—then, quite suddenly, Hughes reneged.

The excuse put forward to Greenspun was that Hughes had discovered that the golf course was watered with recycled effluent water—as indeed most of Las Vegas' golf courses are—and that he was perturbed that "everybody would be contaminated by the germs."

Greenspun could not agree to a total cancellation of the deal—which would have left him with a $4 million loan that would "have taken me a hundred years to pay off"—but he did eventually agree to a complicated compromise. Hughes would buy the golf course after all, for $2.25 million, if Greenspun and his wife would promise to manage it for two years "so his executives wouldn't have to go out and get contaminated." Hughes would not, however, buy the 3,600 acres of surrounding land, but he would agree to new terms on the $4 million loan, giving Greenspun a much longer period to pay it off.

Accordingly, a new loan agreement was drawn up in which Greenspun pledged as security his newspaper and just about everything else he owned. It was pretty straightforward except for one thing: Hughes said he did not want Greenspun's media competitor, the Las Vegas *Review-Journal,* to know about the loan, so it was not formally recorded.

Three years later, when Greenspun no longer regarded Hughes as Las Vegas' great benefactor, and was saying so in the columns of the *Sun,* Hughes allegedly attempted to enforce the terms of the *first* loan agreement—which, according to Greenspun, was supposed to have been torn up.

"I was on my way to the Middle East at the time, and I had to get off the plane at Kennedy Airport because they were going to sell me out in seven days, including my newspaper and all my land and everything else," Greenspun has testified. He retaliated with a lawsuit against Hughes—at this writing, still unresolved—for $142 million.

5: HOW TO BUY
AN AIRLINE

The covetous man pines in plenty, like Tantalus up to the chin in water, and yet thirsty.

—Thomas Adams

Nicholas Bez, Sr., Air West's chairman of the board, its chief executive officer, and its majority stockholder, was a first-generation immigrant for whom the American Dream had come true. There was some confusion among Hughes' men about Nick Bez's origins (memo to Hughes, July 30, 1968: "Bez . . . came to this country from Hungary at age 15 . . ."; memo to Hughes, July 31, 1968: ". . . Bez, born in Yugoslavia 75 years ago . . .") but no doubt about his abilities as a rugged and pioneering entrepreneur. As Maheu put it to Hughes, Bez was a diamond in the rough: "Although he does not have too good a command of the English language, I can assure you that his mother did not bring up a stupid boy. . . ."

Born in 1895 in a stone house overlooking the Adriatic Sea, Bez was the eldest of six children in a family which scratched a living from a small vineyard and from the produce of a few olive and fig trees. At the age of fifteen he left Yugoslavia (not Hungary) and headed for Alaska, arriving there virtually penniless. (Just how poor was also in dispute: Maheu told Hughes that Bez had $12 in his pocket when he landed; another storyteller put the figure at $1.50.) Alaska would not then have been everybody's idea of the land of opportunity, but with a coastline almost four thousand miles long it did have one vast resource: fish. Young Nick became by turns a fisherman, a fishing-boat captain, a fishing-boat owner, a fishing-fleet owner, and, ultimately, a canner of fish. Through that progression he also became increasingly prosperous until, in 1931, he was able to divert both time and money into founding an airline, Alaska Southern Airways. Five years later he sold that modest but successful concern to Pan American Airways and, on the strength of the profits, moved south to the United States proper * and specifically to Seattle, Washington. For a while Bez reconcentrated all of his resources on the fishing business—founding, among other things, the Peter Pan Seafoods Corporation—but in 1946 he decided to take a second crack at the regional airline business.

It would be hard to overstate the importance of the role the airplane played in the development of the western United States after the end of World War II. Ill-served by railroads, the western states relied more heavily on air travel to link its large but isolated centers of population than perhaps any region in the world. Fed by that need, local carriers such as Nick Bez's West Coast Airlines sprouted and flourished dur-

* Alaska did not become a state until 1959, although the territory had been a possession since 1867 when the U.S. purchased it from Russia for about two cents an acre.

ing the 1940s and 1950s. Those were good times to run a little airline: Thousands of war-surplus Dakotas (DC-3's) were on the market at knockdown prices, along with war-surplus pilots and mechanics. But whatever the legend, even venerable DC-3's could not go on forever, and by the early 1960s many small operators, including West Coast, were in trouble. With the introduction of jet airliners, the cost of replacing even a modest fleet soared beyond the means of most little airlines. Yet, without jets, they could not hope to long survive the competition provided by larger carriers on the major intercity routes. The only solutions to the dilemma were to sell out or merge, and in 1960 Bez went looking for a partner.

Pacific Airlines, based in San Francisco, was in much the same position as Bez's West Coast, but its routes were potentially more lucrative. Combined, the two airlines' revenues might have been able to withstand the cost of buying and maintaining jets, and with that in mind, Bez bought out two-thirds of Pacific's shares. Unfortunately, before doing so, he neglected the formality of seeking permission from the Civil Aeronautics Board (CAB). The board, a government agency, regulates the affairs of U.S. airlines—from deciding what routes they can fly to how much they can charge. The CAB also regulates the ownership of airlines, and lacking sanction from the board for his takeover of Pacific, Bez was obliged to give up control.

At least, Bez *appeared* to do so. The new majority owner of Pacific Airlines was a group of diverse citizens made up of an investment banker, a New York lawyer, and four Seattle businessmen. The deal was done with borrowed money secured by notes which Bez at least partially guaranteed. (With appropriate humor, the group called itself SETON—which is "notes" spelled backward.) As a result there was close if informal cooperation between West Coast and Pacific and, eventually, another attempt at marriage.

In June 1967 Pacific and West Coast announced, this time with all due decorum, an intended merger. The trouble was, the CAB might still not approve because neither airline appeared to be particularly well run and, as a general principle, the board tends to believe that two mediocre airlines joined together will equal one bad one. What was needed to make the deal work was a third airline, one with solid management credentials, which could be persuaded to form a trinity.

Bonanza Airlines certainly fitted that bill. Its management was good and so, particularly, were the extensive aircraft maintenance facilities at its base in Phoenix, Arizona. What Bonanza lacked, from July of 1967, was the services of Robert Henry, its key executive for fifteen years, who was persuaded quite suddenly to become president of Pacific. Faced with that loss; Bonanza's management agreed to contemplate a three-way merger, and negotiations began in San Francisco a month later. The resulting agreement, reached in surprisingly short order, was the formation of Air West.

On paper the deal looked impressive, and the CAB gave its approval with little hesitation. The merger became effective on April 17—making Nick Bez, overnight, chairman of one of the largest local airlines in the U.S.—and Air West officially took to the air, with high hopes, on July 1.

It was, from the start, an unmitigated disaster.

The committee which set out to design a horse and came up with a camel could at least claim to have incorporated a useful feature or two. That's more than can be said for the committee that designed Air West. It was made up of twenty-four members—twelve from Bonanza and six each from Pacific and West Coast—who divided into factions, based on old loyalties, that could not agree on how to do almost anything. The supreme example of the inevitable result was a fiasco that became known as the "July 4 massacre."

The day Air West began service to eighty cities in eight U.S. states, Canada, and later Mexico was also the day it introduced a spanking new computer system. It was designed to handle passenger reservations and flight planning; it was supposed to keep track of the whereabouts of planes and crews; it was supposed to monitor cargo shipments, fuel requirements, supplies of food, and even the company's personnel schedules. The trouble was, it did not work.

94

Larry Decker, Air West's vice-president for marketing, wanted to but could never forget what followed. "We actually had our people running out to meet a flight, opening the door and asking, 'What flight are you and where are you from?'"

The computer system designed by IBM had been given a trial run during which it seemed to work well. On that premise, Air West's directors had decided to scrap the communications networks that the three airlines had used before the merger, leaving Air West with no backup. To make things worse, they had, with supreme overconfidence, chosen to launch the new airline at what was the busiest time of the year for air travel, and compounded that by running a large advertising campaign which had stimulated a forty-percent increase in reservations.

The July 4 holiday weekend was pandemonium. "We did not have time to tell the public what the problem was, or even to explain it to our own people," said Decker.

IBM sent about twenty experts to San Francisco to put the system right, but although they worked around the clock they still could not find the problem. The machine would occasionally tantalize the humans working on it by giving signs of recovery, only to fail once again.

Meanwhile, at airports in Arizona, Alberta, British Columbia, California, Idaho, Montana, Nevada, Oregon, Utah, and Washington, Air West arrived early or late or not at all. Passengers with confirmed reservations turned up at check-in desks to discover that Air West had never heard of them and, more often than not, were sent to a departure gate to find no plane. Indeed, the service was so bad and the schedules so chaotic that Air West became known, universally, as Air Worst.

There were, of course, lots of jokes. Senator Warren G. Magnuson, chairman of the powerful Senate Commerce Committee, explained to a luncheon audience in Goldendale, Washington, why Vice-President Hubert Humphrey had been late for the dedication of a dam on the nearby Columbia River. "The vice president was up and waiting at 8 a.m., but he was waiting for an airplane from Air West. I guess many of you know the answer to that." They did. The laughter took several minutes to subside.

The situation was not at all funny for Air West's directors or its nearly four thousand employees. It took IBM three weeks to cure the computer malfunction (the cause remained a mystery). The financial consequences of the chaotic start were staggering for the new airline. Within a month of the launching Air West was, according to Bank of America, in a "precarious situation." Through loans made to Pacific Airlines before the merger, the bank had a large stake in the new airline, and by August it was receiving hourly reports on the financial deterioration. The bank was also getting frequent calls from Shell Oil, which was worried that the bills for aviation fuel might not be paid. And the members of the Air West board were "at each other's throats."

Nick Bez led the flight to panic. Air West had been his concept and he had been "totally in love" with it. Now, four weeks or so later, he was visibly ill, and willing to sell his share of the airline to anyone. But who could possibly want to buy it?

Las Vegas and the rest of Nevada depended on Air West for service to more than fifty cities and, obviously, the collapse of the airline, which seemed imminent, would have had serious repercussions for the city. The deepening crisis therefore received considerable coverage in the local newspapers, and undoubtedly one of the most avid readers of the reports, published almost daily, was Hughes. Earlier in the year, in an attempt to get back into the airline business, Hughes had courted Western Airlines, a solid regional carrier based in Los Angeles, but the negotiations had come to nothing. Air West, in desperate need of help, was a more promising prospect, and in July, Hughes told Maheu to "determine if perhaps this entity might be for sale." There was, as always when Hughes wanted to buy anything, the need to be discreet: "Bear in mind not a word of this must leak out. Bob, I assure you that if my name is linked with Air West, even in

96

the most nebulous way, that stock will shoot up on the market like a rocket."

Maheu began by looking up the names of Air West's board of directors but recognized only one—Patrick J. Hillings—as someone he knew reasonably well. As it happened, Hillings, a former Republican congressman from California, was not in his home state at the time, but in Miami attending the Republican National Convention. Because speed was almost as important as discretion, Maheu mentioned the problem to John Meier, Hughes' scientific adviser, who was a friend of Don Nixon, the brother of the President-to-be. Nixon was in Miami and just might know how to reach Hillings. He did (on the strength of making the contact, Don Nixon would later claim, to no avail, that Hughes owed him a substantial finder's fee) and Hillings recommended that Maheu should approach Nick Bez. He would, he said, be happy to make the introductions.

By the time Maheu and Bez met for the first time on July 31, the seventy-two-year-old Air West chairman looked to be a very sick man. He was flushed, short of breath, and tired easily. Nevertheless, the meeting went on for four hours, because although Bez was only too willing to see Hughes as the owner of Air West, there was a serious conflict as to how that might be achieved. Putting it bluntly, Bez simply wanted out. He suggested that Hughes buy his shares, which amounted to about ten percent of the outstanding stock, and then go on to buy whatever was available on the open market.* Nothing could have been further from what Hughes had in mind. He would later regret it—"God! How I wish I had taken Mr. Bez's stock at 15 dollars a share and not even talked about 100%. That is when all of our troubles started"—but Hughes' instructions to Maheu at the time were to acquire Air West lock, stock, and barrel or not at all.

In order for Hughes to succeed, it would be neces-

* After the merger, Air West had issued 3,727,000 shares of common stock which were traded on both the American Exchange in New York and the Pacific Stock Exchange in San Francisco.

sary, as a first step, for the board of directors to recommend such a deal to Air West's shareholders and the problem for Bez was whether he could deliver a sufficient number of the board's votes. One obstacle, of course, was that the members of the board were "at each other's throats." A good deal of that hostility was directed toward Bez, who was "a very difficult man to work with." On a more rational level, many of the directors believed that, given time, Air West could become not only viable, but extremely profitable. (That was exactly the advice that Hughes had received from his own private source. The Lockheed Aircraft Company had hoped to sell Air West four or five of its TriStar jumbo jets, and in that cause the marketing department had prepared a confidential report on Air West's prospects for Lockheed's president, Dan Haughton. A Lockheed executive, Jack Real, had obtained a copy of the report, "without telling anybody why I want it," and had sent the contents to Hughes. Real later retired from Lockheed and joined the Hughes organization as a "special assistant." He also became, in time, a director of Hughes Airwest.)

Despite the difficulties, Bez agreed to begin sounding out his fellow directors, and Maheu predicted to Hughes that control could be acquired "very quickly" and "without too much difficulty."

Hughes had it in mind to pay the shareholders *more* than the market value of Air West's stock. That is not to say that he intended to pay more than the stock was worth. As he explained his scheme to Maheu, "This plan necessitates that the stock edge downward with the existing continuous bad news and then that we come along with a spectacular offer to pay the stockholders in liquidation a price substantially above the market. Any rise in the market before our offer will adversely affect the plan."

The figure Hughes proposed was around twenty dollars a share—three dollars more than the depressed market price. Nick Bez was hoping for a little more and bargained the price up to $21.50, but there Hughes stuck. By then Bez had allowed some, but by no means all, of his fellow directors to learn what was going on, and they agreed to meet with Maheu in

Seattle for negotiations on Friday, August 9. The meeting turned out to be a little more than the formality Maheu had anticipated.

On Thursday evening the twelve Bonanza directors learned for the first time, "through the grapevine," what Bez was up to. When the Seattle meeting began the next afternoon, a lawyer representing the Bonanza faction was on hand to express their reaction. "Howard, you won't believe it but this bastard attorney from Bonanza is raising holy hell with Bez," Maheu reported to Hughes. "He has served him notice that he will vigorously oppose the deal at $21½ before the board, the stockholders and before the C.A.B."

The Bonanza group believed that selling Air West at that price would be like giving it away. Maheu thought they were "out of their minds" and told Hughes: "The problem comes from . . . Frank Beer, the legal counsel to the Bonanza group."

Beer caused the meeting to go on until almost midnight, and kept Maheu literally on the trot, telephoning progress reports to Hughes at the Desert Inn. Indeed, Maheu excused himself from the meeting so many times, Hughes became concerned that the Air West people might get the idea that his alter ego could not function on his own. Maheu reassured him that "at no occasion have I given the impression of contacting you back and forth."

Bez, for one, could not stand the pace and left the meeting before agreement could be reached. "He apologized for doing so," Maheu told Hughes, "but as you know he was quite sick earlier in the week and on instructions from his doctor he went home and went to bed."

Despite the objections of the Bonanza group, the Friday-night meeting did reach a tenuous accord, and during the weekend Maheu and Bez worked on the details and on the composition of a public announcement to be made on Monday. To help them in that endeavor Maheu was able to call on the services of a New York lawyer named Chester Davis. Of all the formidable advocates retained over the years to defend Howard Hughes' interests, Chester Davis was unquestionably the most formidable.

Born Caesar Simon in Rome in 1910, Davis was the product of an Italian mother and a French-Algerian father. When Mr. Simon died, his widow took her young family to the United States and in due course married Chester Davis Senior. Chester Junior became a graduate of Harvard Law School and a naturalized citizen, in that order, and embarked on a legal career of considerable distinction. In 1961 Davis, by then an established partner in the eminent New York law firm of Simpson, Thacher and Bartlett, was assigned to run the firm's biggest case—indeed, the biggest case in the history of U.S. civil litigation—representing the defense in the matter of *TWA* v. *Hughes*. Subsequently, Davis discovered a "conflict of interest" within Simpson and company in that the firm occasionally acted for parties who were, in the TWA case, on the plaintiff's side. Davis resolved the conflict by setting up his own law firm, which assumed responsibility for Hughes' defense. From that point onward Chester Davis and the multifaceted legal interests of Howard Hughes became synonymous.

At times, it seemed as though Davis' obdurate handling of the TWA case would end in total victory for the airline (although, as we shall see, he was vindicated by the final outcome). But in other areas Chester's tenacity and legal cunning produced some remarkable dividends for Hughes. One example of what might be termed his novel approach to the law was Davis' Joe DiMaggio Bat Theory, which went like this: Davis believed that Hughes' privacy was sacrosanct—"if he doesn't want to see somebody, why the hell should he?" —and, further, that the facts about his life could be protected like a commercial property—"Look at it this way. If you are going to bring out a bat and put Joe DiMaggio's name on it, then you have to pay DiMaggio a royalty."

Davis was not, of course, interested in collecting royalties, but he was determined to prevent others from doing so and to that end came up with the idea of, in effect, patenting Howard Hughes, much like Hughes Senior had patented the oil-drilling bit. In 1965 a Nevada corporation called Rosemont Enterprises Inc. paid an alleged $15 million for what it claimed was "the sole exclusive right to use or publish [Hughes'] name, likeness, personality, life story or incidents therein." All of the directors of Rosemont, save one, were directors of the Hughes Tool Company; the exception, Chester Davis, served as secretary-treasurer, and he also provided the corporation with accommodation at his Manhattan office. During Hughes' lifetime, Rosemont never actually got around to exploiting its "exclusive right," but it did deter all but the most obstinate from publishing books about the reclusive billionaire.

When in August 1968 Davis turned his talents to constructing a legal document that would reflect the progress of the Air West negotiations, he faced a sizable problem. Clearly, Hughes' proposed takeover could not remain a secret any longer, and yet because of the Bonanza faction's strenuous opposition, there was nothing very concrete to announce. Chester Davis, however, is rarely stuck for words.

On Monday, August 12, the world learned that Nick Bez had signed—the day before—an agreement to "use his best efforts to effect a sale of assets and transfer of the business of Air West to Hughes Tool Company" at a price of approximately twenty-two dollars a share. On the face of it, the "best efforts agreement," as it came to be called, was a meaningless piece of legalese (what, for example, constitutes "best efforts"?), but it did contain a clause which, in years to come, was to assume almighty significance. (The clause said that Hughes' offer was subject to the proviso that if and when the deal was consummated, Air West's value must be no less than seventy-five percent of its net worth as of July 31, 1968. The agreement did not specify what the airline's net worth had been in July. Neither did it say what would happen if the proviso was not met.)

The agreement also acted as the catalyst for a formal declaration of war from not only the Bonanza group but also some of the Pacific Airlines faction. After Bez, the two biggest Air West stockholders were Edmund Converse (Bonanza) and David Grace (Pacific), who immediately announced that handing over the airline to Hughes would "not be in the best interests of Air West, its stockholders, the traveling public or the public in general." They promised Hughes one hell of a fight.

Air West's president, Robert Henry, went even further by predicting that Hughes would be the "inevitable" loser. Whatever else happened, he said, the CAB in Washington, D.C., would never approve Hughes' takeover because, "the board has had many occasions in the past to deal with Hughes Tool Company ownership of airlines and generally indicated that it was not successful and not in the public interest."

Henry and his allies would not, perhaps, have been so confident if they had known to just what lengths Hughes was prepared to go.

Jimmy "the Greek" Snyder is fond of telling the story of how he helped Howard Hughes win the battle for Air West.

Besides being the self-acclaimed "oddsmaker to the nation," the Greek also ran a public relations and publicity firm called Information Unlimited in Las Vegas which, in August 1968, got a new client. Snyder, who knew both Robert and Peter Maheu slightly, was having dinner at the Sands Hotel one night when he was invited to the Maheu table. In time, the conversation turned to Air West and Bob Maheu asked Snyder for any ideas that might help the takeover bid. Snyder said he would "put a pencil to it."

Twenty-four hours later, Information Unlimited submitted a written proposal to Maheu for a publicity campaign, along with a list of "political and business leaders who might support a Hughes takeover." Maheu was impressed, but wondered if Snyder could "produce on this" by the end of the year, when Hughes' offer for Air West would expire. The Greek said he could—for $50,000. When Maheu hesitated, the Greek—his old gambling instincts instantly welling to the surface—offered to play double or nothing: If Hughes got Air West by December 31, Snyder would get $100,000; if not, Snyder would get nothing. Maheu eventually decided to settle for the more conventional business proposal, which was, as things turned out, just as well—Snyder would have won his bet, albeit by the skin of his teeth. But then, of course, the Greek did know a thing or two about odds.

He was born Jimmy Synodinos in 1919 in the steelworkers' town of Steubenville, Ohio. After Jimmy's mother had been murdered, the family moved for a while to the Aegean island of Kios, but in 1932 Mr. Synodinos remarried and they returned to Steubenville. It was, according to the Greek, a wide-open town. There were eleven bookmaking joints, a pinball machine in every candy store, and, on Water Street, you could get laid for a couple bucks—"and that was expensive stuff." Steubenville in the Depression was also a very tough town, and for children like Jimmy the only education that counted was learning the art of survival. Jimmy learned fast.

He started in business as a scavenger, finding old bottles, newspapers, and anything else of value, which he traded in at the local junkyard. One day the junkman offered him an old bicycle frame. Piece by piece, Jimmy assembled spare parts into a complete bike, making it irresistible by adding a bright coat of blue paint. All his friends wanted to borrow the bike, which Jimmy let them do for a few days until he had a captive market, when the free rides abruptly ceased. From then on, it cost twenty cents a day to ride Jimmy's bike. He patched together eight more in the next four months and the daily take went up to $1.60.

When the bike-renting business went into decline—some of the customers forgot to return the bikes—Jimmy became a bookmaker's runner, which gave him the opportunity to make a judicious study of the *Racing Form*. It was not long before the Greek was placing bets himself and winning often enough to become a full-time professional gambler. In 1956 he moved to Las Vegas and discovered that there was more money to be made assessing the odds than playing them. The Greek would and has set the odds on just about anything from the outcome of baseball games, fights, political elections, and football matches to the chances of a convicted murderer, Caryl Chessman, going to the gas chamber. (Snyder made Chessman a four-to-nine favorite to go, which he did.)

103

Information Unlimited, Snyder's PR company, could be said to be in the gambling business, too. Its greatest coup was to persuade the aging male chauvinist Bobby Riggs to present a giant Sugar Daddy candy stick to Billie Jean King during their "battle of the sexes" tennis match at the Houston Astrodome in August 1973. Sugar Daddy's manufacturer, Nabisco, was prepared to pay Riggs and King $15,000 each to take part in this brief pantomime. The gamble was whether the network television cameras, which were covering the tennis match, would also cover the presentation ceremony. They did, and according to the Greek, Nabisco got $1 million of publicity for an investment of $30,000. Sugar Daddy's sales went up by nearly thirty percent.

Nothing quite so vulgar was planned for the Air West campaign. Snyder's job was to drum up public support for Hughes' takeover bid, and he reckoned to do that by generating a crusade to "save" Air West. The gamble in this case was whether enough influential people could be persuaded to join the cause.

Alan Bible, Nevada's senior senator, had praised and supported the three-airline merger which had created Air West and there was, therefore, some doubt as to whether he might, after such precious little time, support its takeover. Snyder spoke to Bible by telephone at around noon on September 9, and a note which Information Unlimited sent to Maheu reflects the conversation: "Senator Bible agreed that he would make a statement. Air Line service within Nevada must improve. It makes sense for Hughes to acquire Air West. . . Then Bible said he wanted to talk to someone in Hughes' organization to determine details and status of negotiations. . . ."

Two days later, after talking to Bob Maheu, the senator approved a statement "fully endorsing the Hughes offer of purchase," which, he said, represented "an excellent solution to what has become a deplorable situation." The statement was hand-delivered to Information Unlimited, where it was wrapped up in some catchy prose and issued as a "news release" on September 12. The same day, by kind coincidence, Bible took an Air West flight from Reno to Las Vegas which managed to arrive three hours late, adding a certain piquancy to his words.

The Las Vegas *Sun* gave Bible's statement generous treatment with a banner headline: "BIBLE BLASTS AIR WEST/URGES HUGHES DEAL OKAY." The *Sun* readers were not told, however, that Bible's statement had been initiated and disseminated by a PR company paid by Hughes. The newspaper, or at least its executive editor, Bryn Armstrong, knew: Information Unlimited's "news release" was actually written by Armstrong, who was moonlighting for Snyder for $135 a week.

Bryn Armstrong also won support for the Air West crusade from Nevada's second senator, Howard Cannon, a particularly powerful ally because he was chairman of the Senate's aviation subcommittee. Armstrong's 1968 diary shows that he first contacted a member of Cannon's staff on September 5: "located James Joyce in Reno—Cannon out of country—would push for Hughes support statement soon as returned." On September 16: "4:30 P.M.—met with Jim Joyce (2 hours) and went over entire Hughes presentation and background for statement by Sen. Cannon." Finally, on September 18: "12:00 lunch with Jim Joyce to block out Cannon statement on AW [Air West]."

Information Unlimited found yet another senatorial ally in Warren Magnuson of Washington, who is chairman of the Senate Commerce Committee, which as the senator pointed out, "exercises jurisdiction over transportation matters in the U.S." On September 30 Magnuson sent a letter to the chairman of the CAB calling for an inquiry into Air West and "timely implementation of such remedial action as is consistent." A copy of the letter was given to the press.

Meanwhile, other less eminent but still influential voices, egged on by Information Unlimited, joined the cause. Clark County Assemblywoman Eileen Brookman urged Air West's stockholders to approve the Hughes offer. She dictated her statement over the telephone to Snyder's office, where Armstrong composed a news release. At about the same time, the Mineral County Businessmen's Association (Mineral County is in west-central Nevada) and the managing director of the Airline Passengers Association supported Hughes' bid for Air West. So, too, did the president of the Air Line Employees Association and Las Vegas Mayor Oran Gragson.

There was also a plan to form a "group of prominent southern Nevada residents" which would vote for Hughes, as it were. Information Unlimited actually wrote a press release announcing the event which quoted a nonexistent Joe Smith, "spokesman for the group." The release was never issued because those "prominent southern Nevadans" who were approached refused to play ball.

Jimmy the Greek's role in all of this—and the existence of his retainer with Hughes, paid by the Tool Company at the rate of $12,000 a month—was not public knowledge. Officially, Hughes' public relations, such as they were, continued to be handled by his longstanding PR consultants, Carl Byoir Associates, who dealt with most of the inquiries from journalists concerning the bid for Air West.

The politicians who lent their names to the campaign, of course, had to know that Snyder was working for Hughes. No doubt they sincerely believed that a Hughes takeover would be beneficial for Air West. But there is also no doubt that some of them, at least, were not in a position to be thought of as totally unbiased observers, because they had received considerable amounts of money from Hughes in the form of political contributions.

It is impossible to be precise about which politicians received money or to say exactly how much they got. As we shall show later on, the Hughes-Nevada Operations distributed bundles of hundred-dollar bills to politicians as prolifically as a Baptist preacher dispenses sermons in Selma, Alabama, on a Sunday. What is certain is that senators Bible and Cannon were among those who, during their campaigns to stay in office, could count on considerable financial help from Hughes.

When Bible ran for reelection in 1968, Hughes sent written instructions to Maheu that the senator should receive a campaign contribution of $50,000. When

106

Cannon ran for reelection in 1970, Hughes told Maheu to give him $70,000.*

Those Air West directors who opposed the Hughes takeover became known, naturally enough, as "the dissidents." Privately, they had a better name for themselves: the SHB Committee. Depending on their level of indignation at any particular time, SHB stood for Stop Hughes' Bid or Screw Hughes Blind.

The dissidents were led by Air West's vice-chairman (and former Bonanza chairman) Edmund Converse and numbered twelve, exactly half of the board. In theory, that was enough to produce a stalemate, but at the end of the day, it would be up to Air West's stockholders to decide whether Hughes' bid should be accepted. The major problem for the dissidents was how to combat the effects of Jimmy the Greek's publicity campaign, which with its tempo and volume could hardly have failed to make some impression on the shareholders. And in that endeavor they were, they claim, sorely handicapped by their inability to obtain almost any factual information about Air West's financial condition. For its headquarters Air West used what had been the offices of Pacific Airlines near San Francisco, and the HQ was staffed, primarily, by former Pacific employees. Because the Pacific faction of the board was in the main supporting Bez, the HQ had to be regarded as enemy territory.

Information was not the only thing that the dissidents were deprived of. They also had nowhere to hold strategy-planning meetings except for bars and restaurants, where, according to a Maheu report to Hughes, they were spied upon by "operatives" disguised as waiters, who tried to discover exactly how they intended to SHB.

Meanwhile, Jack Hooper—the former Los Angeles policeman in charge of Hughes' personal security—

* Bible has acknowledged to us that his 1968 campaign received a "very substantial contribution" from Hughes, "somewhere in the range of $50,000." He won re-election, but, surprisingly, resigned his seat "for personal reasons" in 1974. We have attempted to discuss any contributions Hughes made with Senator Cannon, but both he and his campaign treasurer have refused to talk to us.

ordered inquiries to be made into the backgrounds of the twelve dissidents. The flavor of those investigations is perhaps best illustrated by one of the reports which Hooper received on a dissident, George Sage: "Absolutely no criminal record, nor contact with the underworld. His closest friend from college days is ELI DONDIS of 854 Madison Street, Fall River (phone: 672-5332). He (Dondis) works for Wolfson, Zalkind (Brokerage) 105 Banks Street, Fall River. They drink together. No evidence that Sage has any connection with . . . Converse, Grace or Henry [the three principal dissident directors] . . . He is considered to be quite wealthy, has no need for money at the present time. . . ."

In that kind of atmosphere, Air West's board of directors met to hear a formal presentation of Hughes' offer from Chester Davis. When the board did vote, it inevitably split down the middle: twelve for the takeover and twelve against. It was now up to the stockholders to decide.

The laws which govern every publicly owned company insist that proposals of such magnitude as a company's takeover should be voted upon at a special meeting of the shareholders, and Air West's board announced that the necessary meeting would be held at the Thunderbird Hotel, Millbrae, California, on December 27, 1968. In practice, it was unlikely that many of the stockholders, scattered throughout America, would personally attend. But those who did not want to take the trouble could still register their votes—one vote for each share—by signing a proxy. Because Air West's board was evenly divided, it could not offer the shareholders any recommendation as to whether Hughes' offer should be accepted or rejected. There were, however, no such restraints on the directors as individuals, and the opposing factions both lobbied shareholders furiously.

Proxy solicitation material must, according to law, be written with great care. In particular, those supporting the takeover had a legal duty to point out all of the circumstances surrounding Hughes' offer and the likely consequences of its acceptance. In some respects, the Securities and Exchange Commission (SEC) alleges, the pro-Hughes forces fell short of those requirements.

To begin with, the pro-Hughes solicitation material was sent out under Nick Bez's name—"I am writing you this letter, which has been produced at my expense, to present my view . . ."—without the disclosure that it had been prepared by Hughes' men: "Dear Bob [Maheu] Enclosed is a copy of the letter for Bez's signature as I felt it should be revised. As you will note from *your* original, the changes were minor but ones which I feel give the letter more appeal to the average stockholder. Cordially, Jimmy Snyder." (Emphasis added.)

More seriously, the material was—again according to the SEC—"false and misleading" in implying that the shareholders would get around twenty-two dollars a share. The crucial factor in deciding exactly how much the shareholders would get was the "net worth" clause which had been inserted into Nick Bez's "best efforts agreement." The material did point out that Air West was losing money and warned that if that situation *continued,* the "net worth" clause might not be met. What it did not say was that the airline's value had *already* fallen far below the minimum figure stipulated in the proviso.

On July 31, 1968, Air West's net worth had been approximately $21 million. Hughes' offer of twenty-two dollars a share depended on the net worth being, at the time of the takeover, not less than $15.75 million. By early December 1968, when the proxy solicitation material was sent out, Air West's net worth had slumped to $12.25 million.

One reason for the financial decline had been a catastrophic loss of public confidence in Air West following the breakdown of the computer. The publicity campaign had not, of course, helped matters. As a result, Air West's business had fallen off to such an extent that it had run short of cash. It desperately needed an injection of money to keep the operation going until, hopefully, public confidence could be restored, but Air West's major creditor, Bank of America, would not allow any further loans. As least part of the reason for the bank's refusal to help was its concern that Nick

Bez was too ill to be "physically or mentally capable" of running an airline. Yet, a further condition of Hughes' offer was that Bez remain chairman of Air West "as long as he is available" or at least until the CAB had approved the takeover.

Unlike the shareholders, Hughes' men knew that Bez was very sick. In September 1968 he had been admitted to the Mayo Clinic in Rochester, Minnesota, for diagnosis and treatment. The clinic is one of the most highly respected medical institutions in America, and although its patients' records are supposed to be sacrosanct, Hughes' men were able to discover that Bez's condition was "much worse than he or any member of his family have been informed."

Maheu reported to Hughes: "Through our confidential sources we were able to ascertain that he has terminal cancer of the liver and one lung has been affected very badly."

By December 27, Bez had been discharged from the Mayo Clinic and was well enough to preside over the special meeting of stockholders—but only barely. Any physical exertion exhausted him, and he was obliged to spend some of the meeting lying down on a couch.

As had been expected, most of Air West's stockholders chose to register their votes by proxy, but at least one turned up to witness the proceedings at the Thunderberd Hotel. George Crockett, the Las Vegas businessman, owned twelve-thousand shares of Air West stock and counted Howard Hughes among his friends. (The two men had met during the early 1950s when Hughes, on his occasional visits to Las Vegas, used Crockett's house as a base, "generally fixing his own breakfast.") One hour before departing for San Francisco and the meeting at Millbrae, Maheu had invited Crockett to go along in a Hughes private jet. Anxious to see if he was going to collect twenty-two dollars for each of his shares—then valued on the open market at about eighteen dollars—Crockett accepted the invitation.

There was, as things turned out, little Crockett could usefully do at the Thunderbird Hotel except lend moral support. For everybody in the Hughes camp—includ-

ing Chester Davis, who had flown in from New York—
it was a deeply frustrating day. Every proxy that voted
in favor of Hughes' bid was challenged by the dissidents on what Maheu described, in one of his many
messages to Hughes that day, as "all conceivable
grounds." To add to the delay, about a quarter of the
proxies were held up by the Christmas mail and it was
not until eleven forty-five that night, twelve hours after
the count had begun, that Hughes had polled sufficient
votes to be declared the winner. Even then it was the
narrowest of victories—fifty-one percent for the takeover, forty-nine percent against.

There was nothing in SEC regulations which said
that Air West's directors were, when they met the next
day, bound by the proxy vote. To be certain of that,
one of the dissidents had sought advice from an eminent
New York law firm—ironically, Chester Davis' old firm,
Simpson, Thacher and Bartlett—which said: "It is our
opinion that action by the stockholders . . . does not
in any way affect the responsibilities of the members of
the Board to act in accordance with their own best
judgment as to what will be in the best interests of Air
West." Indeed, Simpson and company went on to say,
a dissident who changed his mind simply because of
the stockholders' vote would be "abdicating" his responsibilities.

With that in mind, the dissidents were determined to
stand firm. But that, of course, would only produce
another stalemate—unless one of the pro-Hughes faction could be persuaded to change his vote.

The convert turned out to be John Parker. Fortuitously, a rival bid for Air West had been made at the
last possible minute by Northwest Airlines, a largish
international carrier based in Minneapolis, Minnesota.
Parker felt that more time was needed to study Northwest's proposal* and he joined the dissidents, making
the vote thirteen to eleven against the Hughes bid.

If Maheu and Chester Davis were upset by this sudden turn of events, they did not show it. According to

---

* Northwest's bid was tentative. Unlike Hughes, the airline
did not offer cash, but one of its shares for every four of Air
West's.

Crockett, who returned with them in the Hughes jet to Las Vegas, they passed most of the flight playing cards while Crockett acted as bartender. But this, as the dissidents were soon to find out, was the calm before the hurricane.

Immediately after the apparently victorious board meeting, Edmund Converse, David Grace, Air West President Robert Henry, and another director, Joseph Martin, Jr., had flown to New York to meet with Northwest Airlines' representatives. The negotiations with Northwest were still continuing when the news broke that "disgruntled stockholders" were suing the dissidents.

The first case was filed in the Court of Chancery of the State of Delaware—where, for tax reasons, Air West was registered as a corporation—on December 30. The thirteen plaintiffs said they were the owners of a total of 320,045 shares of Air West common stock. They claimed that in rejecting Hughes' offer, thirteen directors (the twelve original dissidents plus John Parker) had ". . . deprived Air West of a valuable opportunity to sell its assets at an advantageous price and have placed Air West in a precarious financial position which might result in bankruptcy. . . ." The stockholders asked the court to order the directors to approve Hughes' offer and to pay any damages which might have resulted from their "derelict" conduct. The clincher was attached: The plaintiffs asked—and the court immediately agreed—that the dissidents' stock should be confiscated, pending the outcome of the case.

For at least some of the dissidents, the suit was a devastating blow. Joseph Martin, Jr. strongly suspected that they were witnessing the disguised handiwork of Chester Davis, and he wanted to fight, but it was clear to him that the dissidents' ranks had been broken. He found Ed Converse sitting in a hotel suite "in the bedroom, in a chair and you know he was really beat up and he was terribly upset. . . . And Ed was just losing his taste for the game. It was quite obvious . . . that there was no joy in Mudville." There were other dissidents in the room and Martin realized that several of

112

them "had pretty well decided that they were going to cave."

In retrospect Martin says: "I think the lawsuits were crucial . . . because if it hadn't been for the lawsuits I don't think people would have changed their minds until after we had a definite answer from Northwest. To people like Ed Converse, being sued is something that isn't part of his experience. This is a frightening sort of thing to happen. . . ."

Martin's belief that Chester Davis had been responsible for the lawsuit was at least partially justified.

After Air West's board had voted against Hughes, Davis was approached, he says, by several stockholders who asked what could be done to turn events around. Davis obviously could not represent the stockholders, but it just so happened that he had taken along to California a Delaware lawyer named George Coulson. Coulson said he would find a Delaware firm to take the case.

When Davis returned to Las Vegas in the Hughes jet, Coulson went with him and both men checked into the Frontier Hotel. Early the next morning Coulson went to Davis' room with a suggestion that the lawsuit be filed along with a request for the confiscation of the dissidents' stock. Coulson telephoned a Deleware law firm to set things in motion, and he and Davis drafted the complaint that was filed in Delaware the next day.*

Such urgency was necessary because Hughes' offer for Air West was due to expire in two days' time, at midnight on December 31, and he was adamant that it would not be renewed. Possibly directors like Martin who wanted to continue the fight may have hoped that the dissidents' ranks would hold until that deadline had passed. But Howard Hughes was not a man to leave things like that to chance.

George Crockett has been amazingly frank about the part he played in driving down the value of Air West's stock. He has testified he was asked by Maheu to sell

---

* A second lawsuit, phrased in almost identical language, was filed against the dissidents in U.S. District Court, Southern District of New York, on December 31. Both suits were subsequently dropped.

113

his twelve thousand shares at whatever price it would bring on the open market. He says that Maheu told him he would be compensated by Hughes for the difference between that price and twenty-two dollars a share. He sold his shares on December 31, and at Maheu's request, he says, he sent telegrams to the thirteen dissident directors, threatening to sue for damages.

Crockett did all that, he says, "naturally assuming" that Maheu wanted to put pressure on the dissidents "by forcing the price down . . . he wanted to create a panic among the board of directors to influence them to change their minds."

He was also very forthright in asking Maheu for the money owed to him. On January 13, 1969, he sent Maheu an itemized account covering the "loss" he had suffered on the sale of his Air West stock and the expense of sending the thirteen telegrams. It amounted to $87,418.04.

The bill was not paid as promptly as Crockett would have liked, but after he had done a little agitating, $70,000 was added onto the price of some parcels of land which, coincidentally, Hughes was buying from Crockett.

Maheu denies almost all of those allegations. He claims that Hughes somehow discovered that Crockett had suffered a loss on the sale of Air West stock and, feeling sorry for his old friend, instructed Maheu to compensate Crockett. Another old friend of Hughes did not do so well. Hank Greenspun, the publisher of the Las Vegas *Sun,* also sold his (fifteen thousand) shares of Air West stock on December 31, but, unlike Crockett, he was never compensated. (Nevertheless, the SEC alleges that Greenspun was part of the Hughes conspiracy to defraud Air West's stockholders. He vehemently denies the charge, saying that he sold his shares in the belief that the Hughes takeover would not go through and that the price of the stock would, therefore, begin to fall. He also says that, far from profiting, he lost $50,000 on his Air West transactions.)

In any event, by noon on December 31 the price of Air West stock on both the American and Pacific exchanges had dropped by three dollars a share.

A little over one hour later, the first dissident capitulated. John Parker, the recent convert, sent a telegram to Nick Bez saying that he had changed his vote again, and now supported the Hughes takeover. By the end of the day five other dissidents had surrendered.

At Maheu's house on the Desert Inn golf course, which had been the scene of feverish activity, there was barely time for celebration before Maheu and Chester Davis flew to Seattle to get Nick Bez's signature on a purchase contact. The formalities were completed just two hours before the midnight deadline. For all practical purposes Air West belonged to Howard Hughes—although, as we shall see, it was another fifteen months before he took possession, by which time the airline was in liquidation.

In the "wee hours" of New Year's Day Nick Bez got his telephone call from Hughes. According to Maheu, he walked away from the conversation "nine feet tall." He died of cancer a little over a month later on February 5.

6: HHH, LBJ, AND THE BOMB

Hard pounding, gentlemen; but we will see who can pound the longest.
                    —First Duke of Wellington

At exactly six o'clock on the morning of Friday, April 26, 1968, a 1.2-megaton hydrogen bomb, code named Boxcar, was detonated in the Nevada desert just 102 miles northwest of Las Vegas. The device, the largest ever exploded in the continental United States, was buried 3,800 feet underground and the earth

115

tremors it created were picked up on seismographs from New York to Alaska, registering as high as 6.6 on the Richter scale.

The shock could actually be felt as far away as southern California. In Las Vegas buildings trembled and, legend has it, the chandeliers in the downtown casinos swayed for as long as thirty seconds. Legend also has it that Howard Hughes went crazy.

John Meier, a "scientific adviser" to Hughes, had been stationed on the roof of the Desert Inn equipped with a plumb line to measure the sway of the building. Meier says he had taken with him a large friend who, should the plumb line swing more than six inches in either direction, was to stamp on the roof above Hughes' bedroom to warn that the building could fall down. Before that could happen, however, Meier alleges that John Holmes, one of the five male secretaries, ran onto the roof in panic.

"He felt it, he felt it," Holmes is supposed to have shouted. "Get down there immediately and call him, John; the building's going to fall down. He's hiding under the bed." Hughes stayed under the bed—or, at least, so the story goes—for almost two and a half hours.

It is in some details an unlikely tale.* Nevertheless, it is true that Hughes campaigned to prevent the Boxcar test with a determination that bordered on the obsessional, threatening at one time to "dedicate the rest of my life and every cent I possess in a complete, no-quarter fight to outlaw all nuclear testing of every kind and everywhere."

In truth, Hughes was not opposed to nuclear weapons, although he did for a while form a strange alliance with (to his eyes) radical ban-the-bomb groups. What he was opposed to was the testing of

* Meier, who was on the payroll of Robert A. Maheu Associates, was fired in September 1969 because of an overt friendship with the President's brother, Donald Nixon, which caused concern to both Hughes and the White House. At the time of writing he is living in Canada, a fugitive from a tax-fraud charge brought by the IRS. Meier has made extraordinary allegations about Hughes' involvement with the CIA and Watergate, which are discussed in the Epilogue.

those weapons in Nevada for the very practical reason that he felt the tests were damaging his then $70 million investment in Las Vegas.

His failure to prevent Boxcar only served to multiply his resolve, and he told Bob Maheu: "You know what we want to accomplish and you know our resources are unlimited." Hughes proposed that those resources should be offered to Vice-President Hubert Humphrey, who would be given *"full, unlimited* [emphasis in the original] support for his campaign to enter the White House if he will just take this one on for us."

When Humphrey proved to be unwilling—or unable —to "take this one on," Hughes said that President Lyndon Baines Johnson should be offered an outright bribe of one million dollars.

By coincidence, atomic energy and big-time gambling arrived in Nevada at the same time. In 1947, while Bugsy Siegel was opening the Flamingo Casino in Las Vegas, the Atomic Energy Commission (AEC) was establishing, just outside the city, the Nevada Proving Grounds. The two industries expanded side by side, becoming before long Nevada's biggest employers.

With its thousands of square miles of inhospitable desert and a climate more suited to flies than people, southern Nevada provided the ideal location for weapons testing. Each year the AEC detonated up to forty nuclear devices both in the atmosphere and underground* at the Pahute Mesa Proving Ground without raising significant protest. Any misgivings that Nevada and its residents might have felt about safety or the environmental effect were, no doubt, overwhelmingly offset by the ten thousand jobs the AEC provided.

Toward the end of 1966, however, Howard Hughes' arrival in Las Vegas coincided with an announcement from the AEC that it was to begin a series of tests of somewhat greater magnitude than had been carried out at Pahute Mesa before. The first, code named Greeley, was detonated just after Christmas and the

* Since July 1962—in anticipation of the Limited Test Ban Treaty, which was signed in 1963—the United States has refrained from testing nuclear weapons in the atmosphere because of the dangers of fallout.

117

shock waves it created were felt in Las Vegas. A month later another bomb was exploded. It was not, in the nature of these things today, very large,* but some hours after the test a 4,000-foot-long crack opened up across the floor of a section of the proving ground known as Hot Creek Valley. This event—with its implication of a possible connection between man-made and natural disturbances in the earth's crust—increased Hughes' already intractable disapproval of nuclear blasts on his new doorstep. Bob Maheu was dispatched to register a protest.

The AEC was not very obliging. It said that while no more large explosions were planned for the immediate future in southern Nevada, the test program, with a detonation at Pahute Mesa every couple of weeks or so, would continue. Hughes, irritated but unable to do very much about it, bided his time.

The moment for serious protest, and for a campaign which might draw widespread public support, seemed to have come when more than a year later, on the night of April 8, 1968, earth tremors again rattled the windows of Las Vegas. Hughes was outraged. The AEC had given no warning of a major test and, he said in a note to Maheu, "a lot of people must have been scared pissless." With curious logic, Hughes found it particularly outrageous that this "overpowering explosion" should have occurred the night before the funeral of Martin Luther King (who was assassinated in Memphis on April 4). Hughes told Maheu, "Please find out what in God's name went haywire . . . this may be the opportunity we have been waiting for to demand a real stop to this outrageous program."

Maheu's reply, that it was a minor earthquake and not a bomb which had caused the tremors, did nothing to dissipate Hughes' indignation. "That's even better," he wrote. "Now we can raise a hue and cry that can be heard from here to Carson City [Nevada's capital] and back again." Hughes reasoned—"argued" is per-

* This was an "intermediate" bomb in the range of 500 kilotons—meaning its explosive force was equivalent to 500,000 tons of TNT. For comparison, the atomic bomb dropped on Hiroshima on August 6, 1945, had a force equivalent to 20,000 tons of TNT.

haps a better word—that if earthquakes and bomb tests were indistinguishable, at least to him, then "it is too much to expose a metropolitan community to this kind of abuse willfully." And who could say that it was not the constant pounding of bomb explosions that had provoked the earthquake?

Maheu, it must be said, was not the most willing recruit to Hughes' campaign. His sympathies lay with the "peace through (American) strength" ideology. And anyway, he was realistic enough to realize that Nevada would not easily be rallied to a cause that could cost ten thousand jobs. Events, however, denied him any real choice. A week later, with a malevolent sense of timing, the AEC announced Boxcar's impending detonation.

This, said Hughes, was the last straw. "Bob, I know you feel this whole deal is too much trouble but I want you to give this your very utmost all-out effort. I want you to call the Gov. [governor] at once and the Senators and Congressman. You are free to tell them . . . that if they do not cancel this one extra large explosion I am going to the President in a personal appeal. . . ."

It was, of course, exceedingly unlikely that President Johnson would at that moment have been much moved. Beleaguered by the war in Vietnam, racial riots and campus unrest at home, his health failing and his party deeply divided, LBJ would surely have had little appetite for additional controversy. It occurred to Maheu that Vice-President Hubert Humphrey, on the other hand, might be far more amenable to an appeal from Hughes. Vietnam aside, Humphrey had a dovish reputation; there was also the consideration that he had, just days beforehand, announced his candidacy for President and might welcome the chance to make a new and powerful ally. (Johnson had announced on March 31 that "I shall not seek and I will not accept nomination" for a further term in office.)

Maheu proposed to Hughes that, as a beginning, they should ask for a ninety-day delay of Boxcar to allow time for an "independent study" of the risk posed to Las Vegas by the blast. In that moderate cause, he said, they could expect the support of the Vice-President.

Hughes was grateful: "Your taking hold of this bomb deal as you have (when I know it is not a favorite project of yours and you must be doing it in response to my request)—this has meant a great deal to me. I send my sincere thanks." He also, in a series of notes written to Maheu between April 16 and April 26, offered suggestions to help the campaign along.

First, Hughes suggested that Maheu tell the Vice-President "he is free to tell the people in Washington if they don't grant the 90 day delay I am going to the public immediately. I am going to tell the whole story. . . ."

It is not clear from Hughes' notes what the "whole story" was, but he left no doubt as to his own fears: "It is the considered opinion of some people who have studied this matter that the explosions in the past may very definitely have caused the recent earthquake. If so this is a hell of a note in a place that is being developed as a resort which depends for its very life-blood on the tourists who come here voluntarily in open competition with Hawaii and many, many other resorts.

"In other words how can we expect to realize our full potential as a resort if we are scaring people away with bomb-tests and earthquakes."

Hughes claimed, with some exaggeration, that the earthquake had been followed by "an avalanche" of calls to local newspapers from frightened people. "I don't think fear has any place in a resort. People want to go where they can forget the war, the draft and the riots. They want to go where they will not encounter any violence."

With such undeniable logic on his side, Hughes was convinced, at least for a while, that the ninety-day moratorium would be granted. Then, he said, Maheu should personally go to the White House and "endeavor to sell the President on a permanent policy." He was sure Humphrey—"H.H.H."—would be glad to set up the appointment, but in any event Maheu would have no difficulty in getting to see the president. "You have gotten a lot of publicity as my sole representative in important matters and I definitely feel you would be more willingly accepted at the White House than anyone else I know of."

The AEC's response to Hughes' campaign was not altogether sporting. Faced with evidence of some public support for the idea of a moratorium, the agency challenged, at least by implication, Hughes' patriotism. Boxcar, said the AEC, was a "weapons related experiment, designed to improve the nation's nuclear armament capacity" and any delay, even of ninety days, would have "an adverse effect on national defense."

That was, in all conscience, a bit of a tall story—or as Hughes put it, "pure 99-proof unadulterated shit."

He told Maheu: "There is not a word of truth in it. We have an overkill position in the bomb already. Our only limitation lies in the area of means of delivery." Hughes also pointed out that developing test weapons into operational military hardware is a long, arduous process that can take years. If Boxcar's derivatives should be needed in a hurry, he said, the AEC could always make up the time lost during the moratorium by putting in a bit of overtime.

Still, having conjured up the vision that the Russians were coming, so to speak, the AEC was obviously not going to be easily deterred. Hughes decided that only three courses of action offered much hope of stopping Boxcar.

The first alternative, he said, was to apply for a court injunction. "I think it is just a problem of finding the right judge."

Second, "an order from LBJ inspired by Humphries." (Hughes invariably spelled Humphrey's name incorrectly.)

The third alternative was to begin direct negotiations with the AEC, "just like buying a hotel," he said. Hughes theorized that the AEC's scientists were not willing to agree to a moratorium for fear that it would be seen as a tacit admission that Boxcar might pose some threat, however remote, to Las Vegas. Such an admission could lead to an abandonment of the

Nevada test site and the scientists could find themselves "on some God-forsaken Pacific island." Hughes
believed, with chilling cynicism, that "after becoming
used to Las Vegas living they are not about to swap
it for some desert island." What was needed, he said,
was "somebody to wheel and deal with the A.E.C.
and offer them a deal whereby they can continue to
enjoy the pleasures of living in Las Vegas." He did not
specify the deal, but he said it should afford "a
graceful way they can give us the 90 day extension
without injuring their position, without admitting defeat, without admitting by inference that the bomb
they wanted to detonate would have endangered everyone in the community, without embarrassing themselves."

If negotiation with the AEC was the course that
Maheu chose to follow, Hughes wanted one thing
made very clear: Any deal was absolutely conditional
on Boxcar's postponement. "If they ride roughshod
over me and go ahead with this explosion I will have
nothing [further] to discuss with them. They could not
even get an appointment to get in the office. All the
horses and all the tractors in Nevada could not even
get them through this door."

By this time Hughes' campaign against Boxcar had
cast him with some unlikely allies: The Women's
International League for Peace and Freedom, the
Federation of American Scientists, radical students,
ban-the-bomb groups, and liberal professors around
the U.S. joined in his protest. Hughes held faint hope
that public opinion alone could sway the AEC but
he told Maheu that the protest groups should be
"played for all they can do for us."

He also wanted newspaper support and he was
distressed that the Las Vegas *Sun* was remaining "im-
maculately uncontaminated by carefully staying out of
the argument." What could be done, he asked Maheu,
"to persuade Mr. Greenspun [the *Sun*'s publisher] to
jump in and get wet all over?" (As Maheu realized
only too well, neither the *Sun* nor any other Nevada
newspaper could be expected to join a campaign
which taken to its logical conclusion would cost a
sizable number of readers their jobs. Hank Greenspun

did come to believe, however, that in refusing to even consider a moratorium, the AEC had behaved arrogantly, and a couple of days before Boxcar was due to be detonated he wrote a column saying so. When he saw the newspaper, Hughes wrote a note to Maheu which began, "Please call Hank, if he is awake, and tell him I just read his column and I seriously think he ought to get the Nobel Prize for it, it is that great. . . .")

Although some of the banners raised in Hughes' support were perceptibly tinged with red, he did not find his new role as protest leader altogether displeasing. Indeed, he seems to have savored it. He acknowledged that "we may lose the battle to stop the explosion Friday" [Boxcar], but if it went ahead he would "campaign to kill off the entire nuclear test program—to kill it off completely—*but good.*" [Emphasis in the original.] It was clear, he said, that this was a cause many people were waiting to champion and all they required was a leader. "I could easily be that leader," and with that threat in mind the AEC had "damned well better get down off their high autocratic horses and start talking a compromise with us."

The AEC remained singularly unimpressed and the countdown went on. In Hughes' last two messages to Maheu about Boxcar there was a note of desperation.

Perhaps, he said, he should, after all, write a personal note to the President that "we could ask Humphries to deliver—hand deliver—to Johnson." The trouble with that strategy was, he admitted, that LBJ might argue it was too late to stop the test, and if that happened, "we really have had it but good."

His final gambit was to propose a compromise. Maybe the AEC would agree to a shorter moratorium of say, sixty days in return for a promise from Hughes to "pay all overtime and all other expenses required to achieve a completion of any weapons program . . . by the original target date, should the defense department decide they need those weapons."

Boxcar was detonated on schedule. There was no earthquake and no leak of radiation—and, presumably, Russian aggression was deterred.

123

But, as Hughes had promised, one battle did not end the war. Publicly, the campaign against the Nevada test site was, if anything, intensified. Privately, it took on a new and sinister dimension.

By both men's accounts, Vice-President Hubert Humphrey and Maheu met for the first time within the two weeks following Boxcar at the Hilton Hotel in Denver, Colorado. The approximate date and the location of the meeting are about the only things they do agree on.

According to Maheu, Humphrey "indicated that he would give us all the help we needed relative to our fight in the area of atomic energy." In return, Maheu says he pledged a "campaign contribution" of $100,-000—half of it to be paid in cash. The Vice-President, said Maheu, "seemed very grateful." After Denver, "we had several conversations by telephone, and the matter was handled very delicately" until July 29, 1968, when, Maheu alleges, he left a briefcase containing $50,000 in hundred-dollar bills on the floor of the vice-presidential limousine. A check for $50,000 in favor of the Humphrey campaign was, indisputably, donated by Maheu on October 17.

Humphrey emphatically denies receiving $50,000 in cash from Maheu or anybody else. He denies promising Maheu support for Hughes' campaign in return for money. And although he did publicly oppose the Nevada tests, Humphrey denies that his stand was in any way inspired by Hughes.

It is extremely difficult to reconcile these conflicting stories, because of a lack of solid evidence, making it impossible to say where the truth falls. Maheu's story, by far the most detailed of the two, contains some incongruous elements, but then, as he says, a great many of the things that took place in Howard Hughes' world were unbelievable. Humphrey has chosen to allow his defense to rest on blunt denial rather than detailed explanation, on the grounds that a public squabble would gain him nothing. In that, his judgment cannot be denied. His judgment in flirting with the Hughes empire in the first place is more questionable. At the very least his conduct exposed him to the *suspicion* that he was willing to trade his integrity for a crock of Hughes gold. The episode deserves to be explored if only to demonstrate that even astute and venerable politicians like Humphrey can be victims of their own gross naiveté.

After the meeting in Denver, Maheu wrote a memorandum to Hughes which began, "The following reflects the suggestions and procedures set forth by the Vice-President. . . . He feels we should have two objectives—(a) delay the future plans of these big blasts until (b) the propitious moment at which the Administration will urge that underground testing be added to the [Test] Ban Treaty. He feels very strongly that we have a good chance of accomplishing these goals if we follow the steps listed below. He pledges his support and that of the Administration."

Maheu went on to detail the "Vice-President's program," which consisted primarily of a suggestion that Hughes should hire six scientists "who are highly respected by the Administration" to conduct an "independent study." Maheu believed the program could be accomplished within a budget of $300,000 and he added: "During this program, the Vice-President will work with us very closely and confidentially. . . . He is anxious to get your reaction to the above-mentioned plan."

Hughes was not, apparently, overimpressed: "You say, 'What do you think of Humphries' program?' Bob, I am no expert at these things. If I were, we would not have to go to Humphries to start with. Any program is as good or as bad as what he can produce with it—I am certainly nobody to evaluate. . . ."

Neither would Hughes cooperate fully with what he called "Humphries' scientists." It seems that technicians at the Hughes Aircraft Company (HAC) had submitted to Hughes a report in which they said they did not share "Humphries' confidence" that a study would produce sufficient evidence to get the test program stopped. Maheu asked Hughes for the name of the technicians so that he could clear up any "inconsistencies." On May 24 Hughes replied: "I certainly cannot put you in touch with these men and

125

I hope you are aware that I disclosed this report to you in the greatest of secrecy. . . .

"This does not mean I do not trust you. . . . It simply means that my confidantes in the H.A.C. and H.T. Co. [Tool Company] organizations put their very lives in jeopardy with some of the disclosures they make to me, and if they thought this information went to anybody—no matter whom—they would not continue to inform me.

"So, you will just have to proceed with your scientist as you see fit, . . . When his report comes in if it is favorable, that is fine. If it is unfavorable, we have a problem. . . ."

Despite these reservations, Hughes' public campaign against the Nevada test program began to pick up considerable momentum during the summer of 1968. Dr. Alan Ryall, a seismologist in Nevada's neighbor state, Utah, circulated a report in which he claimed that all explosions which registered more than 5 on the Richter scale* were inevitably followed by an increase in earthquake activity. Dr. Barry Commoner of Washington University in St. Louis, Missouri, said that the Hoover Dam, near Las Vegas, could be threatened. Another Utah scientist, Dr. Robert Pendleton, said the people of Utah were being "showered" with radioactive material from the Nevada tests, and in response, the Peace and Freedom Party of Utah marched through the streets of Salt Lake City with placards saying, "Ski in Utah—The Greatest Radioactive Snow on Earth."

While this chorus of protest was growing, Maheu was, he says, endeavoring to fulfill the part of his contract with Humphrey that called for a $50,000 cash donation. The problem, curiously enough, was laying his hands on the money.

It was routine for Maheu to get any cash he needed from Nadine Henley, Hughes' formidable special assistant who ran the Hollywood office at 7000 Romaine Street. She was able to write checks on Hughes' private account with a bank in Houston, Texas, and cash them at a local branch of the Bank of America. But,

---

* Boxcar had registered as high as 6.6 on the Richter scale.

Maheu says, "I needed the money in a hurry . . . and he [Hughes] did not want me at that time to discuss the Humphrey contribution with his officials in Hollywood." On Hughes' instructions, Maheu says, he borrowed the $50,000 from a man named Chester Simms, who was the casino manager at Hughes' Frontier Hotel.

The money was in hundred-dollar bills, and Maheu divided them into ten bundles of $5,000 each. He had agreed, he says, with Humphrey that the cash would be handed over at the Century Plaza Hotel in Los Angeles. But the prospect of carrying so much money on a plane from Las Vegas was one that Maheu found intimidating: "It was the first time in my life that I had participated in a delivery of this magnitude. I considered it an awesome responsibility."

As insurance against a plane crash or robbery, Maheu therefore took only half of the money with him when he flew to Los Angeles on July 28, leaving $25,000 with his son Peter, along with instructions that it should be delivered to him at the Century Plaza the following day.

Humphrey had arrived in Los Angeles six days earlier in an attempt to revive his campaign to win the Democratic presidential nomination. In California's primary election the previous month, he had secured only twelve percent of the vote against Robert Kennedy's forty-five percent and Eugene McCarthy's forty-three percent. Kennedy's assassination (he was shot at the Ambassador Hotel in Los Angeles on June 5 and died the following day) had presented Humphrey with the opportunity to make up lost ground, as it were, but he returned to California with reluctance and some trepidation. The Vietnam war was the albatross that overshadowed Humphrey's campaign—although, in truth, he had played little part in formulating the policies that had prolonged it—and the antiwar protestors were nowhere more active than in California. Humphrey anticipated that revisiting California in the aftermath of Kennedy's assassination would provoke vigorous disturbances, and he was right. Outside the Elks Hall in Los Angeles an anti-Humphrey demonstration got out of hand and the

Los Angeles Police Department, with customary zeal, produced a display of semiautomatic weaponry that almost caused a riot. Inside the hall, pro- and anti-Humphrey groups exchanged punches and the Vice-President was obliged, for safety's sake, to make a hurried exit.

His visit to Los Angeles was to end on Monday, July 29, with a fund-raising dinner at the Century Plaza Hotel. Maheu bought himself a seat at the dinner for $5,000 (paid for by check) and also took a suite of rooms—naturally—on the hotel's seventeenth floor to await delivery of the $25,000 he had left in Las Vegas. He anticipated, he has testified, that there would be a suitable moment during the evening when he could quietly hand over to Humphrey the bundles of hundred-dollar bills.

The messenger charged by Peter Maheu with carrying the second $25,000 from Las Vegas to Los Angeles was Gordon Judd, a lawyer who worked for the Hughes-Nevada Operations as an assistant to Jack Hooper. Judd was given a locked briefcase, and a caution that the contents were "important," and told to deliver it to Robert Maheu, who had the key. When Judd arrived at the Century Plaza, he says, he found Maheu in an ebullient mood and they chatted about The Man and Humphrey. Judd never got to see what was in the briefcase he had carried, but from his conversation with Maheu he had little doubt that it "contained a campaign contribution." (Maheu took the briefcase into his bedroom, where, he says, he unlocked it and added the $25,000 he had transported.)

The Humphrey dinner, a small affair for about thirty people, was held in a meeting room on one of the hotel's underground levels. It began and ended relatively early because Humphrey was to fly that night to San Francisco. Among those present was Lloyd Hand, former U.S. Chief of Protocol (1965–1966) and a friend of both Maheu and Humphrey, who remembered that toward the end of the evening, Maheu approached him and said he wanted to see the Vice-President privately. Hand, who was intending to accompany Humphrey on the journey from the Central Plaza to the airport, invited Maheu along for the ride.

128

Maheu said, "I need to get to my hotel room and get my briefcase. Would we have time?" Suitably assured, Maheu left the dinner for between five and ten minutes and returned, briefcase in hand.

There are several conflicting versions of the subsequent events. The Humphrey motorcade, consisting of limousines and police cars, left the Century Plaza by way of an underground drive that leads from the subterranean levels of the hotel to the street. Most of the witnesses remember Maheu getting into Humphrey's car while it was parked in the underground driveway; on the other hand, Maheu remembers getting into the car outside the front of the hotel after the motorcade had reached street level.

In any event Maheu got into the car, carrying his briefcase, and the convoy set off for the airport. After traveling no more than five hundred yards, it stopped.

Joseph Cerrell, a professional political campaign manager who was in the lead police car, says that the order to stop the motorcade came, via radio, from a Secret Service agent who was in the Humphrey limousine. Cerrell got out of the police car and walked back to the limousine. "I inquired were there any problems; I had not anticipated the premature stop," he has testified. "Maheu indicated there was no difficulty. He'd had conversation with the Vice-President, had seen him, visited him, and was now returning to the hotel."

Maheu says that when he left the car he also left the briefcase containing $50,000.

Describing what happened during the brief ride, he said: "I made some reference to atomic energy problems which Howard Hughes wanted curtailed in Nevada. I left the briefcase on the floor of the limousine. I bid the Vice-President God speed. I said goodbye to his wife and I left. I did not think it appropriate to open up the briefcase, rip open the envelopes and brazenly take out the cash." Maheu says that he felt no need to bring the briefcase to Humphrey's attention; Humphrey had known since the May meeting in Denver that he was going to get $50,000 in cash, delivery had been promised for that night, and during the fund-raising dinner, "I did mention to the Vice-President that I had with me the item which we had discussed previously. . . . I had every reason to believe that Senator Humphrey knew the purpose of why I was going to be in the limousine for such a short period of time."

Humphrey has no recollection of his ride with Maheu. He remembers only that they met "in front" of the Century Plaza. "On that occasion there were present my wife, well-wishers, supporters, U.S. secret service agents, and members of my staff whose names I do not recall. The substance of the conversation between myself and Maheu was that he wanted to wish me well and to be of help. My reply, in substance, was that I thanked him for his offer of support in my bid for the presidency and for participating in the fund-raising reception that evening."

Lloyd Hand's memory seems a little better. He shared the back of the limousine with Humphrey and Maheu during its five-hundred-yard journey and remembers "a conversation between Maheu and the Vice-President principally concerning what Mr. Maheu stated was Mr. Hughes' concern about atomic underground testing in Nevada." He has a vague recollection that Maheu showed Humphrey a memorandum and he remembers the car stopping and Maheu's departing.

On the vital question of whether Maheu left his briefcase in the car, Hand has this to say: "I don't, I simply don't know . . . I have a vague recollection, an impression, that he did."

Gordon Judd, the Hughes-Nevada lawyer, has no doubts on the subject. Waiting in Maheu's hotel suite, he was, he says, attracted by the noise of police helicopters and went out onto the balcony to watch the departure of the Vice-President's motorcade. From his vantage point, seventeen floors up, Judd saw Maheu, briefcase in hand, walk out of the hotel's main entrance and get into a black limousine. He saw the car drive off, he saw it stop, and he saw Maheu get out, minus the briefcase.

A few minutes later, Judd testified, Maheu returned to the suite and said, "Mission accomplished."

If Maheu did leave a briefcase in the limousine, and

if that briefcase did contain $50,000, could Humphrey have simply been unaware of it? Joseph Cerrell, who was in the lead car of the convoy and who has worked on several Humphrey campaigns, belives that to be a credible explanation. "It is possible that if something had been left for him [Humphrey] in the limousine without him being clear in his own mind as to what it was, he could have left it [behind]. . . . That is quite conceivable to me, that he didn't know it was there or understand the magnitude of what was transpiring. This was a day that had started at 7:30 in the morning. There were no restbreaks, no reststops—we went straight through and now it was 9:30 at night. It is very difficult for any person to endure and it's quite conceivable that, as the teenagers say today, his head wasn't all with it."

That theory woud have to allow, of course, that when Humphrey transferred from the limousine to an airplane at the Los Angeles airport the briefcase was unnoticed, left behind, and, subsequently, stolen—without anyone realizing what had happened.

If that is so, then Humphrey's campaign received only $55,000 from Maheu—the $5,000 donation to the fund-raising dinner and the $50,000 donation paid by check on October 17.

And yet, according to Maheu, Humphrey in due course thanked him specifically *for donating $100,000*.

On November 8, 1968, the day after the presidential election in which Richard Nixon narrowly defeated Humphrey, Maheu was asleep at his home in Las Vegas when "my then-15-year-old daughter came into my bedroom to wake me up and tell me that the Vice-President was on the telephone. He, naturally, was disenchanted with how he had been defeated, but he wanted me to thank Mr. Hughes for one hundred thousand, plus the smaller contributions and assured me to inform Mr. Hughes that we could count on his cooperation because, among other things, he philosophically agreed with Mr. Hughes as to the abolishment of underground testing."

The conversation was overheard by Maheu's daughter Christine, who, unbeknownst to her father, listened in on the extension. (It was not, she says, the first time she had eavesdropped: She listened in on some of her father's conversations with Hughes because "I always wanted to hear his voice.")

Christine says, "The telephone rang, and I think it was early in the morning. I can't remember. My dad was sleeping. Whenever he used to get to sleep, I wouldn't wake him unless it was really important, because he only used to sleep maybe three or four hours a night—if he got that; he was lucky to get that. So, anyway, I answered the phone saying, 'Maheu residence' and a voice said, 'Hello, is Mr. Maheu there?' And I said, 'Who is calling, please?' and the voice said, 'Vice-president, vice-president calling.' So then I went and I woke up my father and I told him the vice-president was on the phone. I left the phone in my room off the hook. I didn't wait to see if he picked up the phone or not, I just went back to my room and I picked up the receiver and listened because I was excited that the vice-president would be calling my father. Then the voice—vice president—said, 'I want to thank you, thank Mr. Hughes for the hundred thousand and that I'll continue to be of assistance.' "

Christine has testified that the voice she heard was that of Humphrey because she had heard him on television. She is also certain that the figure mentioned was $100,000 because, "I just couldn't believe it." The only thing that impressed her more during the conversation was that Humphrey "called my dad Bob."

It has to be said that there are flaws in the evidence offered to support Maheu's version of the story.

For example, if—as most of the testimony insists—Maheu boarded the limousine in the *underground* driveway of the Century Plaza, then Judd could not possibly have witnessed the event from a balcony seventeen floors *above*ground. If Judd was mistaken about that, then his claim that he saw Maheu leave the car without his briefcase must be open to doubt.

More seriously, there is some doubt about Maheu's claim that he borrowed the $50,000 from a casino manager because Hughes "did not want me at that time to discuss the Humphrey contribution with his officials in Hollywood." On July 30, the day after Maheu allegedly delivered the money to Humphrey, he met at the Century Plaza with two of Hughes' most prominent California, officials—and discussed a contribution to Humphrey.

Nadine Henley and Bill Gay both say that at the meeting Maheu announced he would need $125,000— $50,000 for Humphrey, $50,000 for Nixon, and $25,-000 to help pay off the debts that the late Robert Kennedy's campaign committee had incurred. (Nadine Henley cashed a $25,000 Hughes check that same day and delivered the money to Maheu. He flew to Washington, D.C., the following day and handed the money over to Larry O'Brien, chairman of the Democratic National Committee, who in turn delivered it to Kennedy's brother-in-law Stephen Smith.) It was not, according to Miss Henley, until September of 1968 that Maheu told her that Hughes had authorized contributions of $100,000 for both Humphrey and Nixon. She send him $100,000 for Humphrey on September 9. At no time, she says, did Maheu claim that he had already paid Humphrey half of it.

Chester Simms, the casino manager who, Maheu says, loaned him the cash that was given to Humphrey, died in 1971 without ever being called upon to give his side of the story. (Maheu says that he repaid Simms during the early part of 1969 out of money he received from Miss Henley.)

We are left, therefore, with three conflicting records: Leaving aside the $5,000 dinner fund donation, which is not in dispute, Nadine Henley's records show that she gave Maheu $100,000 intended for Humphrey; Maheu's records show that he donated $100,000— albeit, not the same $100,000—to Humphrey's campaign; Humphrey's records show that he received only $50,000. If Humphrey did not get it, what happened to the missing money?

Hughes was in no doubt that Maheu stole it. His empire charged in court that after Maheu was fired in December 1970 he was unable to account for thousands of dollars that he received and that he invented —among other things—the story about Humphrey.

If that is so, it was extraordinarily fortunate for Maheu that years before any charges were leveled against him, he should have taken a mysterious car ride with Humphrey which provided such colorful weight to his claim.

One more thing must be said. In the libel trial that Maheu launched against Hughes in 1973, the Summa Corporation * attempted to prove that Maheu had stolen the $50,000. The jury was not asked to decide if Humphrey had received the money—only if Maheu had pocketed it. They found him innocent.

It seemed pretty certain in the fall of 1968 that the next President of the United States would be Richard Nixon, and not Hubert Humphrey. Either way, Hughes would be on the winning side, for he had by then decided to back both candidates at least to the tune of $50,000 each, but perhaps the prospect of a Nixon victory—however appealing it might have been to Hughes in ideological terms—did not bode well for the campaign against the bomb. Humphrey had made it clear publicly that, as President, he would frown upon the nuclear test program; Nixon, on the other hand, had made no such commitment.

That fact may in part explain why Hughes suddenly switched the strategy of his antibomb campaign and focused his hopes on the retiring President, Lyndon Baines Johnson.

Maheu was at home in Las Vegas when he received orders from Hughes to "make an appointment" with LBJ. The President had been unwell. Maheu "called a contact in Washington, D.C. who informed me that the President had had a relapse . . . and was resting at the L.B.J. ranch in Texas." Maheu says that he sought out one of the President's staff and, eventually, received a telephone call inviting him to the ranch.

It says something about Hughes' nimbus that this appointment was made without either Maheu or the President's staff having any idea of its purpose. Hughes said, "I'm not ready to tell you yet," and Maheu even left Las Vegas for Texas totally unaware of his mission.

To guard against unexpected delays, Maheu flew to Dallas in one of the company's executive jets the night

* In December 1972, after stock in the Hughes Tool Company had been sold to the public, the remainder of the Hughes empire became known as the Summa Corporation.

before the appointment, checked into a motel, and called Hughes.

"I wish you would tell me what it is that you want me to discuss with him [LBJ] so I could be thinking about it at least during the night," Maheu said.

Hughes refused. "Call me in the morning, just before you leave," he said. Meanwhile, he wished Maheu a comfortable night's sleep—something which in those circumstances, Maheu says, was "kind of difficult."

Even in the morning Hughes kept his own counsel until time threatened to run out. Finally, "with a few minutes to go, Mr. Hughes called me and told me that my assignment was twofold. Number one, which didn't have much significance to me at that time, he wanted me to feel the President out as to his thinking insofar as a cessation of the war in Vietnam was concerned." (Maheu says, a little spitefully, that he later realized the significance: Hughes wanted the war to continue, he claims, because it would improve sales of Hughes' helicopters to the U.S. Army.)

"Number two, he wanted me to suggest to President Johnson that he, Howard Hughes, was prepared to give him $1 million after he left the office of the presidency, if he would stop the atomic testing before he left office."

At last, Maheu has testified, he knew that his mission was bribery, and on an impressive scale. Not for one moment, Maheu says, did he intend to carry that mission out, but for Hughes' benefit he had to go through the motions and he flew to the ranch to keep his appointment.

LBJ was not there. Overnight he had suffered another relapse (the problem was a heart condition which eventually killed him) and he had been taken to a hospital for treatment. Lady Bird Johnson, however, was on hand to greet Hughes' ambassador and, dismissing her Secret Service guards, took Maheu on an impromptu tour of the ranch to pass the time. It was not until midmorning that Johnson returned from the hospital—much recovered—and not until after lunch and a second tour of the ranch—this one guided by LBJ—that the two men got down to business.

"He brought me to the home in which he was born,

then we retired to his large bedroom and living quarters." According to Maheu, it was the President and not he who first raised the nuclear issue. "He [Johnson] mentioned that he had received a note from Mr. Hughes relative to atomic energy testing. He mentioned that the note had been delivered by an attorney in Washington and that it contained inaccuracies." For fear, presumably, that those inaccuracies might embarrass his fellow Texan, Johnson said that Hughes' note was one presidential document that would not be placed in the Johnson Library.

The President went on to say that the Nevada test program was very important to national security. Maheu agreed: "I told him that a friend of mine who had been connected with the National Security Council since its formation had told me repeatedly that he'd never seen a President or a vice-president who, where national security problems were concerned, did not give them number one priority and place in a very secondary position his own political thinking. I pointed out to him that my friend had had very high praise for Presidents Eisenhower, Truman—all the Presidents—and the vice presidents—Mr. Johnson when he was vice-president, Mr. Nixon when he was the vice-president—that where national security was concerned, everything else took a very secondary position. And I, too, felt that conviction. . . ."

It must have seemed to Johnson a very odd speech. For months Maheu had been prominent as Hughes' conductor of the growing chorus of protest over the Nevada tests. Now, having gained access to the President as Hughes' emissary, Maheu was actually disavowing the campaign. And that was not, apparently, the limit of Maheu's treachery. Far from trying to bribe Johnson, he offered him some of Hughes' money for nothing. "I said to him that Mr. Hughes was very interested in his future and how could he be of help to him?"

Johnson replied that after his retirement his greatest interest would be in the Johnson Library, to be built in Austin, Texas, where the records of his administration would be stored for future study. If Hughes would care to make a contribution, a very small contribution,

136

toward the library fund it would make him very happy.

On that convivial note the meeting ended and Maheu returned to Las Vegas to report that his mission had been abortive. We do not know how he explained his failure, but Hughes donated not one cent to the Johnson Library fund.

The LBJ episode aside, the quality of Hughes' private campaign against the bomb improved significantly during the last few weeks of 1968. While the public protests continued wih razzmatazz and dramatic revelations—for example, of the dangers that threatened not just Las Vegas but "Clark County, northern Nevada, California, Utah and Arizona"—the negotiations that secretly took place in Washington, D.C., were of a distinctly more sophisticated nature than before.

The credit for that belongs to Lawrence F. O'Brien, who was formally retained by the Hughes Tool Company in October 1968 to provide "management consulting and public relations" advice. O'Brien's services did not come cheaply—his fee was $180,000 a year—but then, he was, and is, one of the shrewdest political operators around. He managed John Kennedy's campaign for President in 1960 and Johnson's in 1964. For a while he served in Johnson's cabinet as Postmaster General and was widely expected to manage LBJ's campaign for reelection in 1968. When Johnson announced he was surrendering, however, O'Brien was among the first of those leading Democrats who defected to Robert Kennedy's campaign. O'Brien directed the bandwagon until it was halted so abruptly by the gun of Sirhan Bishara Sirhan.

O'Brien and Robert Maheu met for the first time a month after Robert Kennedy's assassination on July 4, 1968. The pressing reason for the meeting was the $25,000 contribution to the Kennedy campaign that Maheu had committed before Kennedy's death. Although the campaign was obviously over, it still had debts to pay and Maheu assured O'Brien that the commitment would be honored. There was, so far as Maheu was concerned, another reason for the meeting. After the murder Hughes had assumed that O'Brien would be looking for a job and he told Maheu to "make every effort to get Larry and his boys to come on board." At the July 4 meeting O'Brien made it clear that he was not interested in joining the Hughes Tool Company payroll, but he would, he said, be willing to become a consultant. In fact, O'Brien had already decided that he was going to set up his own company, O'Brien Associates, with headquarters in New York, and he was searching for clients. He agreed to submit a written proposal to Maheu on what services he might be able to provide Hughes.

On July 31 the two men met again, this time at the Madison Hotel in Washington, D.C., and agreed that O'Brien would begin acting as a consultant for Hughes after the Democratic National Convention had taken place in August. (Maheu took the opportunity to hand over the $25,000 owed to the Kennedy campaign.) There is no doubt that Hughes was sorely in need of some expert advice. What with Washington's hostile reaction to the antibomb campaign, the Justice Department's attitude toward casino acquisitions, and official opposition to a proposed takeover of the ABC television network, Hughes' image in the capital was certainly in need of a little dusting. Before O'Brien could "climb on board" to handle the job, however, there was an unforeseen delay.

At the Chicago convention Humphrey—having defeated Eugene McCarthy for the Democratic nomination—looked to O'Brien to manage his campaign for the presidency. O'Brien hesitated, not out of lingering loyalty to Robert Kennedy's memory but because of his agreement with Maheu. He said he would only accept the assignment if Maheu could be persuaded to accept the delay it would cause. Humphrey called Maheu from Chicago: "I would appreciate it if you could see your way clear to go along with this," he said. Maheu unhesitatingly agreed. (There were two other commitments which Humphrey renegotiated, one of them to a New York publishing company, Atheneum, for whom O'Brien had promised to write a book. Mike Bessie, the head of Atheneum, would not at first believe that the Vice-President was calling him—he thought he was being hoaxed.)

O'Brien's stewardship of Hubert Humphrey's campaign was a remarkable demonstration of the art of the possible. On September 3, the day after Labor Day—when the presidential campaign traditionally begins—the opinion polls showed Humphrey trailing far behind Richard Nixon. Worse the independent candidate, Governor George Wallace, was not far behind Humphrey—and he was closing the gap. (O'Brien is reputed to have told Humphrey: "Look, I'm going to work my tail off for you, but as your manager I have to say to you—right now, you're dead.") Humphrey's campaign suffered from a lack of money, a lack of organization, and a candidate who, when he took to the road, proved to be a disaster. By contrast, Nixon's campaign was ridiculously overendowed. And yet on Election Day, Humphrey came within a whisker of causing a profound upset. He lost to Nixon by less than one-quarter of one percent of the popular vote, and there are few who would deny Larry O'Brien's role in that achievement.

Miracles of that quality were not really attainable when O'Brien became—as it were—Hughes' campaign manager. With Humphrey's defeat, the battle against the bomb had lost its most prominent ally* and a good deal of public support had dropped off when the AEC was finally goaded into issuing a 311-page report answering point by point the cries of "danger" which Hughes had raised. O'Brien knows a lost cause when he sees one. His strategy, therefore, concentrated on repairing the damage which the campaign had caused to Hughes' always delicate relations with Washington.

The overwhelming consideration had to be money. From the start, Hughes had been out to protect his Las Vegas investments, forgetting, perhaps, that they were a drop in the bucket compared to the income which Hughes' companies received from the U.S. government. Exact figures are hard to come by, but the Philadelphia *Inquirer* has calculated that Hughes—indirectly, of course—received an average of $1.7 million *a day*

---

* Humphrey, who had given up his Senate seat in 1965 to become Vice-President, retired from politics temporarily, becoming a professor at the University of Minnesota. In 1970 he won back his Senate seat and was re-elected in 1976.

139

from the U.S. Treasury.* Ironically, most of that money came from the three armed services in the form of contracts to the Hughes Aircraft Company. It seems safe to assume that the people who dispensed those contracts would have been among those least amused by Hughes' efforts to ban the bomb.

To repair the fences, O'Brien and Maheu set out to make it clear to the White House, the Pentagon, and Capitol Hill that no one was more patriotic than Howard Hughes: To use Maheu's language, when national security was at stake, every other consideration was very secondary. Hughes did not like the Nevada tests—for environmental reasons, of course. But he appreciated, his envoys explained, that the program was a necessary part of America's strategy to persuade the Russians to sign a nonproliferation treaty.

It was, in all fairness, not a bad piece of public relations. Hughes, the superpatriot, prepared to swallow the bitter pill in his country's cause, was a far more inspiring image than the one of Hughes, the entrepreneur, conspiring to protect his real estate.

The one man who was not altogether happy with this policy was Hughes, whose persistent complaints sometimes provoked Maheu's indignation:

"Howard, it appears to me that every time we discuss this issue, I am placed in a position of having to defend myself for the things that the A.E.C., Department of Defense, and the President of the United States may do in correlation to certain things which they claim must be accomplished relative to our long-range relations with Russia. . . .

"I don't mind taking on as adversaries the A.E.C., the Dept. of Defense and the Russians—as formidable as they all may be individually—but frankly and humbly, Howard, I don't have the desire to do all these things at the same time that I have to prove the necessity of my existence to an ally. . . ."

Howard Hughes never really did know when he was licked. The tests continued at regular intervals—as

* The *Inquirer* calculated that in the ten years between 1965 and 1974 Hughes' companies received over $6 billion of U.S. tax money—almost $5.75 billion of that coming from the Air Force, Army, and Navy.

they still do today—and sometimes they rattled the windows of the Desert Inn penthouse.

"Bob—

"Well, the blast went off this AM. Bob, what are we going to do to try desperately to obtain a policy against this conduct by the AEC. . . ."

7: EVERY ONE A WINNER

The King was in his counting house
Counting out his money . . .
> —Nursery Rhyme

The Silver Slipper Casino, just across the Strip from the Desert Inn, is one of Las Vegas' more modest attractions. Outside, a high-heeled slipper, neon-lit, revolves on top of a twenty-foot pole. But amid the glitter of the Castaways, the Frontier, the Stardust, and especially Circus Circus, all of which share the same block, it is easily overlooked.

Inside, it is fashioned, vaguely, after a speakeasy of the Old West. The entertainment is burlesque and, like the food, not very distinguished.

For a while after it opened in 1956, the Silver Slipper gained a reputation as the informal gathering place for Frank Sinatra's clan. But, in April 1964, it also gained notoriety when the management was discovered to have adjusted the percentage in favor of the house, by shaving the craps dice. In Las Vegas terms it is a "grind" casino for small bettors (grinds), and unlike its rivals on the Strip, it doesn't even offer a room for rent.

When Howard Hughes bought the Silver Slipper— for $5.3 million in March 1968—there was some talk of improvements. Hughes told Maheu that he planned to build a block of hotel rooms and a bridge, linking the Slipper to the Stardust next door, but nothing came of the idea. The casino remains what it has always been: the outcast of the Strip, exceptional only in its mediocrity.

Yet, between April 1969 and November 1970 the Silver Slipper contributed money more generously to more Nevada politicians than perhaps all of its swanky rivals put together. From the accumulated losses of the grinds, more than half a million dollars was given away, with extraordinary informality.

The money came from the head cashier's cage, located at the back of the casino, a little to the right of the main entrance. There, twice a day, armed security guards deliver padlocked metal cash boxes containing the takings from the gambling tables. (The customers play with chips—plastic counters—which they buy from the dealers at the tables. The dealers are required to immediately push the cash they receive through slots in the tables into the locked cash boxes below. For obvious reasons, this money is called the "drop.")

The unloading of the boxes is apparently quite a sight. Out of choice, Bob Maheu never participated in a count, but he says, those who have "tell me that it's some kind of an awesome thing to open up these little boxes and see piles of $100 bills that have to be counted."

In the bad old days, before Howard Hughes gave Las Vegas respectability, the experience sometimes proved to be too much for some casino owners. In the privacy of their cages they would allegedly "skim" the cash—pocket some of it—before the count, thus depriving the Internal Revenue Service of its rightful share.

Skimming became much more difficult in 1968, at least in theory, when the Nevada Gaming Commission introduced new counting rules. Since then owners have not been allowed inside the cages unless an employee—with no stake in the casino—is also present. If two owners are present in the cage at the same time, then one of them must have less than a five-percent shareholding.

There is, of course, a curious illogicality about this safeguard: Casino employees are not necessarily any less prone to corruptibility than casino owners. But in any event the important point is that Nevada authorities—and the IRS—are only concerned with what happens to the piles of cash *before* the count. Once it is completed, and once the winners have been paid, the surplus—known, again for obvious reasons, as the "hold"—belongs to the casino's owners to do with what they will.

Howard Hughes' "hold" was used to touch just about every political base in Nevada. For a while there wasn't a race—for Congress, for state assembly, for the governorship, for judgeships, and for local offices —which money from the Silver Slipper did not help to finance.

The genesis of the Silver Slipper fund lay in the suspicion of Robert Morgan that the Hughes Tool Company had, unwittingly made illegal political contributions.

Morgan, an accountant, was hired by the Hughes Tool Company in 1967 as director of finance for the Hughes-Nevada Operations. In practice, that meant that he supervised the financial affairs of the casinos owned by the Tool Company—the Desert Inn, the Sands, and the Frontier Hotel—rather than those owned personally by Hughes.

Beginning in the summer of 1968 those casinos began to incur some extraordinary expenses.

Lawrence Ryhlick, then financial controller of the Sands Hotel, was told by Maheu's deputy, General Nigro, "that there would be a requirement for funds which were personal to the organization and certainly not like a normal type of business expense."

The first "requirement" was for $4,420.07, which, Nigro said, was "to cover the expenses of a political figure." Ryhlick wrote out a Sands Hotel check, cashed it at the casino cage, and gave the money to the general.

A few days later, on July 4, Nigro asked for more. This time, he said, he needed $4,000 to take with him to Washington, D. C., where he would be "talking with a political figure."

On August 2, 1968, the "requirement" was for $20,000. This time, said Nigro, all of the Hughes hotels in Las Vegas would share the burden. Ryhlick dutifully collected $5,000 each from the Sands, the Desert Inn, the Frontier, and the Silver Slipper (which was owned personally by Hughes). He delivered the money—as he had been instructed—to Jack Hooper, the former Los Angeles policeman then in charge of security for both Hughes and the casinos.

There were five more transactions identical to that one. On August 30, October 7, October 17, November 1, and November 19, Ryhlick went his rounds, picking up $5,000 bundles of hundred-dollar bills, delivering the money each time to Hooper.

Ryhlick didn't ask what the money was being used for and nobody told him. In the books of the Sands Hotel he entered the transactions as "business expenses—nondeductible for tax purposes" and the other casinos did the same.

On December 5, 1968, there was a "requirement" for $50,000. This time the call came in the middle of a Sands Hotel staff meeting and it was so urgent that Ryhlick had no time to arrange for the burden to be shared. He drew the entire $50,000 from the Sands cage. (This money, allegedly destined for President-elect Nixon, was supposed to have been delivered to Bob Maheu at his office at the Frontier Hotel by a driver. Maheu says he never got it. As with the $50,000 Hubert Humphrey denies receiving, the mystery of who got it seems insoluble.)

Ryhlick was called upon to provide funds from the Sands once more, on January 31, 1969, when he delivered $16,000 to Jack Hooper.

By that time he was, he says, nervous, and understandably so. He had distributed, in a period of about six months, almost $200,000 with no idea of what the money was being used for and without collecting a single receipt. When the Tool Company's auditors asked Ryhlick to explain these "nondeductible business expenses," he genuinely could not. (Ryhlick knew how much money he had paid out because he had kept a personal record.)

As it happened, Robert Morgan had worked for

the auditors—the eminent firm of Haskins & Sells —before he became the finance director for the Hughes-Nevada Operations. His desk was the logical place for the problem, and that is where it landed. But try as he did to find out what had happened to the money, Morgan was no more able to enlighten Haskins & Sells than Ryhlick had been. The reason, quite simply, was that Jack Hooper, who had received most of it, refused to tell him.

Hooper also refused to tell Calvin Collier, the treasurer of the Hughes Tool Company. Summoned to Houston by Collier and told that Raymond Holliday, no less, wanted to know where the money had gone, Hooper replied, "Mr. Hughes doesn't want you to know." (Hooper has consistently maintained that position through all of the subsequent legal investigations into Hughes' affairs. He received a total of $330,000, but will not say where one penny of it went.)

It says a great deal about Hughes' demagoguery that even executives with the power of Holliday and Collier felt unable to put the question to the one man who, presumably, knew the answers. Instead, Collier went to Maheu. He was not very helpful. He did not know where most of the money had gone, either, he said, "because that's the way Howard Hughes wants it."

The overwhelming concern of the Tool Company was that it might be breaking the law. Of course Hughes could give money to whomever he chose, but corporations—even those, like the Tool Company, with just one shareholder—cannot contribute more than $10,000 to candidates running for federal office. And such contributions *must* be declared.

In those circumstances it was unthinkable for the casinos legally owned by the Tool Company to give away undisclosed but undoubtedly large sums of money to unnamed people. If these secret payouts were going to continue, the money would have to come directly out of Hughes' pocket.

The only property in Nevada with a large enough cash flow which (for income tax reasons) Hughes owned personally was the Silver Slipper. Collier and Morgan between them worked out the details. In April 1969, the fund was born.

At least ninety-one political candidates in Nevada received money from the Silver Slipper. If any of them had wondered what Hughes expected to achieve through such grand patronage, Thomas Bell could have enlightened them.

Bell was a Nevada lawyer with some useful connections. For three years (1955 to 1958) he was on the personal staff of Nevada Senator Alan Bible and became, he says, the senator's protégé. When, in 1967, Hughes sought a local lawyer to help obtain the gaming license for the Desert Inn, Bible, along with Nevada's other senator, Howard Cannon, and the governor, Paul Laxalt, joined in recommending Bell. Perhaps one of his qualifications for the job was that his brother, Lloyd Bell, was undersheriff of Clark County, where Las Vegas is located. The sheriff's department is responsible for investigating those who apply for a gaming license.

By 1969 Bell was working virtually full-time for the Hughes-Nevada Operations. He kept records of his assignments, and in the legal battles that followed Hughes' departure from Las Vegas, he was asked to review them:

I have a file concerning Nevada government—state, county and municipal.

I have a file that reflects my efforts to avoid the personal appearance of Hughes before any governmental agency in Nevada.

I have a file concerning my monitoring and advice to Hughes of all actions in the executive, legislative and judicial branches of government in the state of Nevada that affected him personally. And further I have a file . . . concerning Mr. Hughes' request to stop the A.E.C. (Atomic Energy Commission) tests at Mercury, Nevada.

I have a file asking me to take whatever legal action is necessary to avoid the construction and completion of the Bonanza Hotel.

I have a request from Mr. Hughes, and a file to back it up, to advise him on every single bill introduced into the Nevada legislature and to request the members of the legislature . . . to adopt his

146

views of what bills should and should not be passed in the 1969 session.

I have a file concerning Hughes' request to stop the legislature from increasing the sales tax, the gasoline tax and the cigarette tax in Nevada.

I have either a memo or file or something to the effect to prohibit the passage of legislation that would authorize a licensing of public corporations for gambling in Nevada.

I was advised by Hughes to take the necessary steps to avoid the requirement of his personal appearance before the Nevada Gaming Control Board, Clark County Gaming Control Board or any licensing board for the city of Las Vegas.

I was asked by Hughes to do whatever was possible to arrange for permission for him or his company to acquire the Stardust Hotel. Hughes commissioned me to request the governor of Nevada, then Paul Laxalt, to persuade the federal authorities not to interfere with his acquisition of the Stardust.

I was requested by him . . . to persuade the legislature not to authorize any gaming tax increases.

He requested me to do everything possible to prevent the calling of a special session of the Nevada legislature in 1970.

He requested I stop the Clark County School District integration plan.

He asked me to resist the passage of legislation making gambling debts legally collectible.

He asked me to keep in constant contact with Governor Paul Laxalt concerning all Nevada affairs —legislative, executive and judicial.

I was asked by Mr. Hughes to prohibit the appropriate government agencies from realigning any streets in Clark County without his personal views being first had or given;

to stop any legislation concerning a state income tax and state inheritance tax;

to stop the special Keno tax (proposed) by the Clark County Commissioners;

to urge the prohibition of the construction of any more gambling casinos on the Las Vegas Strip between Sahara Avenue and Tropicana Avenue unless the facilities had at least 500 rooms;

to encourage the governmental officials to deter any further expansion of the Las Vegas convention facility;

to advise him as to the qualifications and background of everyone running for political office and who he should support in the various political races;

to do whatever was necessary to shield him from having to appear personally in any courts of the state of Nevada;

take whatever steps necessary to prohibit any annual sessions of the Nevada legislature and to limit the length of the Nevada legislative sessions; advise him personally on all ordinances or laws regarding obscenity and pornography;

stop any legislation involving censorship or anti-pornography;

do everything possible to slow down further expansion of McCarran International Airport until he personally determined the feasibility of a regional airport in the El Dorado Valley, coupled with a rapid transit system from the valley to Las Vegas;

take whatever action necessary to prohibit rock festivals in Clark County;

advise him as to the legal efforts being made to remove Jay Sarno from ownership and management in the Circus Circus casino and further as to the opportunity to purchase Circus Circus, and advise me that Jay Sarno should not be a licensee in Circus Circus, and I should so advise the governing authorities . . . ;

take whatever steps necessary to prohibit consolidation and/or, annexation of Las Vegas in the county of Clark and the city of Las Vegas;

take whatever steps are necessary to prohibit any further annexation by the city of North Las Vegas; impress the members of the Nevada legislature with his views on consolidation and annexation; attempt to convince the appropriate authorities that there should be no further increase in the assessed valuation of Las Vegas Strip property, except every five years;

request a delay in the selection of an executive director for the Las Vegas convention center until his personal views could be registered;

stop the cities and counties within Clark County from approving the one half per cent optional sales tax;

take whatever action is necessary to encourage the state gaming authorities not to change any of the rules of the various gambling games, and, in particular, roulette;

discourage appropriate state officials from permitting communist bloc entertainers or shows from appearing in the Las Vegas casinos and hotels.

As Bell later testified, that list is incomplete and there were "other matters" that he dealt with on behalf of Hughes. Chief among those was handing out to Nevada politicians and to candidates for political office between $320,000 and $390,000 from the Silver Slipper fund. It is impossible to give a precise figure because the money was scattered like seeds in the wind. Most of the payments were made in cash; no receipts were asked for and no records kept.

Bell says, "Mr. Maheu advised me that the quickest way to get fired by Mr. Hughes was to keep a record of his political affairs and his political contributions. And then he admonished me that I should not have a record that could become available to someone outside the organization."

Nevertheless, he did for a while carry a monitoring list in his wallet. It was the only way of making sure that somebody didn't get paid twice. Eventually, Bell destroyed the list in a paper shredder.

The only semblance of control was that imposed by the accountants, Calvin Collier and Robert Morgan, when they organized the Silver Slipper fund.

The system they established called for Bell and Jack Hooper to maintain floats out of which they would make contributions. To replenish their floats they had to submit a voucher for the approval of either Maheu or General Nigro. The Silver Slipper would then issue a check, cashable at the casino cage.

Because of that it is at least possible to establish from the casino's records how much money Hooper and Bell got. The first withdrawal, on April 21, 1969, was $10,000. In June $30,000 was paid out, $15,000 in July, and $35,000 in August. In September the casino—or, more accurately, of course, its customers—contributed $20,000 and in December, $15,000.

The next year, 1970, began quietly: $10,000 in April, $15,000 in May, and $15,000 in July. Then Hughes' munificence apparently increased dramatically. In August $50,000 was withdrawn, in September $90,000, and in October, the climax—$165,000. In November there were two withdrawals, the first of $15,000 and the second, on November 24, of $20,000. Although few people knew it at the time, the next day Nevada's most active political backer fled Las Vegas, and the state, for good.

The total amount withdrawn from the Silver Slipper in nineteen months was more than half a million dollars. Exactly what happened to most of it is anybody's guess.

Bell never met Hughes nor spoke to him. Generally he got his orders by telephone from one of the five male secretaries—the "Mormon Mafia." Bell says that the conversations would invariably begin, "Mr. Hughes has asked me to ask you . . ." or "Mr. Hughes has directed me to tell you . . ."

Bell was supposed to make his reports to Hughes by the same channels. None of the secretaries took shorthand and, "We'd have to repeat the message a number of times to make sure it was accurate before it was delivered to Mr. Hughes."

Sometimes when he was asked by a political candidate for an unusually large donation Bell would consult with Maheu, but generally the question of who should get how much was left to his own discretion. (Maheu says that he was ordered by Hughes not to play any part in the distribution of the Silver Slipper fund. The reasoning was that, as Hughes' front man, Maheu had to make appearances before the various gaming boards. If ever embarrassing questions about political contributions should come up, he could truthfully answer, "I don't know.")

Deciding who should get contributions was a little problem because Bell's instructions were "to touch every political base in Nevada," and in those circumstances almost every candidate running for office who was credited with a chance of winning could reckon on being offered a donation.

Deciding how much to contribute required a little more effort. "I determined through investigation what other hotels in the area were doing, what other businesses were doing, the general size of those contributions. . . . And then, keeping in mind the size of those contributions it was left in my discretion to make a determination as to the amount to be given to a particular candidate."

A lot of the aspirants came within what Bell described as the $500 class. Then there was the $1,000 class. On occasions Hooper and Bell would confer to fix a candidate's rating and then be together at the payout, which invariably took place at the Hughes-Nevada offices at the Frontier Hotel.

Bell remembers a typical occasion when Thomas Wiesner, who ran successfully for the Board of County Commissioners in 1970, called at the Frontier. Asked to describe what happened, Bell testified, "Well, some general conversation—I can't recall the nature of it. And then Mr. Hooper reaching into his desk drawer and giving to Mr. Wiesner a sum of money in $100 bills as a political contribution—I can't remember whether it was $500 or $1,000. Mr. Wiesner thanking him and Mr. Hooper saying he was happy to be able to do it and 'good luck.' Almost in all cases, that was the general gist of the conversation with those candidates."

Few of the candidates counted the money, or signed a receipt, or even subsequently acknowledged the contribution. Bell did receive a few thank-you notes—"Thank you for the help during my campaign"—but he only remembers one that mentioned the amount of money that had been donated.

Even when much larger sums than $500 or $1,000 were being dispensed, there was little ceremony.

Between 1966 and 1970 William Morse, a Las Vegas lawyer, was chairman of the Clark County Republican Committee, and as such he was active in raising money for Republican candidates in state elections. Fund raising in Clark County was hard work. Typical donations ranged between $10 and $50, and the biggest single contribution Morse can remember receiving was $250. To provide its candidates with campaign funds, the Republican Committee relied primarily on backyard barbecues.

Hughes' entry into the Nevada political arena changed all that. Morse has testified that he "somehow got word" that his committee was to get a contribution from Hughes. He made an appointment with Bell and Hooper, and one Saturday afternoon—after a round of golf—he called at the Frontier Hotel.

"I went into the office, and we passed the time of day and we had a drink or something and they said, 'Well, here's your money' and it was in an envelope. And I didn't count it or count it down with them. I just looked at the envelope and put it in my pocket. After the pleasantries of the day and 'How did you shoot?' and 'What was the score on the golf course?' I left."

According to Morse, that envelope contained $12,000, in hundred-dollar bills secured with a rubber band. According to Bell, it was $15,000. There is also a dispute between the two men as to when the donation was made. Morse says that he paid the money into one of the Republican Committee's bank accounts, but any of his records which might have settled the argument did not survive.

In view of the manner in which the Silver Slipper fund was operated, it is hardly surprising that there should now be controversy over just how many hundred-dollar bills there were in some of those packages liberally dispensed at the Frontier Hotel. And the discrepancies that have surfaced are considerable.

Robert Broadbent, who ran, successfully, for the Board of County Commissioners and, unsuccessfully, for the post of lieutenant governor, says he got $12,000. Bell says it was $20,000.

James Brennan, unsuccessful candidate for Clark County Commissioner, says he is "pretty sure" he got $3,000. Bell has testified it was $4,000.

David Branch, a candidate for the Nevada State Assembly, says he got $1,000. Bell says it was $2,500.

Robert List, successful candidate for Nevada attorney general in 1970, says he got $6,200. Bell says it was $9,500.

James Ryan, who ran unsuccessfully for Clark County Commissioner, has testified he got $5,000. Bell says it was $10,000.

And so it goes. The most significant contradiction concerns Ed Fike, Nevada's lieutenant governor from 1967 to 1970, who also ran, unsuccessfully, at various times, for both the U.S. Senate and the governorship. Bell says that he financed Fike's campaigns to the tune of $45,000. Fike says he got $25,000.

In fairness it has to be said that Bell both anticipated and dreaded these kinds of disputes. (And with good cause: in the course of a lawsuit between Hughes' Summa Corporation and Maheu, Bell was in effect accused by Summa of stealing from the Silver Slipper fund between $58,100 and $79,600, "depending on how you count it.") Several times, he says, he raised the problem of his own "exposure" with Robert Morgan, the Hughes-Nevada director of finance. To protect himself Bell wanted to make the contributions by check, but there were very good reasons why that could not be sanctioned.

According to Bell, "Cash was the best way to do it, so as not to expose Mr. Hughes to what I would call political extortion, by letting one candidate know what another candidate got. And it was best, so far as Mr. Hughes was concerned, to not let every candidate know what every other candidate got, because some got more than others. And some were running for comparable offices and therefore a check would have been a bad way of doing it."

Indeed it would. Hughes wanted to back every winner in almost every race and to guarantee that the Silver Slipper fund was used to bet on just about every horse in the field. Hughes could have expected little gratitude from the winners if they had realized that their rivals had received equal, if not greater, patronage.

There was also the consideration, said Bell, that "many of the politicians in Nevada didn't want to take a check. They preferred to take cash. They didn't want to be identified as receiving a donation from a particular contributor and cash was the most appropriate way to make it."

Eventually, at Bell and Hooper's insistence, some donations were made by check when the candidate did not object. However, some of those candidates also got cash. Asked to identify them, Bell refused, saying, "Well, I claim client-attorney privilege on that."

There is no evidence that the Silver Slipper fund was illicit or that the Nevada politicians who benefited from it were corrupt. But the deeply cynical way in which that fund operated made a mockery of Nevada's political and legislative institutions. Hughes cared little about political ideologies, party affiliations, or the qualities of the candidates. All that mattered was that he be on the winning side. He was out to buy favors, secretly and with hundred-dollar bills, and whether the favors came as a quid pro quo or not, he got them.

From the testimony of the men who worked for Hughes, it is clear that he regarded Nevada as a personal kingdom. Eventually he became disillusioned, feeling, he said, like a man "with a mass of seaweed and other entanglements wrapped around him, holding him back." But it is not difficult to understand why he believed, for a while at least, that from the governor downward, he had Nevada in his pocket.

In one sense Paul Laxalt—now Senator Laxalt—and Howard Hughes "arrived" in Nevada at the same time. Laxalt, the son of a Basque-American shepherd and by profession a lawyer, was elected governor of the state in 1966. He took office in January 1967, shortly before Hughes began to take over a considerable proportion of Nevada's second largest industry.

The governor has weighty influence in matters concerning Nevada's gambling policy, so Laxalt's attitude toward Hughes' ambition was of some importance. He proved to be a vociferous supporter. According to his friends, that was because he had been shown, by the Justice Department in Washington, D.C., documentary evidence of organized crime's stake in Las Vegas which "scared him to hell." Laxalt had returned to

Nevada convinced that Hughes represented the road to salvation.

When Hughes' appetite for new casinos seemed at one stage unquenchable, Laxalt did—in response to considerable public criticism—summon a special session of the Nevada Gaming Policy Board to determine "if we are on the brink of a monopoly." But when crucial questions were raised at that session, such as what would happen to all the casinos—and all the jobs they represented—when Hughes died, Laxalt intervened. "That's asking to look into a person's will," he said. "We have no right to make this type of inquiry."

To anyone who asked, Laxalt made no apologies for his attitude. "Mr. Hughes' involvement here has absolutely done us wonders. I just returned from a trip to the East where I spoke to some industrialists in midtown Manhattan and their questions no longer are concerned with the Mafia, the skimming, the underworld. . . . People come here now feeling they can come here in respectable, safe circumstances."

To enhance that newfound respectability, the Hughes-Nevada staff played an extensive public role in the state's civic affairs, joining the Governor's Manpower and Economic Development Conference, the Governor's Gaming Task Force, and the Governor's Advisory Council on Tourism.

And a strong personal friendship developed between Laxalt and Maheu. When the Maheus held a party, the social columns of the local newspapers usually recorded that "the Paul Laxalts were there." The two men also became frequent tennis partners. (Among those who were cynical of Hughes' declared intentions to bring development to Las Vegas, there was a joke that the only thing he'd build would be a tennis court for Maheu and the governor. Disregarding Maheu's $350,000 house, they were right.)

The net result of this rapport was the extraordinary preferential treatment accorded Hughes. During Laxalt's term in office Hughes was allowed to acquire more casinos (seven) than any other operator in Nevada without even fulfilling the normal licensing requirements.

There is no suggestion that Laxalt's vocal and practical support for Hughes was improper or that he gained personally from it. He did, when his term as governor was nearing an end, accept an offer from Maheu to become Hughes' personal attorney. That, however, came to nothing.

The only personal benefit he seems to have sought was ephemeral. He complained to Maheu that it was embarrassing for him to have to admit that he had never spoken to Hughes, and after some prompting, Maheu arranged a telephone call with The Man. Laxalt thus became one of the handful of people to have spoken with Hughes since 1954, and the Las Vegas *Review-Journal* headlined the event in blue ink. (There are cynics who say that the governor was hoaxed by Maheu. Laxalt admits he has no way of proving the ownership of the voice he heard, but his belief that it belonged to Hughes is unshakable.)

There is, however, evidence that Laxalt used his contact with the Hughes-Nevada organization to win substantial financial support from the Silver Slipper fund for Republican political candidates.

Thomas Bell, the fund's main distributor, says, "From time to time during Paul Laxalt's administration he asked me to convey to Mr. Hughes the desirability of making political contributions to certain candidates, not in any specific amounts. I conveyed this information on to the penthouse to Mr. Hughes through his aides and I received replies back, not for any specific amounts, but to comply with Paul Laxalt's wishes.

"He [Laxalt] actually visited me personally with reference to supporting particular Republican candidates, namely Chick Hench, Ed Fike, Bob List . . . Bob Broadbent. I believe he even requested support for Cameron Batjet, candidate for the supreme court, Bill Radio, Zel Lowman, Wilson McGowan, Woodrow Wilson. . . ."

William Morse, the chairman of the Republican Central Committee, received his $12,000 (or $15,000) donated at Laxalt's request, and, Bell has testified Laxalt also asked him to support Robert Broadbent, candidate for lieutenant governor, "as best Mr. Hughes could." Bell raised the question with Maheu, who said, "because of Paul Laxalt, and what have you, go ahead and do the best you can with him but try to hold it down."

Laxalt's most notable efforts were on behalf of Ed Fike, who in 1970 was the Republican nominee for governor. According to Bell, Laxalt "pushed very hard" for funds for Fike. "I informed Bob Maheu of Paul Laxalt's urging for additional contributions for Fike. I think I mentioned to Maheu that we had already given [Fike] twenty thousand and he wanted another thirty or forty. Bob Maheu told me to do the best I could to hold him down." (In that year's primary election Mike O'Callaghan, a teacher who had lost one leg during Army service in the Korean War, emerged as the very strong Democratic contender for the governorship. Up to that point he had received no financial support from the Silver Slipper, but during the remainder of the race he received $25,000 in contributions from Bell. At the polls he defeated Fike by a small margin. In 1974, O'Callaghan was reelected by a near unanimous vote.)

There is also evidence that Hughes believed Laxalt to be, in effect, an agent of the Hughes-Nevada Operations and that he wanted the governor to use his influence in ways which went far beyond the bounds of propriety. One episode in particular serves to illustrate what Hughes *thought* he could demand.

Toward the end of 1967 Maheu began negotiations on behalf of Hughes to buy two casinos in northern Nevada belonging to Bill Harrah. The casinos, one in Reno and one on the south shore of Lake Tahoe, were prime properties and Maheu's initial bid was $50 million.

But the negotiations proceeded only very slowly and Hughes became impatient. In February 1968, he told Maheu that Laxalt should be called in to handle the negotiations with Harrah.

Sometime around February 15 Hughes wrote a note to Maheu which, in part, said: "Now re Harrah, you and I know he will never call so please do call him now, and if he still unwilling to make up his mind, please ascertain the whereabouts of the Gov. and his plans for PM. . . . Also before you hang up with Harrah, if he is negative, please find out where he will be all afternoon, so you are in a position to tell the Governor where to reach [him]."

Three weeks later, on March 7, Maheu received a proposal from Harrah. It was, in Maheu's words, a "complete shock." In effect Harrah said he was only willing to sell the Lake Tahoe casino, but the price would still be $50 million. For that Hughes would only get the property. Harrah would retain his name and the right to perhaps open another casino, if he chose, to compete with Hughes for Lake Tahoe's gamblers. Maheu sent the proposal to Hughes with a note which read, "Boy, the economics don't make any sense. I have to believe that this guy is completely out of his fucking mind."

Hughes scrawled his reply on the bottom of Maheu's note. "Please tell all of the above to the Gov. . . . I only insist Harrah hold to his original price of $50,000,000 for both clubs and since he chooses to keep the Reno club I only ask that an appropriate deduction be made. . . . Please try to persuade the Gov. to try to persuade Harrah to hold to the scheme of pricing he has been discussing with us all these weeks. . . ."

Five days later Hughes followed up with another note to Maheu. "I feel the Gov. should point out to Harrah the obvious unfairness [of] this complete reversal of his position. . . . I feel the Gov. should explain to Harrah that you don't treat friends in this way. Let's have the Gov. working on this. . . ."

Maheu denies that he passed on to Laxalt any of these requests, and he denies that Laxalt played any role in the Harrah negotiations. "Laxalt and I became very good friends," he said. "But I always felt that when I asked him for something it was something that we merited and I did not get involved in any area in the misuse of power which is something that I vehemently attempted to avoid. . . ."

If that is true, then Maheu must have lied to Hughes —or at least led him to believe that Laxalt was willing to moonlight as an unpaid emissary. There is another

Hughes note, also written in March 1968, which expresses even more explicitly what Hughes thought:

"Bob . . . I want you to go to see Nixon as my special confidential emissary. I feel there is a really valid possibility of a Republican victory this year. If that could be realized under our sponsorship and supervision every inch of the way then we would be ready to follow with Laxalt as our next candidate. . . ."

8: MR. PRESIDENT

Maybe you've cheated
Maybe you've lied
Maybe you have finally lost your mind
Maybe you're only thinking 'bout yourself
—*Mr. President*, Randy Newman

While conflict and confusion surround the details of Howard Hughes' political contributions to just about everybody, it is possible in most cases to boil the contradictions down to manageable proportions. For example, Hubert Humphrey either did or did not receive $50,000 in cash on July 29, 1968. If he did get the money, it was intended to buy his support for Hughes' antibomb campaign.

By comparison, the story of Hughes' payoffs to President Richard Milhous Nixon is so enmeshed in deceit as to be almost indigestible. About the only certainty is that Hughes was more generous toward Nixon than to any other politician. But exactly how much of Hughes' money the President got, when it was paid, why it was paid, and what Nixon did with it are questions that can only be answered with conjecture.

One reason for that, as we have tried to demonstrate,

is that the Hughes coffers leaked money as copiously as a sieve. There was, seemingly, no end to the sources of or the conduits for cash, and the problem facing any student of Hughes' political munificence is that just when it seems that all the bagmen, and all their sundry fonts, have been identified, another distributor or another fund pops up. It is a bit like toying with Pandora's box: You open it at your peril, for out will come not evil, perhaps, but certainly multiple confusion.

Mercifully, the saga of the Nixon contribution begins simply.

On October 23, 1968, Robert A. Maheu Associates wrote out seventeen checks totalling $50,000 to various committees supporting Nixon's bid for the presidency. Sixteen of them—the Nixon for Victory Committee, the Nye County [Nevada] Committee for Nixon, Victory '68 Committee, Friends of Nixon Committee, Supporters of Nixon, Good Government with Nixon Committee, Nixon for President Committee, Clark County [Nevada] for Nixon-Agnew, Campaign '68 Victory Committee, Nevadans for Nixon Committee, Southern Nevadans for Nixon, Citizens for Nixon-Agnew, Clark County, Nixon's the One Committee, Campaign Sixty-Eight Committee, Las Vegans for Nixon-Agnew, and the Nixon-Agnew Committee of Southern Nevada—got checks for $3,000. The other one—Youth for Nixon Committee—got only $2,000, not, presumably, out of any discrimination toward the young but to make the total contribution a nice round $50,000. Everyone agrees that this money came from Hughes' private bank account, administered by Nadine Henley: On September 9, 1968, she had given Maheu Associates a check for that amount with the intention that it should benefit Nixon's presidential campaign.

That was Hughes' only orthodox donation to Nixon. From then on we are dealing not with checks and the adequate records they create but with the more typical currency of Hughes' political patronage—untraceable hundred-dollar bills.

Sometime in the late summer or early fall of 1968, after Richard Nixon had won the Republican party's nomination for President, Charles "Bebe" Rebozo began seeking funds for the campaign of Nixon and his running mate, Spiro T. Agnew. Rebozo was not an official Republican fund-raiser nor was he a member of Nixon's staff or any of the campaign committees. He was, however, a uniquely close friend to Nixon. And when it came to the fast pursuit of lots of dollars, there were few men better qualified than Bebe Rebozo.

Charles Gregory Rebozo was the youngest child of a Cuban cigar maker who moved to Miami to live and raise his family. Young Bebe was voted the best-looking boy in the class of 1930 at Miami High School, and after that triumph he began a varied career as tire salesman, gas station manager, tour guide, and airline steward. It was land that provided Bebe with his big break. Anticipating the Florida land boom, he bought some beachfront property cheaply, selling it at a considerable profit when prices began to skyrocket. He repeated the same trick several times, and by 1968 was over halfway to becoming a millionaire. (During the five years of the Nixon presidency, he achieved that status several times over. By his own account, his wealth increased to $4.5 million, and among his extensive interests he is now chairman, president, and principal stockholder of the Key Biscayne Bank.)

In any search for campaign funds it would have been natural enough, given Howard Hughes' interest in so many political races, to look to him for a hefty contribution. But Rebozo, not normally a reticent man, was extremely leery about forging any tangible link between Nixon and Hughes—and with good historical reason.

In 1956 Hughes had made a loan of $205,000, on extremely generous terms, to then Vice-President Nixon's brother, Donald, to bolster his fast-food business, which specialized in a triple-decker sandwich called a Nixonburger. In 1960, when Nixon was running for President against John Kennedy, the details of the unrepaid loan were revealed by the syndicated columnist Drew Pearson (despite Bob Maheu's energetic efforts to kill the story), and the curious episode came to haunt Nixon's campaign. In San Francisco's Chinatown, for example, the presidential hopeful, wearing a full-faced smile, posed for a picture with

161

some Chinese children who were holding a banner; unbeknownst to Nixon, the Chinese characters on the banner said, "What About the Hughes Loan?" At the luncheon which followed the rally, Nixon opened a fortune cookie to find the message—this time in English—"Ask Him About the Hughes Loan." Every fortune cookie in the place contained the same demand.

Bebe Rebozo has said he has no doubts that Hughes' loan to Don Nixon cost his brother the 1960 election and "it didn't help in 1962" when Richard Nixon ran, unsuccessfully, for the governorship of California. Understandably, then, in approaching Hughes for money during the 1968 campaign, Rebozo felt the need to be circumspect.

As it happened, one of the Republican campaign committees in Washington, D.C., was headed by Richard G. Danner. He had known both Rebozo and Nixon for a long time and, indeed, claimed to have been the catalyst of their now famous (or notorious) friendship.* More relevantly, Danner had an important contact with the Hughes organization. At the height of World War II he had been head of the FBI's office in Miami, and among the 250 special agents he had directed was Edward Morgan—the Washington lawyer whose name has cropped up so many times in our story. Rebozo called Danner, who called Morgan, who called Bob Maheu to ask the question: How much, if anything, was Hughes going to give Nixon?

The reply that came back down the line from Maheu was a promise of $50,000—payable *in cash* (and, therefore, not to be confused with the $50,000 which Maheu intended to contribute by check to the various Nixon campaign committees).

For reasons that are quite unclear, it was not thought appropriate to simply have the money delivered to

* Danner met Nixon in 1947 when the then senator was vacationing at Vero Beach, Florida. For something to do, Danner suggested they go on a fishing trip with a boat-owning friend of his, Rebozo. During the trip Rebozo remembers exchanging less than a dozen words with Nixon, whom he assumed had been miserable. However, he later received an enthusiastic thank-you note from Nixon, and many more trips followed.

either Danner or Rebozo by some trusted courier. Instead, in September 1968, a meeting to discuss the mechanics of the delivery was set up in New York City. It never took place, because at the last moment Rebozo discovered that besides himself, Morgan, and Danner, two other men were planning to attend—and he wanted nothing to do with either of them.

It was bad enough, from Rebozo's viewpoint, to learn that Don Nixon planned to be there; far worse was the announcement that the fifth participant at the meeting would be a man with a name pronounced like the word "mire."

Throughout his lifetime Hughes kept coming into contact with men whose names sounded like "mire" and they almost always brought him trouble. Gabe *Meyer* was the name of the man Hughes killed; Stanley *Meyer* was a wheeler-dealer who would—in 1971—play an important role in the creation of a bogus Hughes autobiography; John *Meier* was Hughes' "scientific adviser," who in due time would reveal the billionaire's alleged links with the CIA; and then there was John *Meyer,* perhaps the most troublesome of all.

In August 1947, during the U.S. Senate's investigation of Hughes' wartime activities, the pressing questions had been how Hughes had obtained $60 million worth of warplane contracts from the government and then failed to deliver a single plane. On the question of how the orders had been obtained, John Meyer was thought to be something of an expert. During the war he had been Hughes' "public relations consultant," and his duties included "picking up the check" for people, including government officials, whom Hughes wanted entertained. Meyer's expense records, subpoenaed by the Brewster Committee, showed that in five years he had picked up checks totaling $164,000. One not untypical item was the $100 paid by Meyer to a lady named Dolores Tatum who spent the evening of October 14, 1946, entertaining Interior Secretary Julius A. Krug. Meyer was summoned before the Brewster Committee to explain in more detail his fascinating exploits, but before his testimony could be completed he was ordered by Hughes to leave Washington, and he disappeared.

Actually, the fifth proposed participant of the New York meeting was John *Meier,* the scientific adviser. But the only Hughes man with a name like "mire" that Rebozo had heard of was John *Meyer.* On that misunderstanding, he called the meeting off.

It has to be said that superlawyer Edward Morgan could not have been too upset by the abrupt cancellation. Although he had played a significant part in putting Rebozo in contact with the Hughes organization, he subsequently lost some of his appetite for the transaction. He was, he says, unhappy at the prospect of a large amount of cash being handed over to Rebozo rather than to an official campaign committee: Putting it bluntly, he wanted some kind of guarantee—such as a signed acknowledgment—that the $50,000 would reach Nixon. Because no satisfactory guarantee was apparently available, Morgan told Maheu that he wanted nothing more to do with the affair.

The lack of the services of both Rebozo and Morgan may explain, in part, why it was not until *after* the election, and *after* Nixon's victory, that the first attempt was made to deliver Hughes' cash contribution to a campaign by then over.

Roughly one month after the election, President-elcct Nixon attended the Republican Governors' Conference held December 4–7 at the Canyon Hotel, Palm Springs, in the southern California desert. According to Maheu, Nevada Governor Paul Laxalt arranged for a rendezvous with Nixon at the desert home of publisher (later U.S. ambassador to Britain) Walter Annenberg, and on December 6, Maheu has testified he arrived in Palm Springs clutching a manila envelope containing ten bundles of hundred-dollar bills.

Maheu checked into a hotel—the reservation having been made by the Secret Service—and waited for the appointed hour. When it came, he and Laxalt got into their rented car and drove to Annenberg's house. "We approached the front of the house and Governor Laxalt went inside, came back out and said that the schedule had been disrupted by some emergencies," Maheu says. Evidently the emergencies were so pressing that Nixon could not even spare a few moments to receive Maheu's manila envelope, and the appointment was canceled. Maheu and Laxalt, no doubt feeling just a little bit sheepish, turned their car around and went back from whence they had come.

(There is some irony in what subsequently became of this particular $50,000. Having failed to deliver it to Nixon, Maheu says that he took it back to Las Vegas, kept it for a while in a hidden vault under the staircase of his home, and then, early in 1969, used it to pay back the loan from Chester Simms—which, allegedly, had been made for the benefit of Hubert Humphrey.)

The determination of Hughes' organization to give Nixon his due did not dissipate, but after the Palm Springs fiasco it became apparent that what the Hughes-Nevada Operations lacked was someone in whom the new President might have confidence. Consequently, Maheu began to seriously court Richard Danner as a prospective employee.

Danner's career had been somewhat varied—FBI agent, political campaigner, car dealer, and lawyer—but unlike many of Maheu's recruits to the Nevada operation he did possess some experience of the resort business, having been at one time safety director and city manager of Miami. In December 1968 he was asked to go to Las Vegas to talk with Maheu and Maheu's deputy, General Nigro. The following month Danner took his wife to Las Vegas so she could see where her husband's career might take them. She must have liked it, for in February 1969 Danner accepted Maheu's offer to become managing director of the Frontier Hotel and Casino. According to Maheu, Danner also accepted an additional assignment: "He was paid a salary or a fee above and beyond the going rate of our managing directors so that he could become the conduit to the Administration via Rebozo."

Not surprisingly, Danner was regarded as a very valuable employee indeed. He lived at first in a suite at the Frontier, which was redecorated and modernized at a cost of more than $100,000. And when the time came that Danner's mother-in-law needed special care, it was the Hughes-Nevada Operations that picked up the bill, which during one period amounted to $3,-933.08. Explaining the circumstances in a note attached to his expense account, Danner said: "I had a choice of either keeping her here at the hotel or putting her in the [Las Vegas] Convalescent Center and because of her age and infirmity it would have presented a very difficult proposition here."

In return for this generosity, Danner worked hard, particularly on his extracurricular assignment. According to his expense accounts for 1969 and 1970, he made several trips to visit Nixon and/or Rebozo in Washington, D.C., New York, Key Biscayne, Florida, and San Clemente, California. In the course of those trips, according to Danner himself, he took the opportunity to hand over to Rebozo *two* payments of $50,000 *each*.

Leaving aside for a moment the puzzle of why Hughes' cash contribution to Nixon should have been double the original offer, it would be useful to determine when the money was actually handed over; the dates might provide some clue as to just which causes the contributions were intended to benefit. Unfortunately, the participants in the Nixon affair do not share the same recollections.

The one thing Danner is certain of is that he delivered $50,000 to the so-called "Western White House" on July 3, 1970—eighteen months after Nixon became President. Recalling the circumstances, Danner says he took an Air West flight to Santa Ana, California, very early that day and rode in an airport limousine to Nixon's San Clemente residence, where he met Rebozo. They had breakfast and then he and Rebozo went into the guest room Rebozo was using, where, with no one else present, Danner handed Rebozo a brown manila envelope containing ten $5,000 packets of hundred-dollar bills. Danner took the same limousine back to Santa Ana and caught an Air West flight to Las Vegas.

As to when the other $50,000 was paid, Danner is of two minds. When he was first interviewed about the matter by IRS agents he said that he had delivered the money to Rebozo in Key Biscayne, Florida, in August 1969—almost a year *before* he made the San Clemente payment. In a subsequent interview with the IRS, however, he changed the date to August 1970—a month *after* the San Clemente payment. His expense accounts do indeed show that on August 19, 1970, he flew from Las Vegas to Miami—using an Air Travel credit card to pay for the ticket—and rented a car. (Danner says that he then drove to the Key Biscayne Bank and met Rebozo in his office, handing him an envelope containing the $50,000. Rebozo casually examined a few of the bundles of hundred-dollar bills and then left the office for a few moments, taking the envelope with him. When he returned he told Danner that he had put the money in a safety deposit box which "he kept separate from his personal belongings and records, for political contributions." Danner returned to Las Vegas the next morning.)

However, while Rebozo agrees with Danner that one payment was made in July 1970 (at San Clemente), he says that he received the other $50,000 in "late 1969." Maheu goes along with that, saying he was present when the July 1970 payment was made and he remembers Rebozo acknowledging the fact that this $50,000 was the second and final installment. But, by everyone's agreement, the money for the second installment came from the Silver Slipper Casino fund—and Thomas Bell, who actually withdrew the cash, says he did not give it to Danner, for transmission to Rebozo, *until October 1970*.

So, the only certainty is that Rebozo got $100,000 of Hughes' money long after Nixon became President and yet long before he began his campaign for reelection. Why?

Danner says the money was intended to help Republican candidates running in the 1970 congressional elections. "Mr. Rebozo initially told me that he would furnish me the names of Congressional candidates needing financial assistance and we would contribute directly to their campaigns. He later changed the instructions and told me to give the $100,000 to him and he would handle the distribution of the funds and would give me the names of the recipients if I wanted them."

Rebozo's story is totally different. He says it was always intended that the money should be set aside and saved for Nixon's reelection campaign in 1972. Therefore, he says, he kept the money in a safe deposit box (number 224) at his Key Biscayne Bank, waiting for the appropriate moment to hand it over to a Nixon campaign committee. The moment did not come in 1972, because by then Maheu and Hughes were engaged in a ferocious public battle and "I didn't want to risk even the remotest embarrassment of Hughes' connection with Nixon." Rebozo says he left the $100,-000 in box 224 untouched, hoping that things would have "cleared up" in time for the money to be used for the 1974 congressional elections or the 1976 presidential race. However, in May 1973 Rebozo was briefly interviewed by the IRS about Hughes' money,* and after consulting with both Nixon and Richard Danner at Camp David—the presidential retreat in Maryland —he decided to return the money to the Hughes organization. It was duly returned, via the Marine Midland Bank, in New York, on June 25, 1973.

Not everyone has found Rebozo's story totally believable. In particular the doubters—which included investigators for the Senate Watergate Committee and the IRS—were skeptical of Rebozo's claim that Hughes' money had lain untouched in the safety deposit box and that the hundred-dollar bills he eventually returned were the same ones he received.

One reason for the skepticism was that when box 224 was opened—in the presence of an FBI special agent—the supposedly untouched fund of $100,000 had grown to $100,100, adding a new dimension, perhaps, to the truism that money makes money.

There was also the solid evidence, uncovered by the Watergate Committee, which showed that Rebozo maintained and administered a "secret fund" for Nixon's personal benefit. In March 1972, for example, the fund contributed $4,562.38 toward the cost of a pair of diamond-studded earrings which Nixon gave to his wife for her sixtieth birthday. And between 1968 and 1972 Rebozo paid more than $45,000 (presumably from the fund) toward the cost of remodeling and

* The IRS had actually found out about the payments from Danner a year earlier but it postponed its investigation until after Nixon had been reelected President because of a top-level decision to avoid interviewing "sensitive political figures" during the election campaign.

redecorating two houses which Nixon owned at 500 and 516 Bay Lane in Key Biscayne. Many Senate investigators had little doubt that at least some of this money came out of Hughes' $100,000. (Under federal law it is not illegal to use campaign funds for personal purposes, but if that is what happened, Nixon should have declared Hughes' contribution on his tax returns as unearned income. He did not.)

Whatever the money was used for, there remains the curiosity, harder to satisfy, of exactly what Hughes hoped to gain in return for his $100,000. Richard Danner insists that no specific *quid pro quo* was sought; instead, he says, the contributions were intended to be a gesture of friendship "to allay any Nixon Administration fears that the Hughes organization was anti-Nixon. We felt that there might be such fears since Lawrence F. O'Brien was on retainer to the Hughes Tool Company." If there is any truth in that, how stupendously ironic it is that Nixon's downfall should have been brought about by the burglary of Larry O'Brien's Watergate office, for the purpose of the break-in was almost certainly to discover how much O'Brien knew about the financial links between Hughes and Nixon.

However, there is circumstantial evidence to suggest that at least $50,000 worth of Hughes' generosity toward Nixon was motivated by less ephemeral considerations.

In early 1970 Hughes was considering the purchase of one of Las Vegas' largest and best-known hotels, the Dunes. One possible stumbling block was the likely opposition of the Justice Department, which, Maheu and his men rightly believed, would object to Hughes' acquisition of the Dunes on the same antitrust grounds that had been used to prevent his purchase of the Stardust in 1968. Richard Danner was therefore assigned to circumvent that obstacle by going right to the top—Nixon's Attorney General, John Mitchell.

Michell and Danner met at least three times in Washington, D.C., during the first few months of 1970. Back in Las Vegas after one of those meetings Danner discussed the progress of the negotiations with Maheu. Thomas Bell—the chief distributor of the Silver Slipper fund—was called in and told that "certain political obligations had to be met as a result of the trip which Danner had just made." The obligation was apparently $50,000, which Bell was told to make available to Danner for delivery to Rebozo.

After his next meeting with Mitchell, Danner told Maheu that the Attorney General had advised that Hughes should go ahead with the negotiations to buy the Dunes. Mitchell has denied telling Danner anything of the sort. What the Justice Department's attitude would have been must remain a matter of speculation, because the Dunes negotiations floundered when Hughes refused to pay the asking price.

But that hotel was not the only item on Hughes' shopping list when Bebe Rebozo received, according to his own account, the first $50,000. In late 1969 Hughes was still trying to complete his acquisition of Air West. And to do that, he was badly in need of a little sympathetic help in Washington, D.C.

Back in the summer of 1968, when the plan to acquire Air West had been little more than a twinkle in Howard Hughes' eye, Washington lawyer Ed Morgan had asked that he be allowed to informally "waltz this deal by" the Civil Aeronautics Board (CAB), which has to approve any deal made. Accordingly, Morgan had approached board members for their reaction to Hughes' proposed reentry into the airline business. He reported back to Maheu that no strident opposition seemed to exist.

That was not too surprising, because historically CAB *members*—political appointees, nominated by the White House and sanctioned by Congress—had been extremely tolerant of the unorthodox way in which Hughes ran his airlines; the opposition to Hughes had traditionally come from CAB *staff*. In 1960, for example, during the battle for control of TWA, it was a CAB lawyer who threatened public hearings into the airline's plight unless Hughes surrendered. When Hughes did concede, it was CAB staff who worded the announcement that he would never be allowed to regain control "without a searching inquiry into the public interest factors."

Similarly, in 1962 it was CAB staff that mounted spirited opposition to Hughes' takeover of a financially troubled New England carrier, Northeast Airlines. The staff lost that battle because an independent examiner told the board that Northeast would collapse into bankruptcy unless Hughes was allowed to have the airline.* But the argument produced one of the more abiding commentaries on the way Howard Hughes did business. Annoyed by the Hughes Tool Company's refusal to produce information about its finances and its plans, a CAB lawyer named Paul Seligson wrote to Chester Davis: "Mr. Hughes and Toolco are trying to force the Board to view their transactions through a looking glass of their own design. This course can only result in a distorted view of the facts and a decision grounded upon the logic of Alice's friends in Wonderland."

By 1969, when the CAB began to consider Hughes' bid for Air West, Paul Seligson had become a gamekeeper turned poacher. He was now among the small army of lawyers hired to argue *for* Hughes. But there remained at the CAB plenty of lawyers who still believed that Hughes had no place in the airline business. That view was all the more firmly held because Hughes was not seeking only control of Air West, but the right to operate it as a private, wholly owned entity.

In deciding whether a change in airline ownership "will not be inconsistent with the public interest," the CAB is required by its charter to inquire deeply into the character of the would-be owner—which, in the case of Air West, was the Hughes Tool Company. However, it was not the outright owner of the Tool Company, or any of its executives, who went before the board, in public session, to answer questions, but Bob Maheu—who had no connection with the company and who knew as little about its affairs as he did about running an airline.

That, of course, was no accident. Hughes had nominated Maheu as his spokesman precisely because he

---

* In 1964, in an attempt to regain control of TWA, Hughes disposed of his fifty-percent interest in Northeast. It remained financially troubled until 1972 when Delta Airlines bought it.

could answer any embarrassing questions about the Tool Company's policies or finances with a sincere "I don't know." (For the sake of appearances, Chester Davis had suggested that Maheu should be made a token director of Toolco, but foreshadowing the rancorous argument to come, Maheu declined on the grounds that he refused to serve under its chief executive, Raymond Holliday.)

Maheu carried what he regarded as "this burden" extremely well, although there was a moment when he threatened to abandon the CAB hearings, return to Las Vegas, and resign. During one recess Bill Gay somewhat injudiciously showed Maheu a memo that Hughes had written to Chester Davis warning that Maheu's headline-grabbing tendencies needed curtailing. By his own account, Maheu was furious, calling Hughes "an ingrate." Gay was, however, able to calm the hurricane by agreeing that Hughes was indeed an ingrate and a breaker of promises, too boot. Suitably placated, Maheu went on with his testimony to the CAB, and through the treatment he was afforded, it became increasingly obvious that once again the board would give Hughes what he wanted.

Things might not have gone quite so smoothly if the members of the board had known that the one man who had serious doubts about the advisability of Hughes' acquiring Air West—was Howard Hughes. In a memo written to Maheu just before the CAB hearings began in March 1969, Hughes said: "I am hesitant because I think it has evolved into a lousy deal for me financially at this time." If Maheu could only do something about the $137.6 million judgment in the TWA case that was threatening, "I would feel better," Hughes said, "but, with that hanging over my head, I just can not go on spending money as if there were no tomorrow."

Even if the Air West deal did go through, there was considerable doubt in Hughes' mind about who should run the airline. Maheu was, perhaps, hoping that he might be given the office of chairman; in any event, he believed that the operating executives should be General Nigro—who had his Air Force experience to rely on—and a man named Francis Fox, former general manager of Los Angeles International Airport, who had been hired by Maheu in late 1968 in anticipation of the Air West acquisition.* But Nigro and Fox were, to Hughes, "Maheu's men." And although no one could yet have realized how deep the rift would run, Hughes was by 1969 beginning to entertain some doubts about his alter ego. (The beginning of a Hughes memo to Maheu written in February 1969 illustrates the conflicts that were arising: "Bob, You yourself have said this is a most important moment. Since it is, will you please do me one most important favor and refrain from reading between the lines and writing your own interpretation of my message. Please, I beg you, take them for just what they say. Nothing more. . . .")

Unaware of the problems simmering on the back boiler, the CAB approved Hughes' takeover of Air West on July 15, 1969. Because Air West had foreign routes (to Canada and Mexico), it was necessary for the President to consider any foreign policy implications of the change in ownership and confirm—or veto —the board's decision. Nixon gave his blessing within six days.

In theory the takeover of Air West had now been accomplished, save for the formalities. However, Hughes' lawyers developed an interest in the fine print of the CAB's approval, and at five-forty P.M. (Eastern Time) on July 23 Chester Davis found the flaw: As far as the CAB was concerned, the Hughes Tool Company was now an "air carrier." That meant that the Tool Company itself, and not just its new division, was subject to CAB jurisdiction. "I believe," Davis wrote to Hughes, "you will conclude that such a result is undesirable."

"Undesirable" must have ranked as the understatement of 1969. If the Tool Company had become the owners of Air West, its books—like the books of all other scheduled airlines in the U.S.—would have been open to CAB scrutiny, and that was an imposition to

* Fox, Maheu, and Nigro had all been classmates and friends at Holy Cross College. Fox was hired as "Director of Aviation" of the Tool Company, pending the outcome of the bid for Air West.

which Hughes had never, and would never, submit. Furious backpedaling, designed to delay the takeover date, commenced.

At this point, most of Air West's beleaguered directors bailed out. Some had begun selling their stock as early as January 1969 when the purchase agreement was signed, but in July and August the trickle became a flood with sixteen of the board members heading for high ground. As a consequence, the value of Air West's stock dropped to ten dollars a share.

Selling out, for whatever they could get, may not have been the most noble recourse, but in all conscience Air West's directors were faced with an awful dilemma. They had signed an agreement which, because of the net worth clause, in effect guaranteed that Air West would be worth at takeover time at least $15.75 million. Yet, by the end of June 1969 the airline's net value was $16 million *below* that figure—giving it a *negative* value—and it was falling every day. As Maheu put it in a note to Hughes, "There is no way that these bums can meet the terms of their agreement. . . ."

At that time Maheu was strongly advocating to Hughes that the takeover be abandoned. "I realize fully well that because of Chester's foresight we have protection by virtue of the net worth criteria. On the other hand, I have very serious compunctions as to our position vis-a-vis the individual stockholders when they grasp the full realization that they will be paid considerably less than $22 per share. . . ." Rather than risk the shareholders' wrath by paying far less than twenty-two dollars a share, Maheu proposed what he called Operation Extricate.

If Hughes had followed the advice, he would probably have avoided a great deal of future agony, but nothing, it seemed, could dilute his passion to get back into the airline business.

At nine P.M. on August 14 he announced to Maheu "my final decision re Air West: I will contract immediately to take delivery of the airline July 1st 1970." Until then, Hughes said, "I will give the present management the undisturbed opportunity to run the airline in any way they see fit." That would mean, of course, that the existing management would be responsible for any losses incurred up to the end of June 1970 and for any further decline in the airline's net worth. If management was concerned about that prospect, said Hughes, "let them lay a few people off and take some steps to cut the losses."

So far as the problem with the CAB was concerned, Hughes said he was willing to gamble on Maheu's "political ability" to "obtain such changes in the present decision . . . as may be absolutely necessary." Actually, as things turned out, it was Chester Davis who found a way of allowing Hughes to acquire Air West while leaving the Tool Company's books securely closed. His solution was to create a new entity, the Hughes Air Corporation, wholly owned by Hughes, of course, but also wholly independent of any other part of the empire.

In October 1969, Hughes Air applied to the CAB for permission to acquire Air West. There surely could have been no doubt in the board's collective mind that this virgin corporation—which turned out to have a board of directors almost identical in composition to the board of the Tool Company—was nothing more than a device, designed to circumvent the CAB's legal duty to fully investigate those who chose to own public-service airlines. Nevertheless, the CAB gave its approval for the takeover without a murmur of complaint, and President Nixon followed suit.

It has to be pointed out that at around this time—according to Rebozo (and, before he changed his story, to Richard Danner)—Hughes paid out $50,000 for the intended benefit of Nixon. It would be going too far to say categorically that this $50,000 was an outright bribe, paid to insure the success of Hughes' bid for Air West. But, equally, it would be naive to underestimate the degree to which "influence" was the hard currency of Nixon's Washington.

Even Ed Morgan, Hughes' Washington lawyer, who had balked at the idea of giving Nixon money unless an acknowledgment could be secured, saw nothing wrong in recommending that Hughes should appoint to the presidency of Air West one of the five members of the CAB who had approved the acquisition. On

May 13, 1970, Morgan sent Maheu a "confidential" memo reporting that in March he had been to lunch with CAB member Robert T. Murphy, who had been a classmate at Georgetown Law School. During lunch they had talked about Murphy's future. "In this same context, he mentioned Mr. Hughes' acquisition of Air West," Morgan wrote. "It soon became apparent that he was exploring the possibility of an association with Air West as its President."

Morgan claimed that everybody in American civil aviation "loves" Bob Murphy and continued: "Murphy has always been our friend. He would like to become a member of the Hughes organization. Making him President would add great class to Air West."

Murphy did not join Air West. Indeed, he says, he did not tout for the job and had the sole ambition of remaining a member of the CAB,* which was probably as well, for by early 1970 Air West was in no position to benefit from any amount of class.

In February, Air West told its stockholders that if the deal with Hughes was to go through, the company would have to make "substantial adjustments" to its balance sheet in order to meet the net worth clause which Chester Davis had had the foresight to compose back in 1968. As a result of those "adjustments," the stockholders would get "materially" less for their shares than the twenty-two dollars they thought they had been promised. The only alternative to that, the stockholders were told, was bankruptcy: Air West was finally and irredeemably broke.

Faced with that choice, the stockholders once again voted in favor of the Hughes takeover and waited to see just how "material" their loss was going to be. It was, as things turned out, almost fourteen dollars a share: Instead of twenty-two dollars, Hughes paid a little over eight dollars.

The mechanics of how the eight-dollar figure was arrived at were extremely complex, but in basic terms this is what happened: Hughes bought the assets of Air West for $89 million, which was roughly the figure

* In 1972 Murphy left the CAB. He is currently general counsel and executive director of the Association of Local Transport Airlines in Washington, D.C.

he always said he would pay; to meet the net worth clause, however, Air West was obliged to designate $48 million of that money as an "asset"—and promptly delivered it back to Hughes; another $8 million of the purchase price was set aside to meet various "contingencies," leaving just $33 million for distribution to the shareholders. Expressed another way, Hughes got the airline lock, stock, and barrel for about $41 million—well under half of what he originally said he would pay.

In the opinion of the Securities and Exchange Commission the catastrophic fall in Air West's net worth between August 1968 and March 1970, which allowed Hughes to save himself a useful $48 million, was no accident. Specifically, the SEC charged that Hughes, with the help of accomplices, had conspired to defraud Air West's shareholders by

• orchestrating an illicit publicity campaign to destroy public confidence in Air West;

• manipulating the price of the stock;

• issuing "false and misleading" proxy solicitation material;

• intimidating the dissident directors through lawsuits secretly instituted and financed;

• Deliberately delaying the takeover until Air West was all but bankrupt.

Air West became Hughes Airwest in April 1970 and took to the skies with a brand-new livery. Under the new management things soon began to improve, and within two years the airline was making money. Since then it has consistently made a profit and now carries almost four million passengers a year, earning more than double the annual revenue (currently about $170 million) it did before the takeover.

Meanwhile, in total contrast, other parts of the Hughes empire began to encounter extreme turbulence. The storm warning had been posted on December 23, 1969, the day before Howard Hughes' birthday, when U.S. Federal Judge Charles Metzner confirmed that Hughes owed TWA $137,611,435.95, plus the entire costs of the case, amounting to approximately $10 million. There would, of course, be an appeal to the Supreme Court, but that was the last resort; if it failed, Hughes would be forced to find almost $150 million in cash—or watch his empire be dragged into involuntary bankruptcy.

It is no exaggeration to say that the TWA judgment hung over the Hughes empire like the sword of Damocles. The kind of internal pressures it created would have tested the mettle of any group of business executives; on the disparate and unorthodox group which Hughes had recruited to serve him, the pressures were, literally, unbearable.

9: DONNYBROOK

My center is giving way, my right is in retreat; situation excellent. I shall attack.

—Marshal Ferdinand Foch

Donnybrook Fair was an annual carnival first held in the year 1204 on the site of what is today an expensive residential district three miles southeast of Dublin in the Republic of Ireland. Over the centuries the fair grew in size and popularity but also in disorder until it became known less for cheerful commerce than for the fights which invariably developed. By the time the fair was suppressed in 1855, Donnybrook had become synonymous with a noisy, nasty free-for-all.

Appropriately enough, then, the confrontation at which the simmering conflicts within Hughes' empire boiled over became known, according to Bill Gay, as the Donnybrook Meeting. It was an indoor affair, and there were no fisticuffs, but this Donnybrook was as mean-tempered as any drunken brawl.

The meeting was held in the presidential suite of the Century Plaza Hotel in Los Angeles in the summer of 1970, and besides Gay, the head of the "Mormon Mafia," the participants were Raymond Holliday, chief executive of the Tool Company, Chester Davis, Bob Maheu, and Francis Fox, the Tool Company's "Director of Aviation." The main attraction was a shouting match between Davis and Maheu, not now the good friends they had once seemed. The two stood an arm's length apart and over and over, like actors in a play short on dialogue, repeated their lines:

Davis (with vehemence): "Tell me what the facts are, just tell me what they are."

Maheu (with equal vehemence): "If I tell you we have a commitment, we have a commitment."

As their mutual stubbornness and temper increased, the mood became infectious. Gay and Holliday, who were ostensibly there as mere observers, also got into an argument. "I can't remember what the hell it was [about]," says Gay, but after a while "I said, 'Oh shove it' and I just walked out."

In retrospect it is easy to see why Hughes' empire should have been torn apart and almost destroyed by rancorous struggles of which Donnybrook was the first manifestation. What is surprising, perhaps, is that it held together for as long as it did, for no ship ever had a more ill-assorted crew.

In the engine room, so to speak, were the orthodox business executives such as Ray Holliday and Calvin Collier of the Tool Company and Lawrence "Pat" Hyland, a self-taught but brilliant scientist who from 1954 onward ran the Hughes Aircraft Company.* Although they were left to run their businesses pretty much as they saw fit, they were always subject to the captain's unpredictable whim. And, for the Tool Company executives in particular, that meant becoming involved, from 1966 onward, in a host of side ventures for which they had no experience or appetite, but over which they were expected by Hughes to exert control.

Elsewhere on the ship were the abstentious Mormons

* In 1953 Hughes donated the ownership of Hughes Aircraft to the Hughes Medical Institute, a Miami-based nonprofit organization which dispensed funds for medical research. Not all the profits from the company went to the institute, however. The amount of money that flowed to Miami in any year was determined by the institute's sole trustee: Howard Hughes.

179

who abstained from everything except the pursuit of power. Bill Gay, the leader of this faction, enjoyed a somewhat ambivalent relationship with Hughes. (Specifically, Hughes held two grievances against Gay. One concerned a business venture, Hughes Dynamics, which Gay began—without Hughes' consent, according to Maheu—and which lost $9 million before it was closed down. Second, he blamed Gay for the breakdown of his marriage to Jean Peters, which ended in divorce in 1970. That became clear when Gay's daughter, Mary, was to be married and Maheu suggested that Hughes should give a generous wedding present. Hughes replied, ". . . apparently you are not aware that the path of true friendship in this case has not been a bilateral affair. I thought that when we came here and I told you not to invite Bill up here and not permit him to be privy to our activities you had realized that I no longer trusted him. So Bob, you suit yourself . . . I'm not going to ask you not to but I surely am not very happy about it. It certainly does not have my encouragement. My bill of complaints against Bill's conduct goes back a long way and cuts very deep. Also it includes a very substantial sum of money, enough to take care of any needs of his children several times over. . . ." A few hours later Hughes sent Maheu another note: "Bob, I have read your message about Bill again, and the more I read it the more angry I get. I certainly cannot get very sympathetic about Mary Gay . . . when Bill's total indifferance [sic] and laxity to my pleas for help in the domestic area, voiced urgently to him, week by week through the past 7 to 8 years, have resulted in a complete, I'm afraid irrevocable, loss of my wife. I am sorry, but I blame Bill completely for this unnecessary debacle. . . . I don't usually discuss this subject, but the whole episode you describe to me seems very insignificant indeed compared to the instances when I feel he let me down—utterly, totally, completely.") But for all that, Gay—a dropout from Brigham Young University who began work for Hughes as a "staff assistant" at the age of twenty-six—never lost his title, senior vice-president of the Tool Company, nor his authority.

Maheu says that Hughes dared not fire Gay because "Gay knew too much about his personal life." Be that as it may, the Mormon, operating from his own office in Encino, California, was never far from the center of the action. Hughes evidently did try to prevent Gay from being "privy to our activities," but with the five Mormon secretaries intimately aware of what was going on, that was a hopeless endeavor. And, it has to be said, when the chips were down it was Gay (among others) upon whom Hughes relied to get rid of Maheu.

Nadine Henley was in a class by herself. She was originally hired, in 1940, as a secretary by the chief engineer of Hughes Aircraft. Hughes spotted her during one of his infrequent visits to the Culver City plant and she became his personal secretary in 1943. As Hughes increasingly withdrew from the world, he increasingly relied on Nadine Henley, for she ran the Communications Center at 7000 Romaine Street that provided his links with his empire. As head of the "president's staff" she also had been responsible for recruiting a good percentage of the "Mormon Mafia," including Bill Gay and three of the five male secretaries—Howard Eckersley, John Holmes, and Roy Crawford. And, of course, Miss Henley (she was actually married but preferred to use her maiden name) administered Hughes' personal bank account, having the authority to sign checks.

When Hughes left Los Angeles, originally for Boston and then for Las Vegas, she lost personal contact with Hughes, but 7000 Romaine Street became the link between the Desert Inn penthouse and most of the outposts of the Hughes empire, and her influence never ceased to be omnipresent.

In a different way, Chester Davis was also in a class of his own. Besides being a formidable advocate, he had the ability to get on with every faction of the empire—at least for a while.

And then up on deck, having a ball, there were Maheu and his amiable crew: Jack Hooper, the tough ex-cop; Ed Nigro, the Air Force general who had been lured away from the Pentagon by the bright lights of the Strip; the former G-men; the ex-IRS agents; the colorful consultants like Jimmy the Greek and Moe

Dalitz; and the flock of lawyers—most of whom no longer practiced law. Las Vegas might have been made for them.

Through their enthusiastic efforts Hughes became, in a couple of years, the third biggest employer in Nevada and easily the state's biggest investor and gambler. While pursuing their self-appointed mission to clean up the town, they muddied just about every political race by scattering money around like so much confetti. And some of them, at least, took the time out to live the life of Riley.

It is not too difficult to imagine how all this was viewed by the cold-eyed men from Houston or by Nadine Henley or by the Mormons, some of whom found themselves serving as directors of casinos where smoking and drinking were the least of the excesses.

It was, in short, a recipe for disaster: The example of Noah's Ark notwithstanding, leopards and donkeys just do not mix.

Raymond Holliday says that the most persistent complaints about Maheu concerned his extravagance. From as early as September 1968 Holliday, as chief fiscal officer of the Hughes empire, received protests, he says, from Nadine Henley, Bill Gay, Richard Gray —the Tool Company's attorney in Las Vegas—and, occasionally, from Chester Davis.

It was not the size of Maheu's fee that caused irritation, because everyone recognized that out of the $10,000 a week he received he was required to meet expenses, including a fairly substantial payroll. What really jarred were the "extras."

To begin with, there was Maheu's home. Originally, when the family first moved to Las Vegas, the Maheus lived in a house—formerly occupied by Moe Dalitz— which was situated on the Desert Inn's golf course at the back of the hotel. By most standards, the house would have been thought comfortable enough and it came rent free, but Maheu and his wife were "very unhappy" about its proximity to the hotel. Maheu therefore proposed that a new house be built on two plots of land, adjacent to the golf course but farther away from the Desert Inn's tireless and tiresome customers. Hughes approved: "Bob, Please go ahead and buy the two lots in the name of the Hughes Tool Company. And please proceed to build likewise at the company's expense. I think we might get the building job done more economically if the architect and the builder think it is for you at your expense. . . ."

While the house was to be built "economically," that did not mean that it should be cheap. According to Maheu, Hughes wanted the kind of house "that he himself would like to live in," which, interpreted by Maheu, turned out to be nine thousand square feet of mock French Regency mansion, costing some $350,-000, not including furnishings.

In November 1969, with the Maheus in rent-free residence, they gave a party to celebrate—an event that was reported, somewhat breathlessly, by the Las Vegas *Review-Journal* under the headline "MAHEUS ENTERTAIN":

> "Mr. and Mrs. Robert Maheu entertained for a large group of their friends in their beautiful new home on the Desert Inn golf course last Sunday evening. Cocktails and a buffet supper were served in the wide, covered patio adjacent to the pool. The large foyer has parquette flooring and two curved stairways leading to the second floor. . . . Of modified southern mansion architecture, the Maheu home is one of the largest and most beautiful in southern Nevada. Muted pastel shades have been used throughout the home. The buffet table, decorated with flowers and sculptures, extended the full length of the pool. . . ."

Unfortunately, even the most beautiful homes in southern Nevada can become uncomfortable when the desert sun is at its height, but occasionally the Maheus were able to escape to their lodge at Mount Charleston, about forty miles from Las Vegas. Besides being a little cooler because of its 8,000-foot altitude, the $50,000 lodge (with a helicopter pad for a patio) offered a fine view of Charleston Park Restaurant, which Maheu and Jack Hooper bought with a $400,000 interest-free loan from Hughes. (The restaurant was managed by Ed Wight, formerly chief steward of the presidential jet, Air Force One.)

Then there was the $1,250-a-month penthouse apartment at the Balboa Club, Newport Beach, California, which was so handy for entertaining "important contacts" because of its close proximity to the Western White House at San Clemente. If visitors to apartment E-8 could drag their eyes away from the spectacular atrium they could, by leaning over the balcony, see the $200-a-month berth where Maheu kept his boats—first the 35-foot motor-sailer *Alouette* (which was given away to charity) and later the 59-foot sports fisherman, *AlouetteToo,* which cost $120,000.

The expense of keeping the boats and the salary of *AlouetteToo*'s full-time skipper were paid by Hughes because, Maheu says, they were used almost exclusively to entertain important people such as the then Vice-President Spiro Agnew. Agnew enjoyed his voyage—"Mrs. Agnew and I want to thank you for helping to make our cruise aboard *AlouetteToo* most enjoyable. The trip to Catalina [an island off the coast of southern California] was one of the high points of our visit to California. Sincerely, Spiro T. Agnew"— but when Hughes saw some snapshots taken during the ride he was, according to Maheu, "ashamed that the vice-president should be on such a small boat"—and he ordered a bigger one built, at a cost of $330,000.

But Maheu's greatest "extravagance" and the greatest source of irritation to the old guard of the empire was the $1.25 million DeHavilland 125 executive jet which Maheu bought, with the Tool Company's money, in 1968. Even Hughes was annoyed about the plane, if only because he had a preference for Lockheed Jet-Stars, which made up the rest of his executive fleet: "You've kept the airplane six months in defiance of my absolute firm instructions to return it or sell it. . . ." Maheu, however, argued that selling the plane would make him "appear like a real jackass" to his staff, his friends, and his business associates. When Hughes persisted, Maheu told him, "If you want to get rid of this plane, you handle it. . . ." The plane stayed.

All of this—and the houseboy, and the full-time gardener, and Maheu's office at the Frontier, which took so long to decorate because of the need to find for the walls cowhide pelts with matching brands—made some considerable impression on the folks of Las Vegas. Maheu's mansion became known as Little Caesar's Palace, and while there were some who meant it unkindly, most were in awe of this loquacious and hospitable man who tore around Las Vegas like an amiable typhoon, knowing and greeting just about everybody—"Howdy, pardner . . . *Bonjour, mon ami* . . . Hello, there . . . *Arrivederci.* . . ." Not surprisingly, Maheu, rather than the inaccessible recluse he represented, became the target of flattering attention: "My mail was unbelievable, the mail was delivered to the office in sacks. At one time we kept track of the telephone calls that I could not return and they averaged, over a period of 90 days, 104 telephone calls a day that I could not return."

None of that could possibly have endeared Maheu to the Old Guard. Compounding their consternation was the fact that, at least for a while, Hughes too was among his most fervent admirers. Indeed, at one time, Hughes promised to give Maheu something he had consistently denied everybody else: stock in the Hughes Tool Company. Maheu was (justifiably as it turned out) worried about his future security and he mentioned his concern to Hughes. In reply he received a note that said, in part: "If I give you my word to find the solution promptly, such as a voting trust from the Hughes Tool Co. stock, and if I put the formalities into a state of effectiveness for your scrutiny without unreasonable delay, will you consider it done as of now, so your mind will not be filled with these thoughts in the near future? I will assume an affirmative answer and proceed accordingly." For Hughes, who would not give even his most senior executives a written contract —they could all be fired at a moment's notice—that was a staggering concession. Of course, the promise was not kept, but just to have received it made Maheu unique. (Aware of the distinction, Maheu made several copies of the memo and hid them in various places, for posterity's sake.)

Hughes also showed Maheu considerable deference —"I'm sort of anxious to know who we're going to support for President, and how much. . . ." —and he tolerated Maheu's more outrageous losses of temper which sometimes resulted in Hughes receiving extremely insolent notes: "Unfortunately no one has an exclusive to having a busy day. I started writing the memo to which you refer . . . before sunrise and with the many interruptions in phone calls from the penthouse and your requests for immediate answers to innumerable items I was unable to complete the memo until this afternoon. It is now 5:15. I've not shaved, showered nor have I had breakfast or lunch and I have given you my undivided attention as I usually do. . . ."

When the two men did fight, Hughes was usually anxious to make up—"Dear Bob [instead of the normal "Bob"], Welcome back. . . ." Maheu, too, knew a couple of things about the art of reconciliation: ". . . I can assure you, Howard, that it is never my intent to hurt you in any way whatsoever, and when I write one of these stupid things, I really wish you would attribute most of the contents to my blowing off steam, but certainly with no deep-seated malcontent [sic]. . . ."

If, therefore, extravagance had been the only complaint against Maheu, it seems likely that he would have remained more or less invulnerable to the Old Guard's attacks. His fundamental mistake, and it was no less than that, was to give every appearance that he was out not simply to gain power in the empire but to build a new one.

So far as Maheu was concerned, it seemed, the Hughes-Nevada Operations was an autonomous entity that owed almost no allegiance to the Tool Company. Maheu says that everything he did emanated from Hughes' instructions, but evidently he went too far. Specifically, what scared Hughes was his growing impression that the staff of this new empire—most of whom were paid by the Tool Company—owed their loyalty not to the organization, or to The Man, but to Maheu. It must have seemed all too reminiscent of the Noah Dietrich affair,* and Hughes began to express his

* Dietrich's acrimonious departure from Hughes' empire created all kinds of problems because many of the Tool Company executives owed their first loyalty to him. (See Chapter 3.)

fears: "You have said you must inspire this loyalty to you to get the job done. I won't attempt to argue that now, but my immediate personal group of five very most trusted senior executives [the male secretaries], men who've been associated with me for many, many years . . . when these men are so fearful of being in the posture of disclosing some scrap of information which might displease you, I feel this is going too far. . . . The conscious feeling of tension that my close friends and associates feel when the conversation touches on you or anything concerning you, is so evident that I cannot help but be aware of it. . . ."

Yet Maheu showed little respect for the dangers he was courting by, as Hughes put it, "building an organization within an organization"; far from it, he actually tried to expand his influence by invading business territory which Hughes had designated as belonging to the Tool Company. It was a fatal mistake.

Whatever Maheu may have wanted, the Hughes-Nevada Operations, of which he was the chief executive officer, did not exist except as a fancy title on some letterheads. It did not own or operate anything: The hotels and casinos belonged either to the Tool Company or to Hughes personally as did all the other properties in Nevada.* It had no payroll and even its offices at the Frontier Hotel were owned, down to the cowhide pelts on the wall, by the Tool Company, which

* The arrangements were, naturally, complicated. The Desert Inn, the Landmark Hotel and Casino, the Castaways, the Frontier Hotel, and the leasehold of the Silver Slipper Casino were owned by the Tool Company along with the Las Vegas TV station, KLAS, the Krupp ranch, and parts of the North Las Vegas airport. The Tool Company leased the Silver Slipper to Hughes personally for $566,000 a year. The Sands Hotel was owned by Sands Incorporated, a Nevada corporation in which Hughes individually owned all of the stock. Sands Incorporated also owned a subsidiary corporation, Hotel Properties Incorporated, which leased the Castaways and the Landmark from the Tool Company for an annual rent of $2,300,000. In return, the Tool Company leased—and operated—the Sands Hotel from Sands Inc. for an annual rent of $2,720,000. Harold's Club in Reno was a separate Nevada corporation, but that was also a subsidiary of the Sands.

also held the title to Little Caesar's Palace and the ground it stood on.

Maheu was listed as "chairman of the board and president" of some of the hotels and casinos—and some of the gambling licenses were issued in his name —but, by his own account, he had little or nothing to do with their day-to-day operation.

After some vacillation Hughes had also made it very clear that the new acquisition, Hughes Airwest, would be ruled by the Tool Company men. Maheu was made a director of Hughes Air (the airline's formal owners)—perhaps as some recognition for all the work he had done in helping to acquire it—but all of the other members of the board, save Chester Davis, were Tool Company directors, with Ray Holliday taking the title of chairman. Maheu's strong recommendation that General Nigro and Francis Fox should be Airwest's chief operating executives was ignored.

Despite these warning signs of the way things were going, Maheu went to the first board meeting of Hughes Air, held at the airline's headquarters at San Mateo, California, in April 1970, determined to influence its destiny. Specifically, he was determined to see that Hughes Air should take over a helicopter commuter service called Los Angeles Airways.

The idea of buying L.A. Airways had originally occurred in 1968 at roughly the same time that Hughes had made his first tentative moves toward Air West. On the face of it, L.A. Airways was not a very attractive property. In May 1968, and again in August, it had suffered crashes which had claimed the lives of forty-four people and those tragedies had exacerbated its already severe financial troubles. Nevertheless, because of the sprawling nature of Los Angeles and the isolated location of the international airport, a helicopter commuter service had some potential and, Maheu has testified, Hughes was seriously interested in buying the outfit. The 1968 negotiations were only suspended—again according to Maheu—because it was thought it would be asking the CAB too much to approve two Hughes takeovers at the same time. L.A. Airways was, therefore, put on the back burner, so to speak, until the Air West deal had been nicely cooked.

Now, at the first Hughes Air board meeting, Maheu proposed that the negotiations with L.A. Airways be restarted. After making a few introductory remarks, he left the detailed presentation to Francis Fox (who had been invited to attend the meeting as a courtesy). The presentation did not go down well. In fact, it did not go down at all, for none of the directors—with the exception of Maheu, of course—would contemplate the idea for a moment. In their view, the rescue of Airwest, on which they were about to embark, presented more than enough problems. As Bill Gay put it, they felt they needed L.A. Airways "like we needed a hole in the head."

If a further deterrent were necessary there was also the very real consideration that, at that particular moment, the Hughes empire was faced with the possible embarrassment of a lack of ready cash. It seemed likely that before allowing Hughes' appeal against the judgment in the TWA case to go to the Supreme Court, Judge Metzner would insist that Hughes post a substantial cash bond, and if that happened, no one was really sure where the cash would be found. Certainly it did not seem the most propitious moment to invest $7 or $8 million in cash—which is the amount L.A. Airways would probably have needed to survive. Raymond Holliday and Calvin Collier (the Tool Company's treasurer) both dismissed Maheu's proposal as being out of the question, and without even bothering to take a vote, the Hughes Air board moved on to the next item of business.

It therefore came as something of a surprise to Chester Davis to learn, a couple of weeks later, that Hughes was apparently about to publicly announce his intention to buy L.A. Airways. Davis was in the Bahamas on a business trip when Maheu telephoned to say that he was planning to issue a press release announcing the negotiations. Maheu also said that Hughes had agreed to make a loan of $4 million, on generous terms, to a man named Sidney Wyman, who was a part owner of the Dunes Hotel in Las Vegas. Hughes had been interested in buying the Dunes (as we have said, Richard Danner was assigned to overcome the objections of the Justice Department) and the negotiations had been conducted with Wyman. The deal had fallen through because Hughes would not pay the asking price of around $50 million, but, Maheu said, Hughes still felt he had an obligation to Wyman and a $4 million loan was the way he intended to repay it.

This news not only surprised Davis, it alarmed him. Since the Hughes Air board meeting he had managed to persuade Judge Metzner against insisting that Hughes post a cash bond in order to appeal. He had done that by explaining the shortage of "liquid funds" and by promising that the Tool Company—formally the defendants in the TWA case—would not dispose of any major assets (like cash) until the appeal had been decided. Davis suspected that the judge would not now be amused to read in his newspaper that Hughes was cheerfully spending cash he was supposed not to have. Davis begged Maheu to delay the issue of the press release until he could send Judge Metzner one of his more masterful letters explaining the very special circumstances.

He need not have bothered. At about the same time as the judge was reading Davis' letter, Hughes was reading Maheu's proposed press release. According to Davis, The Man "blew his top": "What the hell is all this about? I don't want to buy L.A. Airways." Hughes also said he did not want to lend Sidney Wyman $4 million.

That should have been the end of the matter, but Maheu would not give up. He told anybody who would listen that it was unbelievable that Hughes "wanted to renege on an obligation that he had made to one of the pioneers in aviation [the owner of L.A. Airways] and drop this poor gentleman on his head." More than that, Maheu told Davis that if need be he would mortgage his wife and children and sell his boat but "by God, hell or high water the deal would go through."

This talk of an "obligation" was worrying. What obligation? So far as Davis and the Tool Company board were concerned, this was the first indication that any commitment to L.A. Airways existed.

At Hughes' request, Davis began a hasty investigation of the troubled little airline and the nature of any negotiations Maheu may have conducted with it. It did not take him long to discover that several banks had made loans to L.A. Airways—under the distinct impression that its money had been secured by a guarantee from Howard Hughes.

The pressing concern of Davis, Holliday, and Gay at the Donnybrook Meeting was to find out more about the "commitment" that Maheu had apparently made. But the more insistent Davis became, the more stubbornly Maheu stuck to his reply: "If I tell you we have a commitment, we have a commitment."

The low drama might have gone on interminably but for the intervention of Francis Fox, who had accompanied Maheu to the meeting. He broke the deadlock by inviting Davis to his hotel room, where, Fox said, he might be able to "explain a little more clearly." In the less heated atmosphere of Fox's room, Davis at last discovered some of what had happened. Maheu's deputy, General Nigro, acting as head of the Sands Hotel, had signed a letter on hotel notepaper in the summer of 1969 which the Valley National Bank of Phoenix, Arizona, had taken as a guarantee of a $2.8 million loan to L.A. Airways. There was also the possibility that in January 1970 the City National Bank of Beverly Hills, California, had loaned L.A. Airways $750,000 on what it thought was an indirect guarantee from Howard Hughes.* General Nigro had taken this action because, in his and Maheu's opinion, Hughes was duty bound to keep the little airline going until takeover negotiations could resume.

That information would surely have been sufficient to get almost anyone else in the Hughes empire summarily fired, but Maheu could still have survived. (Nigro, discouraged by his failure to get the job of running Airwest, had resigned as Maheu's deputy in

* The exact nature of Hughes' commitment, if any, to L.A. Airways is a matter of considerable dispute. In October 1970, after its helicopters had been grounded by a lack of cash, L.A. Airways filed a $16 million breach of contract suit against the Tool Company and against Chester Davis as an individual. At the time of writing, the case is still unresolved.

March 1970 and gone to work for the rival Del Webb organization which owned several hotel-casinos in Las Vegas. The general died, after a short illness, in 1972.) Maheu's position had been eroded and his "excesses" were going to have to be curbed but, manifestly, Hughes did not want to lose his alter ego. He assigned Chester Davis—who, Donnybrook aside, had enjoyed a friendly relationship with Maheu—to try to bring about a reconciliation.

After Donnybrook, Maheu had spent an increasing amount of time away from Las Vegas, most of it at his Balboa Club apartment at Newport Beach, and it was there, in July 1970, that Davis went to try to make peace. He took with him a list of ten items that needed sorting out. He also took with him Bill Gay, who, far more than any other Tool Company director, sympathized with Maheu's predicament. Perhaps that was because Gay knew what it was like to be out of favor with Hughes. (When, in 1967, Gay had attended the celebration that marked the takeover of the Desert Inn, he was obliged to hide from press photographers for fear that Hughes—who had told Maheu, "I don't want Bill here"—would find out.) Gay and Maheu had also, since the early 1960s, been partners in a host of private investments—in Venezuelan oil, a sawmill, land in Utah, a ski resort, the asbestos and cattle businesses in Australia, various stocks, and in Orange Radio Inc., which unsuccessfully tried to acquire the license of a Los Angeles radio station, KRLA. None of those ventures had made any money, but the two men were close enough for Gay to want to help.

In total contrast to Donnybrook, the July meeting was extremely cordial. The three men played tennis and then went for a cruise around the marina. After half an hour or so on the water they went below to the cabin and got down to business.

According to Davis, this was "a last-ditch effort to bring Mr. Maheu in line with respect to several matters that were causing internal problems." Chief among those matters, of course, was the charge that Maheu had tried to build his own empire—"an organization within an organization"—and had flatly refused to acknowledge the authority of the Tool Company directors. In the course of doing that, said Davis, Maheu had gone way beyond the limits of his own authority by making commitments such as those to L.A. Airways and Sidney Wyman. What it boiled down to was that Maheu would have to begin to toe the line by establishing "a more coordinated and unified relationship" with the Tool Company's directors.

Maheu was sweet reason: "Yes, it would be helpful," he said. "I would like to have that. I'll have to give it some thought and see what we can do."

On the question of making commitments Maheu was even more conciliatory: "I'll give you one promise and that is that I will never again undertake any activity, any negotiation, without first getting consent in writing from the board of the Tool Company."

But on the second promise Maheu imposed one condition—namely that Davis should "help me to accomplish the L.A. Airways deal and get the loan for Wyman." Davis, who says that at the time of this meeting he still did not know all the facts surrounding the "commitments," promised to do what he could. At least, that is what Maheu remembers him saying. Davis' recollection is that he said, "I will support what I can support."

Anyway, Maheu and Davis, as well as Gay, left the July meeting convinced that most of the problems had been ironed out and that Hughes' empire was about to enter an era of internal harmony. It was an illusion, and it did not last long.

Of all the enemies Maheu had made, none could be counted upon to defend what they saw as Hughes' interests more vigorously than Ray Holliday and Nadine Henley. And, it is now plain, by 1970 both had long decided that Maheu's ambition and Hughes' interests did not coincide.

Miss Henley and Maheu had first crossed swords in 1966 when she had refused to put Peter Maheu on Hughes' payroll as anything more than a "trainee." (Peter therefore remained on his father's payroll.) From that point, their relationship had at best been "strained" until late in 1969 when it became openly hostile: Miss Henley began challenging Maheu's accounts of what he had done with the money she had given him—out of Hughes' personal account—for political contributions. Finally, in early 1970, as she later testified, she refused to give him any more money until the "discrepancies" had been straightened out.

The blow had come at a particularly bad time for Maheu. He was, he claimed, $59,000 out of pocket on the contributions he had made for Hughes during 1969 * and, more seriously, Maheu Associates was being required by the IRS to pay heavy taxes on all the money that had passed through its books. He needed, he said, $100,000 immediately, but Miss Henley refused to pay. She said she had referred the matter to Hughes.

In May 1970, with the IRS becoming insistent, Maheu had appealed directly to Hughes for the money although "begging is very difficult for me." Met by silence, Maheu sent a second note: "Can I be assured of receiving the reimbursement for contributions by this weekend? I hate to be asking again, but, Howard, I really must know." There still being no answer from the penthouse, he wrote again: "Howard, I realize the weekend is not over but I understand that the communications in the federal pen [penitentiary] are not very satisfactory. Seriously Howard, I will feel so much more comfortable if you could assure me that arrangements have been made for my reimbursement on political activity."

In the nick of time Maheu was given his $100,000, but, Miss Henley says, she was told by one of the Mormon aides not to give him any more money without Hughes' specific approval. She was also told, she claims, that Hughes wanted her to look back through the records of money paid to Maheu over the years to see if there were any other "discrepancies." According to testimony she later gave, there were. And in the summer of 1970 she sent the details to the penthouse.

Ray Holliday's contribution to the internal debate about Maheu's future was a little more subtle but no less damaging.

* Maheu says that he often made contributions—in the name of Maheu Associates but really on Hughes' behalf—in advance of receiving the funds from Nadine Henley.

Since becoming the head of the Tool Company (executive vice-president—there was no president) in 1961 he had enjoyed a large amount of autonomy, mainly because Hughes had little interest in the oil-drilling business. Holliday therefore reported to Hughes, he says, when he felt like it. In August 1970 he felt like reporting on the progress of the Nevada operations.

His "Financial Report" to "HRH," dated August 24 was a devastating document. Without making a single specific allegation, it nevertheless, by "summarizing the income or loss for Nevada operating entities from the date of acquisition by years," ripped Maheu's credibility. Maheu may not have been involved in the day-to-day running of the Nevada operations but he called himself the chief executive officer, and as such he carried responsibility.

Holliday's report said that between April 1967, when Hughes bought the Desert Inn, and July 1970 Hughes had lost $12,723,016 in Nevada—which, by anybody's reckoning, was not a good return on an investment of $200 million. Worse, Holliday predicted, "If the 1970 losses continue at the present rate it appears that the overall loss for 1970 will be on the order of $13–14 million compared to $8,444,051 for 1969."

Maheu claims that those figures were rigged in a deliberate attempt to discredit him with Hughes, but he would have had a hard time proving it, for the books were kept by the Tool Company.

This might, therefore, have been a suitable moment for Maheu to try to begin mending the fences, as he had promised Davis and Gay he would do. Instead, Maheu chose first to go incommunicado: He boycotted board meetings of Hughes Air; he again left Las Vegas for Newport Beach and his boat; when Davis telephoned the boat, asking for Maheu's help on a new project, he was told—by the boat's skipper—that *anything* he had to say should be directed to Maheu's lawyer.

And then, with breathtaking bravado, Maheu went on the attack.

In the circumstances that existed it is difficult to imagine a more reckless endeavor than a frontal assault on Chester Davis' professional competence based on, of all things, his handling of the TWA case (which, at the end of the day, Davis won handsomely). It is certainly true that Maheu had a license to interfere. He had been given it originally by the Tool Company's board, which in October 1968 had made him the company's "agent and attorney in fact" in the TWA matter. That franchise had been reinforced by a Hughes memo dated January 1970: "I repeat, Bob, you have *full* [emphasis in the original] authority." But all of that had happened in calmer days. To use that license in the climate that prevailed in October 1970 was nothing short of suicidal.

Why did Maheu do it? He says that his only concern was the protection of Hughes' interests, which he believed would be best served by removing Davis from the TWA case. That does not explain why he did not attempt to remove Davis until two years after he was first given the responsibility for the lawsuit and almost a year after Judge Metzner had confirmed the $137 million judgment against Hughes.

Perhaps the most rational explanation is that by October, Maheu no longer thought that Davis was to be trusted. Rightly or wrongly, Maheu had left the July meeting at Newport Beach convinced that Davis had promised his support for the L.A. Airways deal and the loan to Wyman. Bob Maheu was not a man to regard a breach of promise lightly: "I had been born and reared in a world where a man's word means something. . . ." Yet, so far as he could see, Davis' promised support had failed to materialize, and by October, Hughes was adamant in his refusal to undertake either proposition.

In any event, on November 4 Maheu went to Washington, D.C., with Richard Danner and Gregson Bautzer, a Hollywood lawyer who before Chester Davis' arrival on the scene had handled many sensitive matters for Hughes. In Washington they were joined by Ed Morgan, and the four of them went to see Clark Clifford, formerly U.S. Secretary of Defense in the Johnson Administration, now a high-powered lawyer.

The first proposal presented to Clifford, which he

found acceptable, was that he should become Hughes' lead counsel for the purpose of the appeal to the Supreme Court against the TWA judgment. What Clifford did not find so attractive was the accompanying proposal that Chester Davis and his firm—Davis & Cox—should play no part whatsoever in the appeal. The reasoning, presented by Maheu and Ed Morgan, went something like this: Davis' strategy had been to refuse to produce a defense to TWA's charges against Hughes on the grounds that there was no case to answer. A judgment by default having been entered, it was clear that Davis' strategy had "failed" and, the argument went, the appeal should be based on the grounds that Hughes had had no opportunity to present a defense. Obviously, that would have been an impossible position to take if Davis and his firm were still involved in the case. So Davis, the expendable scapegoat, would have to go.

Clark Clifford doubted the legal wisdom of the maneuver.* He also knew it would be no light matter to remove a lawyer of Davis' eminence—and determination—from the biggest civil case in U.S. history, and Clifford counseled against the idea.

Nothing could dissuade Maheu, however. Stopping briefly in Houston to tell the Tool Company what he had in mind, Maheu returned to Las Vegas and fired off a short telex message to Davis saying, "You are not to be officially identified with the appeal of the TWA judgment and neither your name or that of the firm is to appear on the appeals brief."

Davis' reply was equally short, and under the circumstances, moderate. He pointed out that his lack of involvement in the appeal could "raise unnecessary questions in the mind of the court with a possible adverse effect." He said he did not understand "the good and sufficient reasons" why Maheu had taken this ac-

* As things turned out, Davis was very much involved in the appeal, which ended in his total vindication. On January 10, 1973, the U.S. Supreme Court handed down its decision, which, by a vote of six to two, said in effect what Davis had always maintained: that there was, indeed, no case for Hughes to answer. The court said that the CAB had overseen Hughes' management of TWA and had, therefore, "immunized" him against any violations of antitrust laws.

tion, and he urged that Maheu should "cease interfering with counsel in charge of, and responsible for, the case."

Maheu's reply to the reply, sent on November 12, was a great deal longer and, to say the least, tactless. He said it was "strange and unseemly" for Davis to persist when his handling of the case had brought only "catastrophically adverse financial and other injury to the defendants." Maheu said he regretted the necessity, but "I must insist that you now step aside and permit counsel in charge of appeal to proceed along the lines decided. . . ."

Davis did not bother to respond. He telephoned Ray Holliday to arrange for a special meeting of the Tool Company's board—and he bought himself an airplane ticket to Houston.

10: WATERLOO

When an irresistible force such as you
meets an old immovable object like me . . .
—*Something's Gotta Give*, Johnny Mercer

Bob Maheu tried not to show it, but by the beginning of December 1970 he was a deeply worried man. He had had no real contact with the Desert Inn penthouse since he had asked for permission to go with his wife to Stuttgart, Germany, where they planned to enroll their youngest son, Billy, in school. Hughes had told him to stay home. That was five or six weeks ago, and since then his messages, dictated as usual to one of the five male secretaries, had brought no written response. When he had pressed for answers, the secretaries were noncommittal; when he became insistent, they said Hughes was ill and would be incommunicado for a while. Finally, the telephones in the penthouse simply went unanswered.

"There were pretty lonesome days," Maheu says, and he was not alone in his apprehension. Even the office staff at the Hughes-Nevada Operations felt in the "atmosphere" that something was drastically wrong. Was there anybody up there in the penthouse? Was Hughes ill—or dead?

There was ample reason for concern about Hughes' health. Through Jack Hooper, Hughes' security chief, Maheu was aware of most of the comings and goings at the penthouse and he knew that from early 1969 onward Hughes had required periodic blood transfusions for anemia. A small room in the penthouse had been converted into a clinic for the purpose of administering those transfusions. And, Hooper says, he had spent a great deal of time keeping a check on those who donated blood: Hughes insisted that his donors not drink liquor and that each of them lead a wholesome, clean life.

The unsullied blood coursing through his veins would revive, for periods, the anemic Hughes, but by the autumn of 1970 his condition was clearly deteriorating, and he was little more than a living skeleton. He had pneumonia and chronic constipation, and the DeHavilland 125 jet (which Hughes had objected to owning) was making regular trips between Los Angeles and Las Vegas, ferrying a doctor who was entered in the plane's log under an assumed name. There was also a local doctor, Harold L. Feikes, a heart specialist, attending Hughes, and he was particularly discouraged by Hughes' loss of weight: At a fraction under six feet four inches tall, Hughes weighed just ninety pounds—about sixty pounds less than his normal weight.

Given all these reports, Maheu says he could not help but be perturbed at the abrupt loss of communication with the penthouse. It even crossed his mind that Hughes could have died and that, for some reason, the Mormon Mafia was attempting to conceal the fact. It was a wild idea, perhaps, but then, extraordinary events had surrounded Hughes' life; there was no particular reason for believing that the facts surrounding his death would be different.

To add to the speculation, on December 2 the Las Vegas *Sun* announced in a banner headline, "HOWARD HUGHES VANISHES." The story that accompanied was seriously deficient in facts, but it reported—and accurately as it turned out—that Hughes was gone from the Desert Inn penthouse. (Later, Hughes suggested that Maheu planted the story. He denies it.)

In any event, by December 4 Maheu was sufficiently concerned to have asked superlawyer Ed Morgan to travel to Las Vegas for a high-level and secret conference. Also at the Frontier Hotel offices for the meeting that day were Greg Bautzer, the Hollywood troubleshooting lawyer, Pat Hyland, the head of Hughes Aircraft, and Richard Danner, Hughes' link to the Nixon Administration. They were deciding what they could possibly do to penetrate the wall of silence, when a telephone call came through from Chester Davis. He was in Los Angeles and he wanted Morgan and Danner to fly there immediately for a conference of great importance which, he said, was about to take place.

At two P.M. that afternoon, after a hurried journey of some three hundred miles, Morgan was ushered into the presence of Davis, Bill Gay, Raymond Holliday, and Calvin Collier.

Danner was left in another room of the Century Plaza's suite 1901, cooling his heels for about twenty minutes, while Davis—as spokesman for the group—explained to Morgan that Maheu was fired. It was hoped, Davis said, that Maheu would "gracefully bow out and clear the way" for the gentlemen Morgan was now talking to. But, gracefully or not, he must resign "before sundown" that day—or he would be publicly fired.

Morgan, not a man easily flustered, was more than a little taken aback, and said he thought Maheu might be similarly surprised. He also thought that Maheu might require some sort of explanation.

"Well," said Davis, "this is Mr. Hughes' wishes. That's the reason."

Asked for a few more details, Davis would only

say that there was "general dissatisfaction" with the entire Nevada operation. When that explanation did not suffice, he finally lost patience, vehemently slapped the side of his chair with his hand, and said, "The reason is that Mr. Hughes wants him out."

Ray Holliday was a little more forthcoming—although he, too, was clearly impatient—revealing that Maheu was not to be the only victim. There was an "enemies list" of Maheu men, "something like 150 or 155 people who will be terminated as a result of this action," Holliday said. As it happened, Richard Danner had just been summoned into the room and was still trying to decide exactly what was going on when Holliday turned to him: "You're number five on the list," said Holliday, "and I wish you were higher."

That was, it turned out, a joke—a little touch of levity to lighten the otherwise serious proceedings. Danner was one of the few "Maheu men" who would survive the purge and, indeed, benefit from it in that he was promoted to general manager of both the Sands and the Castaways. But at the time he did not find it very funny.

Bill Gay was also not in any mood to appreciate the humor. He told Morgan of his "great personal regret" for what was happening. He and Bob had been long-time friends, he said, and he felt a high regard for both Maheu and his family. There was, however, no alternative to what had been decided: Friend or not, Bob had to go.

Morgan had been aware, of course, of some of the events that had led to this confrontation, and being an astute lawyer, he must have expected that Davis would not lightly regard Maheu's attempt to take over the TWA litigation. He was, therefore, naturally curious as to whether this "sundown" ultimatum was official. Did it have Hughes' blessing, or was it an elaborate bluff by the Old Guard? Davis replied that he had authority from Hughes *in writing* but he was not about to show it to Morgan. On that rather unsatisfactory note, the confrontation ended.

When Maheu got the news by telephone from Morgan, he was "stunned." He was still "stunned" when Morgan and Danner arrived back in the Frontier's offices and when, a few minutes later, a United Press International reporter stuck his head around the door to say that rumors of Maheu's dismissal were already on the wire. Maheu recovered sufficiently to say that he had no comment. Morgan, always the pragmatist, advised him to hire a lawyer. It was now a couple of hours before sundown.

There was apparently never any thought in Maheu's mind that he should quit without a fight. For one thing, he felt "the days of the Old West were no longer applicable—a *High Noon* or *OK Corral* movie approach was not one I thought we should indulge in where such serious matters were at issue." (Curiously enough, Ray Holliday felt the same way, although for very different reasons. He would, he says, have fired Maheu with one telephone call: "I would have just cleared it up fast. There wasn't anything to discuss." Chester Davis, however, was determined to put on a show—and, after all, Maheu had told Davis to talk to him through his lawyer.)

Maheu also entertained sincere doubts about Davis' ability to fire him, especially since Davis had refused to produce the written authority from Hughes which he claimed he possessed. Then there were the gaming licenses, held in Maheu's name, to consider. Even Nevada, with its willingness to bend the rules in favor of Howard Hughes, might not tolerate such an arbitrary transfer of responsibility.

And, anyway, where was Hughes? The sudden turn of events had finally convinced Maheu that Hughes was no longer in the Desert Inn penthouse. But where he had gone, how he had gone, and particularly, why, were all sinister mysteries.

Last, but probably not least, there was Maheu's pride. However much he might decry Old West tactics, he is not a bad verbal gunslinger himself. "No one," he said, "is going to come into Las Vegas or any other place I live and give me until sundown to get out of town."

Anyone heading for a showdown could do worse than to take along for company, as Chester Davis did, the men from Intertel.

International Intelligence Incorporated, to give it its proper title, was not ('and is not) a run-of-the-mill detective agency. Its board of directors included a former commissioner of Scotland Yard and a former commissioner of the Royal Canadian Mounted Police, and among its operatives were the former chief of the U.S. Justice Department's organized crime strike force in Detroit, the former security liaison officer for the U.S. State Department, the former supervisor of the organized crime intelligence squad of the IRS, the former director of enforcement of the U.S. Bureau of Customs, the former supervisor of intelligence for the FBI, the former counsel for the U.S. Senate's antitrust and monopoly subcommittee, and, for good measure, J. Edgar Hoover's only nephew. In 1970 it was rather new in the private-eye business and its services did not come cheaply, but by the time Intertel began working for Howard Hughes it had established a reputation for a willingness to become involved in situations that others might have deemed prudent to avoid.

Intertel's creator was a lawyer named Robert Peloquin, who in 1967 was chief counsel for the Justice Department's inappropriately named Organized Crime Strike Force. (It is, of course, an *anti*-organized crime force.) In that capacity Peloquin was approached by James Crosby, president of the Mary Carter Paint Company, which was in the process of expanding into a business more exotic than the manufacture of paint. Mary Carter was buying its way into the gambling industry on Paradise Island in the Bahamas, and while Crosby found the prospect exciting, he was, he told Peloquin, "scared to death."

What concerned Crosby was the threat of interference with his new venture from other casino operators in the Bahamas, specifically those who controlled the gambling dens at Lucayan Beach on Grand Bahama Island. A recent British Royal Commission* had established beyond much doubt that organized-

---

* The Bahamas was then a British Crown Colony. In 1969, under a new treaty, it became the Commonwealth of the Bahama Islands, and since 1973 it has been an independent nation.

crime figures—including Meyer Lansky, known for his stature as "The Little Man" and for his mental agility as "The Genius"—were involved in certain Lucayan Beach casinos and had paid millions of dollars in bribes to government officials. The heat created by the Commission's report would undoubtedly cause the mobsters to seek fresh pastures.

To make matters potentially worse, Crosby was obliged under the terms of his gaming license to hire for his casinos only people with previous experience in the Bahamas gambling industry. He did not, he told Peloquin, want it written on his tombstone that he had "been to bed with the Mafia," and so would the Justice Department help him out of his dilemma by screening the staff?

Since its formation in 1963 the Organized Crime Strike Force had spent a considerable amount of its time delving into the Mafia's interests in the Bahamas, and undoubtedly it had accumulated a great deal of knowledge that would have been helpful to Crosby. But, Peloquin said, the Justice Department could not with any propriety set itself up as the sorting house for a private employer.

As a result of Crosby's approach, Peloquin's Strike Force did conduct some kind of investigation into the likelihood of Mafia infiltration, but it was apparently a cursory affair which left Crosby both disappointed and worried.

However, as it happened, shortly afterward Peloquin decided he had served long enough as an official crime fighter. In August 1967 he resigned from the Justice Department along with a senior colleague, William Hundley, and together they founded a law firm in Washington, D.C. It was not long before Crosby became a client—and Peloquin accepted the Paradise Island assignment that previously he had been obliged to turn down.

By then Crosby had sold the paint business, and Mary Carter's name with it, and reorganized his surviving interests into a new company, Resorts International Incorporated, which Peloquin and Hundley sanitized. Not surprisingly, they were apparently very successful at preventing any Mafia invasion of Paradise

Island, and they also became very skillful at circumventing other hazards—skimming and cheating, for example—that threaten any gambling enterprise. In March 1970 they decided to market those talents by forming Intertel, "a management consultancy firm." Peloquin became president and Crosby chairman. Resorts International was the principal stockholder.

One of Intertel's first clients was the Hughes Tool Company. The financial report on Hughes-Nevada which Holliday had "felt" like sending to Hughes in August, and which showed catastrophic losses, suggested almost irresistibly that Hughes had been robbed. Casinos are in the *gaming* business; it is the customers who gamble—some winning, most losing—never the house, which with the percentages firmly in its favor, will *always* win in the long run. (Jimmy Snyder in his book *Jimmy the Greek** described casino gambling as a "nonprofit sport" which he despised: "It's a killer. It's working on the weakness of people." He said that the odds varied from game to game and from casino to casino but they were always firmly in favor of the house.) Holliday's revelation, therefore, that all of Hughes' casinos, with the exception of the Sands and the Silver Slipper, had consistently lost money raised grave suspicion. In October 1970 Robert Peloquin met secretly with Holliday, Collier, Davis, Nadine Henley, Bill Gay, and Gay's assistant, a man called Kay Glenn, and agreed that Intertel would analyze the books of Hughes' casinos. Those books had already been examined by the Tool Company's auditors, Haskins and Sells, but it was reckoned that Intertel's men would be more likely to spot the kind of irregularities to which casinos are inherently prone.

That discreet investigation of the books was still not complete when Intertel was asked by Davis to fulfill a more urgent assignment. On December 4, with sundown approaching and with no indication of Maheu's surrender, Davis and the Old Guard took a private jet to Las Vegas and took with them Peloquin and some of his men.

Davis and company chose for their battle head-

---

* Published in the U.S. and Canada by Playboy Press, 1975.

quarters the eighteenth floor of the Sands Hotel, next door to the Desert Inn and just across the Strip from the Frontier, where Maheu and his men were preparing for the showdown. On the ground floor of the Sands hundreds of party-goers celebrated the hotel's eighteenth anniversary, unaware of the drama that surrounded them.

The first shot that marked the beginning of the battle was fired by, of all people, those eminent auditors Haskins & Sells. At a little after ten o'clock that night about twenty auditors moved into Hughes' seven casinos, announcing to the cashiers that they intended to carry out a "surprise audit." Spot checks are not in themselves unusual in the gambling business and casino managers could usually expect to undergo a couple a year, but there were some characteristics of this "surprise audit" that were very surprising indeed.

To begin with, the teams of accountants were escorted, albeit discreetly, by agents from Intertel who were prepared, if need be, to counter any interference from the regular security forces, controlled by Jack Hooper. And having gained access to the cashiers' cages, the auditors began stuffing money and markers (IOUs) into bags and sealing cash drawers with adhesive tape. Clearly, this was something more than a standard audit.

Although few people knew it at the time, the arrangements for the "surprise audit" had been made back in September with the Houston office of Haskins & Sells by Calvin Collier, treasurer of the Tool Company, a fact that gives some indication of just how long the Old Guard had been planning its coup. Collier had told the auditors to be ready to move into the casinos at very short notice, and contingency plans had been made to supplement Haskins & Sells' Las Vegas staff by temporarily importing help from other offices. However, the go-ahead signal had not been given until noon that day, December 4, when Collier telephoned Harold Robertson, Haskins & Sells' head man in Las Vegas.

Robertson had kept his own counsel until about six o'clock that night, when he called together his staff and the extras who had been specially imported.

He warned them not to discuss the matter with anyone, not even their wives, because the audit must be a complete surprise. He also warned them that they would have to stay in the cashiers' cages all weekend (December 4 was a Friday) until the banks opened on Monday morning and the money could be deposited.

At first all went well for the auditors, perhaps because surprise had truly been on their side. They gained access to the eight cages (the Landmark Hotel had two) without much difficulty, but by around midnight at least some of the casino managers had become seriously concerned. It was standard practice to keep large sums of cash in "banking drawers" at the rear of the cages, and it was these that the auditors were sealing. The "working drawers" at the front of the cages had not been sealed, but it was unlikely that they would have contained enough money to pay off a big winner of, say, $30,000 or $40,000. It is an essential part of the Las Vegas "magic" that those who do win should be paid cheerfully and *promptly,* and there was no question but that the authorities would not have looked kindly on a casino which, for any reason, failed to pay its dues upon demand.

That was reason enough for some of the managers to alert Maheu, who, surrounded by his men, was still at his Frontier office plotting strategy. There was no doubt in Maheu's mind that this was not an audit but an attempted—and, so far as he was concerned, illegal—takeover, and the presence of Intertel agents only served to strengthen that conviction.

Maheu called Nevada's Governor Paul Laxalt for his opinion, which was that such unorthodox events might well endanger Hughes' gaming licenses. With that ammunition, Maheu went on the attack, telling his casino managers to evict the gentlemen from Haskins & Sells—or, as Maheu preferred to describe them, the "Mongolian monks" who, he said, had appeared "out of Mars."

But some of the "monks" would not leave and instead called their boss, Harold Robertson. He rushed over to the Frontier Casino—but Jack Hooper's security guards would not let him into the cage. They would not let him use the phone, either. Robertson went to a public telephone and called Richard Danner (who was, of course, the manager of the Frontier) and appealed for reason. Danner said that Robertson and his men should get out. So, too, did the under-sheriff of Clark County, Lloyd Bell, when he arrived at the Frontier. And Lloyd's brother Tom Bell, who was still Hughes' personal attorney in Nevada, firmly aligned himself with Maheu.

When the auditors still hesitated, Lloyd Bell said he was going to call the sheriff in. That was enough for Robertson, who, figuratively speaking, laid down his guns. He ordered his men out of the cages, and eventually they all left—though in some cases very reluctantly—taking the Intertel men with them.

By four A.M., except for the incessant clattering of the dimes and quarters dropping into the slot machines, all was quiet in Las Vegas. First round to Maheu.

As we have said, the major point at issue was whether Davis had Hughes' authority for the takeover.

He did. On November 14 Hughes had signed a proxy, witnessed by one of his male secretaries, Levar Myler, and notorized by another, Howard Eckersley, who was, handily, licensed as a Nevada notary public. The proxy appointed Chester Davis, Ray Holliday, and Bill Gay "my true and lawful attorneys for me and in my name and stead to vote and to otherwise exercise all rights I may have as a stockholder . . . with respect to any and all shares . . . at the time standing in my name. . . ." The proxy gave the trio the authority to do anything except sell or transfer Hughes' stock or change the names of any of his corporations. Armed with that carte blanche, the Tool Company's board of directors had, on December 3, voted unanimously to dispense with the services of Maheu and Jack Hooper.*

However, one of the greater curiosities of this strange affair is that for a long while Davis refused to produce his license to fire. He would not show it to Morgan and Danner at the Century Plaza Hotel, and

* The Tool Company's board had revoked Maheu's authority in the TWA case on November 12.

when he arrived in Las Vegas for the showdown, he would not show it to Tom Bell.

During the Friday evening Bell had received a telephone call from Robert Morgan (who controlled the finances of Hughes-Nevada for the Tool Company) asking for a meeting. When Bell arrived half an hour later at the rendezvous point in front of the Sands Hotel, Robert Morgan and Calvin Collier got into Bell's car.

The Tool Company men asked Bell to go with them to the eighteenth floor, where Davis and Holliday were waiting to discuss how Maheu might best be ousted. Bell said he would only enter the Sands if, in advance, he was shown "a document of authority under which the new group could take control of the Nevada operations." Morgan and Collier said they would report back to Davis, and left Bell sitting in his car. They returned a few minutes later to say that Bell would not be shown any written authority unless he *first* promised to help get Maheu's name removed from the gaming licenses. Bell, who was, after all, charged with representing Hughes' interests in Nevada, said he could not possibly make that promise until he was satisfied as to what Hughes really wanted. There being no agreement, and nothing more to discuss, Bell left.

Bell's puzzling experience, and the attempted take-over of the casinos, convinced Maheu that Davis was bluffing—he did not have Hughes' authority. So, on Saturday, with an indignation born out of total conviction, Maheu sought the help of the courts to repel the invasion. Bell, still acting as Hughes' lawyer, said it would be perfectly proper to ask a judge to issue a temporary restraining order against Davis and company. It would, however, be necessary to post a bond of around $2,500.

With that course agreed and the cash (taken out of Maheu's bank account) in hand, Bell set off to find a judge. Conveniently, Judge Thomas J. O'Donnell lived nearby in an apartment building on Desert Inn Road. Having once shared a business interest in some real estate, the two were friends. Judge O'Donnell was, as Bell had predicted, perfectly willing to issue a temporary order, but he would not, he said, accept a bond as low as $2,500. With such serious issues at stake, $10,000 would be required.

That demand caused some embarrassment to the Maheu forces, because they did not have $10,000. But Howard Hughes did. Maheu signed a marker and the money was withdrawn from the cashier's cage of the Frontier Casino. At five twenty-five P.M. Judge O'Donnell issued an order temporarily restraining Davis, Holliday, Gay, et al. from interfering with the lawful business enterprises of Howard Hughes. Round two to Maheu.

Meanwhile, the Clark County sheriff and a group of his men broke into the Desert Inn penthouse. There was nobody there.

Jack Hooper's guards, stationed round-the-clock on the ninth floor of the Desert Inn, had been there to prevent people getting in, not out. That, evidently, is why they had not seen Howard Hughes leave what had been his home for four years, almost to the day. On November 25, Thanksgiving Eve, while Hooper's guards were distracted or away from their posts, some of his aides, carrying Hughes on a stretcher slipped through a fire-escape door, walked down nine flights of stairs inside the north end of the Desert Inn, and escaped into the cold desert night.

Waiting for them in the parking lot of the Desert Inn, near the fire-escape exit, was a small fleet of black limousines—which Hughes and his aides ignored: They were decoy cars, designed to draw attention away from the more anonymous station wagons in which the getaway was to be made. The charade was unnecessary, because no one took any notice of what was happening. (Some alert soul did, however, notice the black limousines and took down the details of their license plates. Later, when a check was made, it turned out that the limousines were registered to Hughes Productions at 7000 Romaine Street, Los Angeles.)

The fleet of black limousines headed south; the station wagons, and Hughes, headed northeast to Nellis Air Force Base, five miles or so out of Las Vegas, where a four-engined JetStar, especially leased from Lockheed for the occasion, was waiting.

All that Hughes and his secretaries took with them on the plane was one filing cabinet and some luggage. Everything else, the debris of four years in the penthouse, had presumably been disposed of. According to Nadine Henley, who knows about such things, "We have a regular procedure whenever Mr. Hughes moves that everything not pertinent or of great moment is destroyed."

From Nellis the JetStar flew to Albuquerque, New Mexico, where it was refueled. Hughes was in good spirits: He told his secretaries, "so far, so good—unless one of you is a hijacker." Then on to Nassau International Airport in the Bahamas, where Hughes transferred from the JetStar to a helicopter for the twelve-mile journey to Paradise Island. A little after dawn on November 26, 1970, just over eight hours after leaving the Desert Inn, Hughes was safely ensconced on another ninth floor, this one containing the three presidential suites of the Brittania Beach Hotel, which had been reserved for more than one year at a cost of $1,000 a day. And almost nobody knew he was there.

Given that Hughes had decided to leave Las Vegas, it was not totally surprising that he should have headed for the Bahamas, an archipelago of some three thousand islands, islets (cays or keys), and rocks scattered in the Atlantic about three hundred miles off the coast of Florida. In the late 1950s Hughes had spent a good deal of time there; indeed, the Bahamas was where Maheu and Hughes had begun, by telephone, their quixotic relationship. And when Hughes had been desperate to leave Boston in 1966, it was a toss-up as to whether he would choose Las Vegas or the Bahamas. On no more than a whim, the islands had lost out, temporarily, but Hughes had retained his interest in the Bahamas, and over the years Maheu, Hooper, Danner, Davis, and John Meier, the scientific adviser, had all been asked at one time or another to go there and investigate a project Hughes had in mind. (The Tool Company, too, had had some interest. For years it had leased the Bahamian islet Cay Sal, close to Cuba, on the promise that it would provide development. The lease had, however, been canceled by the Bahamas government when the Tool Company failed to live up to its promise.)

In 1968 and 1969 it had seemed to Maheu almost certain that Hughes would move to the Bahamas. He had become increasingly frustrated with what he saw as the restrictions placed on his activities by the Nevada authorities—and the aggravation provided by the unstoppable bomb tests—and he had told Maheu: "I just wish we could find some place where we could start out with a clean sheet of paper and build a community that would be exactly the way we think it ought to be."

Hughes had added to that impression by telling Danner (who had good connections in the Bahamas through Bebe Rebozo) to try to get the Tool Company's lease on Cay Sal renewed and expanded "to include every key and rock from Bimini to Orange Cay and on the south to that formation of rocks and cays." And more than once Jack Hooper had been called upon to make arrangements for transportation and accommodation.

But toward the end of the decade the political situation in the Bahamas changed dramatically. The predominantly white United Bahamians Party which had controlled the islands as long as anyone could remember lost that control to the predominantly black Progressive Liberal Party. With a clear mandate from the population, eighty-five percent of which was black, the new government under the leadership of the Bahamas' first black prime minister, Lynden Pindling, shrugged off the colonial ties and headed for independence.

It would be going too far, perhaps, to say that Hughes was a racist. But, to say the very least, his views were ambivalent. For example, writing to Maheu about the employment of blacks in his Las Vegas casinos, Hughes said: "Now, Bob, I have never made my views plain on this subject. And I certainly would not say these things in public. However, I can summarize my attitude about employing Negroes very simply—I think it is a wonderful idea for somebody

212

else, somewhere else. I know this is not a very praise-
worthy point of view, but I feel Negroes have already
made enough progress to last the next 100 years, and
there is such a thing as overdoing it."

With that kind of attitude, it is understandable that
Hughes should have been somewhat perturbed by a
report he received from Maheu sometime in 1970 on
present-day life in the Bahamas. The report, which
Maheu had commissioned (and which, for reasons we
find unfathomable, had been entitled "The Downhill
Racer"), was discussed by Maheu and Hughes in a
telephone conversation. (The conversation was tape-
recorded—by whom is a mystery—and Peter Maheu
later found the recording in a filing cabinet.)

Hughes, having read the report, said that even if
the author were only eighty percent right, "It's still
something that should cause us to think a long time
before investing a lot of money down there." However,
never one to give up hope, Hughes wondered what the
chances were to "wrap up the government down there
to a point where it would be, well, a captive entity in
every way. Do your people feel that that's possible or
are you dubious about what could be done with the
government down there?"

Maheu: "Well, the big problem that we find,
Howard, is that there's a very reactionary group within
the colored that feel that [Prime Minister] Pindling is
not moving fast enough against the whites."

Hughes: "That's not toward the left, you mean?"

Maheu: "Right."

Hughes: "Well, then by reactionary you mean left
reactionary?"

Maheu: "Right."

Maheu: "I understand—I just found out late this
afternoon, for instance, just to give you an idea of
how they do react—that a group of them went to a
Kentucky Colonel place and didn't like the way they
were treated and the next night blew up the Goddamn
place."

Hughes: "What do you mean, Kentucky Colonel
—where?"

Maheu: "Chicken—in Nassau."

Hughes: "In Nassau? Do they have it down there?"

Maheu: "Yes."

Hughes: "And somebody went to one of these and didn't like the way it went—didn't like the way they were treated and blew the place up?"

Maheu: "Right."

Hughes: "Well, I agree that gives us cause to hesitate. . . ."

The Downhill Racer report had come as a complete shock to Hughes—". . . a bombshell. I certainly wouldn't have planned to go down there and set up shop if I'd have known that the tension was this extreme or that there was this kind of thing in the wind."

Maheu: "Yeah. I'm afraid, if you remember the numbers it's about 80 percent colored."

Hughes: "Yes, I studied that very carefully. . . . In Puerto Rico they used to think coloreds too."

Maheu: "Right, but they've not been as mistreated by the whites over the years."

Hughes: "Well, why in the hell—the Nassau crowd hasn't been mistreated, they've been riding in the carpet of luxury, haven't they?"

Maheu: "Not really."

Hughes: "I thought the tourist trade down there had been terrific until recently."

Maheu: "Yes but you have to remember . . . the Bay Street boys [nickname for the former white government] were really rough on the colored."

Hughes: "They were? I thought the colored people down there—all the hotel employees and all—seemed to thrive as far as I could make out."

Maheu: "Yes, but they weren't happy."

Hughes: "The prices have always been high down there but tips have been good and I always thought the colored people had it pretty good around Nassau. I know that out in the off islands, the back islands, they have had it a little tougher but I don't see that they would be inclined to blame that on anybody. It would be a geographic situation. Well, anyway, if there is deep-seated hatred there we'll just have to go somewhere else. . . ."

Later in the conversation, still bewildered by the "deep-seated hatred," Hughes said: "Well now you

214

take a place like Bentley. I never saw anyone mistreated in Bentley and I never saw any colored people down there having a bad time of it. Now that's more a sort of fishing and tourist community and good God in heaven they were all living very prosperously there. . . . Well anyway, so much for the Bahamas."

Given that conversation, it is understandable that Maheu believed that the trip to the Bahamas had been canceled. And in August or September of 1970 Jack Hooper had reported to Maheu that the trip was definitely off.

But once the Clark County sheriff had established beyond doubt that Hughes had left the Desert Inn, the Bahamas did seem the most likely destination. For one thing, there was, as Maheu knew, the standing reservation at the Britannia Beach Hotel. And, to add weight to that thesis, present in Las Vegas were not only the men from Intertel but James Crosby and his partner, Jack Davis, the major stockholders of Resorts International, which owned the Britannia Beach Hotel. Crosby and Davis had arrived in Las Vegas with Chester Davis on board the executive jet. And although they had seemed to do little else but play tennis since their arrival, their very presence indicated to Maheu that they had some interest in the drama that was unfolding.

So the best guess was that Hughes had gone to the Britannia Beach on Paradise Island. The question that remained was had he gone their willingly?

Peter Maheu was assigned to find out. The experience he brought to the job was not inspiring. He had worked for the CIA but only as a guard of agency buildings. His training had consisted of a course on the art of picking locks such as might be found on CIA filing cabinets to which careless secretaries had lost the key. It could hardly be expected that that talent would help him find—and, if need be, rescue—Hughes. Still, maybe his father was able to give him some tips, and Peter did have for company Dean Elson, former head of the FBI office in Las Vegas, now working for Maheu Associates. (Before this caper Elson's most exciting case had been the successful

FBI investigation of the kidnapping of Frank Sinatra, Jr.)

Peter, calling himself, in true spy tradition, Mitchell not Maheu, and Elson took the DeHavilland 125 executive jet to Miami, where they hired six local private investigators, headed by a veteran gumshoe named Edward DuBois.

Then they chartered an airplane to fly to Paradise Island and photograph from the air the Britannia Beach and the Emerald Beach hotels, one of which, they were sure, must contain Hughes. Back in Miami they hired a yacht and finalized their plans for a sea-borne invasion of Paradise Island and the "rescue" of Hughes. Meanwhile, in Las Vegas, Robert Maheu alerted NBC television reporter Roy Neal because "if, in fact, Mr. Hughes was being held against his will [we wanted] him to enter the island with us, with a film crew, for the sole purpose of not only being able to protect Mr. Hughes but to protect ourselves from charges of kidnapping and blackmailing, and any other charges that may arise."

While Peter Maheu and Elson remained in Miami, the six detectives, plus two of Maheu's men imported from Las Vegas, traveled to Paradise Island and checked in at the Britannia Hotel, where they were able to secure rooms on the eighth floor. They soon became convinced, rightly, that Hughes was just one story above them, but they still had no way of knowing if he was there voluntarily.

Edward DuBois, the head gumshoe, went to the office of the Bahama attorney general to inquire if it would be illegal to bug the ninth floor with electronic listening devices. Assured that under the circumstances Bahamian law would tolerate such activity, DuBois returned to the Britannia Beach, where he and his men found a busboy who, for a fee, was willing to smuggle a bug into Hughes' suites. According to Bob Maheu, "They had placed the listening device on the tray of one of the room servicemen and the bug was en route to the room when it got caught."

Unfortunately for DuBois, the Bahamian police, alerted by Intertel, did not share the view that bugging was permissible. One of Maheu's men from Las Vegas was monitoring other bugs affixed to the eight-floor ceiling when police and Intertel agents, led by a former U.S. Secret Service agent, burst into his room.

The "rescue" team was arrested, held for twenty-four hours, and then unceremoniously deported to Florida.*

Meanwhile, Peter Maheu had returned to Las Vegas at the urgent request of his father.

Having lost the first two rounds of the battle, Chester Davis was now striking back: He had called a press conference to announce to the world that Maheu was fired, along with Jack Hooper and his entire security force, who for the time being were to be replaced by men from Intertel.

Bob Maheu still hoped that he would be able to resist the takeover through the courts. But he was not about to take any chances.

Monday, December 7 was a day Terry Marsden would not easily forget. She was a secretary at the Hughes-Nevada offices at the Frontier, and having arrived for work at the normal time, she had barely had time to collect her indispensable first cup of coffee and sit down at her desk when another secretary, Judy Hook, rushed into her office and began unloading the filing cabinets.

Soon everybody in the office was at it, grabbing files, papers, even that morning's unopened mail, loading it into cardboard boxes, and stacking those in the hallway. "There seemed to be a certain amount of confusion," Terry said. "No selection was taking place. Just packing and off." According to another observer, an assistant to Maheu named Robert McDonald, the scene was reminiscent of "a Chinese fire drill."

The evacuation of paper went on most of the morning, with the bulging boxes being taken out on dollies

* A Miami grand jury subsequently investigated the caper, but it did not return any indictments. Hughes, however, was outraged by the affair and later said: "It certainly seems to me it was a criminal action, whether it was a kidnap attempt or a wiretapping attempt . . . it certainly seems to me that it falls in the criminal category—and probably a felony, certainly not a misdemeanor."

to the Frontier's back parking lot, near the tennis courts, where they were loaded onto a van.

Yet another load was following that route and was midway across the parking lot when, at about noon, several carloads of Intertel agents—and reporters— roared onto the scene, causing the dollies to be smartly reversed.

Safely back inside the Frontier, the staff locked themselves inside the offices, but, according to Peter Maheu, the Intertel agents "began banging on the door attempting to gain entrance. It was . . . a hard situation to describe in words. There was no way you can place some words on the chaotic situation the office was in at that time."

Even viewed sympathetically, the plunder of the files was a desperate gambit, and it is not really clear what Maheu hoped to gain. He says that he told his son to remove only those files that pertained to the business of Maheu Associates, afraid that Davis might confiscate them and also "fearful that copies of very dangerous and sensitive memos from Hughes" might be there, which ought not to fall into "the hands of strangers." But Maheu's files were thoroughly mixed with Hughes' files, and no real attempt was made to distinguish between them: Acting under Peter Maheu's instructions, the staff had grabbed and packed everything in sight.

In any event, with the Intertel men banging down the doors of the Frontier offices, it was obviously time to go. Robert McDonald and another of Maheu's assistants, Al Bishop, ran for the van, which contained most of the haul, and drove away. They spent the first five or ten minutes driving aimlessly around Las Vegas, checking on whether they were being followed, but also deciding where on earth they should go. Peter Maheu had simply told them to get out of the state because his father wanted the files removed from Nevada's jurisdiction. After a bit of thought they decided on California and, says Bishop, "then we immediately headed for the Interstate and the Nevada line."

They made it and at about eight-thirty that night began unloading the files into the warehouse of a small electronics company* in Irvine, just south of Los Angeles. It was a total waste of effort.

Maheu's theory that the documents could be removed from Nevada's jurisdiction was half-baked because what counted, of course, was *his* whereabouts and he never stirred from Las Vegas. That *he* was, therefore, still very much within the state's jurisdiction was confirmed even while McDonald and Bishop were still making good their escape down Interstate 15. A second Nevada judge, Howard W. Babcock, entered the battle for control of Hughes' empire. On Monday afternoon, at the behest of Davis, Judge Babcock ordered the immediate return of the files. (When Davis first heard of the plunder of the files, he reportedly looked up at the ceiling of his room in the Sands —which he believed Maheu had bugged—and yelled, "If you are up there, you son of a bitch, you're going to jail.")

It is tempting to believe this was all an elaborate plot—a cunning scheme devised by Maheu as a cover to give him the time and opportunity to remove some vital document from the files. If it was, it didn't work. Overlooked by Maheu's men and left behind at the Frontier offices for Intertel to claim was a master index of 6,500 cards which listed and identified almost every piece of paper that had been removed.

Maheu's escapade did have one positive result. To obtain a restraining order against Maheu, Davis was obliged to at last produce the much-vaunted proxy about which he had been so coy. He showed the original to Judge Babcock and a photocopy was given to Maheu, albeit not by Davis but by Governor Paul

---

* The warehouse was owned by a company called ELPAC which Maheu controlled. ELPAC's chairman was Richard Danner, then still very much a member of Maheu's team, who was on hand at Irvine to help unload the documents when McDonald and Bishop arrived. Danner kept the key to the warehouse and suggested that, as some kind of a reward for their efforts, McDonald and Bishop should spend the night in the luxury of Maheu's Balboa Club apartment at Newport Beach.

Laxalt, who was desperately trying to mediate between the two sides.

Laxalt was concerned that the fracas, with its increasingly nasty overtones, would do serious damage to Las Vegas's new "clean" image which he had worked hard to foster. And so he shuttled back and forth between the two factions, trying to obtain the concrete evidence of Hughes' wishes that Maheu was demanding.

The proxy turned out to be insufficient proof. Except for three signatures, the one-page document was typewritten, whereas—as Maheu had cause to know better than anyone—Hughes invariably communicated through *hand*written notes. The proxy was, therefore, in Maheu's opinion, an obvious forgery.

The governor was not really in a position to form any opinion himself about the validity of the proxy, but he was totally convinced by the next piece of evidence Davis offered. Very early on Tuesday morning Laxalt and the district attorney of Clark County, George Franklin, were asked to go to the eighteenth floor of the Sands to take a telephone call—from Howard Hughes. The voice they heard assured them that Davis' takeover was genuine, and that there had been no kidnap. "I'll be home shortly. In intended to go on a vacation fourteen months ago and will return to Las Vegas and spend the rest of my life there," the voice said.

Laxalt, who had, of course, spoken to Hughes on the telephone once before, was in no doubt that it had been Hughes on the line. He said The Man had sounded in good humor and had confirmed that he was staying at the Britannia Beach Hotel: "He even joked about being on the ninth floor again," Laxalt said. But when, at four A.M. Laxalt arrived at Maheu's house to pass on the news to his old tennis partner, he was met with intractable skepticism. The only thing that would convince him, Maheu said, was to receive a telephone call himself from the Britannia Beach Hotel. That was, apparently, asking for the impossible. (Maheu says, with considerable justification, "I still can't understand why Hughes didn't just pick up the phone and tell me himself.")

The next day, in a last attempt at arbitration, Laxalt called a meeting at the El Morocco Motel in Las Vegas which Davis, Gay, Holliday, and Maheu all attended. Maheu was asked to sign a statement saying that he was "satisfied" that Hughes was in good health and had therefore agreed to step down quietly. In return, he was told, the Tool Company would sign a statement absolving Maheu from blame of any "irregularities" that may have occurred during his stewardship of the Hughes-Nevada Operations. He rejected the offer out of hand, saying he was far from satisfied about the state of Hughes' health.

It was now up to the courts to decide what Howard Hughes wanted. Both sides asked for an injunction against the other, and both sides produced handwriting experts of approximately equal eminence who said that Hughes' signature on the proxy was (according to Davis' man) genuine and (according to Maheu's) a forgery.

And then, in rapid succession, Davis delivered two fatal blows. The first was a letter, not typed but handwritten, on three pages of yellow, ruled, legal-size paper.

Dear Chester and Bill—

I do not understand why the problem of Maheu is not yet fully settled and why this bad publicity seems to continue. It could hurt our company's valuable properties in Nevada, and also the entire state.

I believe my company is one of the biggest employers (if not the biggest in the state, and surely what damages an entity employing this many Nevadans is bad for the state itself.)

You told me that, if I called Governor Laxalt and District Attorney George Franklin, it would put an end to this problem.

I made these calls, and I do not understand why this very damaging publicity should continue merely because the properly constituted board of directors of Hughes Tool Company decided, for reasons they considered just, to terminate all relationship with Maheu and Hooper. I asked you to

221

take whatever action is necessary to accomplish the objectives briefly outlined above.

I ask you now please to inform the members of the board of Hughes Tool Company of my desires and feelings in respect to this matter.

It is not my wish to try to tell the board what action should be taken. That is their job. But it seems thère has been some uncertainty as to where I stand, and I want this cleared up at once.

I do not support Maheu or Hooper in their defiance of the Hughes Tool Company Board of Directors, and I deeply desire all concerned to be fully aware of this immediately.

I ask you to do everything in your power to put an end to these problems, and further I ask you to obtain immediately a full accounting of any and all funds and/or property to which Mr. Maheu may have had access.

As I have said, this matter has caused me the very gravest concern, and is damaging my company and all the loyal men and women associated with me in the very deepest and far-reaching way.

My sincere regards,

Howard R. Hughes

Although the letter was addressed to Davis and Gay, it was actually delivered, with their permission, to the Clark County district attorney's office by one of Hughes' secretaries, Howard Eckersley, who said he had brought it from the Bahamas. When the letter was produced in court, Maheu's handwriting expert, Charles Appel—formerly head of the FBI's document laboratory—testified that the letter had been written by someone "not in a natural condition," but it was obvious that Maheu's case was collapsing.

And then, with melodramatic suddenness, Davis produced on the witness stand another of the secretaries, Levar Myler, who swore to the authenticity of the proxy.

Myler said that after Hughes had signed thc proxy in the Desert Inn penthouse on November 14 he (Myler) had kept it "for a few days" in his briefcase and then placed it in a safe deposit box which he and his wife maintained at a Las Vegas bank. On December 3, Myler said, he was at the Britannia Beach Hotel with Hughes when a copy of the Las Vegas *Sun* had arrived bearing the headline "HOWARD HUGHES VANISHES." Hughes had been furious, believing that Maheu had inspired the story because Hank Greenspun, the publisher, "would not have dared to print any such thing without Bob encouraging him." Myler said that Hughes then ordered him to release the proxy to Davis and company, which he did by telephoning his wife and asking her to drop by the bank. She had done so on December 4 and the proxy had been taken by courier to the Century Plaza Hotel.

Myler's testimony irresistibly suggested, of course, that Hughes had not finally made up his mind to fire Maheu until after the Las Vegas *Sun* had reported Hughes' disappearance. But that was now irrelevant. On December 20 the federal district court ruled that Davis, Holliday, and Gay possessed the authority to summarily fire Maheu.

Just before Christmas, the emperor's alter ego was evicted from Little Caesar's Palace.

11: THE LAST LAUGH

When ye build yer triumphal arch to yer
conquerin' hero, Hinnissey, build it out of
bricks so the people will have somethin'
convanient to throw at him as he passes
through.

—Mr. Dooley's Triumphal Arch,
Finley Peter Dunne

It took a while, but eventually, on January 7, 1972,
Howard Hughes came out of hiding and said publicly
at a press conference why he had fired Robert Maheu:
"Because he's a no-good, dishonest son of a bitch
and he stole me blind."

The circumstances surrounding the revelation were
typically bizarre. Hughes sat in his ninth-floor suite at
the Britannia Beach Hotel in the Bahamas, heard but
not seen. Twenty-five hundred miles away seven
journalists sat in a Los Angeles hotel room asking
questions of a weedy, disembodied voice that came
over a couple of loudspeakers, while television cameras
recorded the unintentional comedy.

Allowing for breaks to reload the cameras—Hughes:
"You want me to hold? Or will you call me back?"—
the telephone conference went on for two and a half
hours and then it was the journalists, sweating profusely
because the air-conditioning had been turned off, who
called a halt. "I'd be happy," said Hughes, "to talk to
you just as long as you want."

He was also happy to elaborate a little on his
charges that Maheu "stole me blind. I don't suppose
I ought to be saying that at a news conference, but I
just don't know any other way to answer it. You

wouldn't think it could be possible, with modern methods of bookkeeping and accounting and so forth for a thing like this with Maheu could [sic] have occurred, but, believe me, it did, because the money is gone and he's got it."

Hughes was right: He should not have said it. The allegations against Maheu provoked lawsuits, more bitter than anything Hughes had experienced before, which are still not settled and which removed any chance that he might, as he had promised, stop being "quite as reclusive."

On the face of it, the conference at which Hughes broke his fourteen-year silence had nothing to do with Maheu. Its purpose was to denounce as a fraud and a hoax a 230,000-word "autobiography" of Hughes that McGraw-Hill had announced it would publish in March 1972 and for which it claimed to have paid Hughes an advance against royalties of $650,000. The perpetrator of the hoax was a moderate—in terms of both talent and success—writer named Clifford Irving.

But at the time of the news conference, neither Hughes nor his aides, nor his lawyers nor the men from Intertel believed that Irving was the *architect* of the hoax. Although Hughes stopped short of saying so directly, they suspected—wrongly—that Maheu had devised the plot: "I can say to assume that it's all an accident certainly takes a whole lot of assuming."

And so Hughes set out to demolish not only the credibility of the "autobiography" but that of its supposed architect as well. The story of Hughes' final years is fielled with ironies, but none greater than this: In destroying one monster, the hoax, he created another, far more ferocious, that pursued him and pursued him until he was dead.

If Maheu was at all "responsible" for the hoax then so were Chester Davis, Ray Holliday, and Bill Gay, for it was the battle for control of Hughes' Las Vegas empire that gave Clifford Irving the idea. In December 1970 the Shootout at the Hughes Corral received wildly disproportionate coverage in the American and foreign press, providing confirmation—if any

225

were needed—that Howard Hughes was still very hot copy. It occurred to Irving, an expatriate living on the Mediterranean island Ibiza, that a book about Hughes, containing enough inside information, would be a best-seller. That idea also occurred to a number of better writers than Cliff Irving, but none of them could think of a way of acquiring the hard facts necessary to write a credible biography. Conjuring those facts out of imagination, which is what Irving intended to do, was not a particularly novel idea either. What made Irving's fiction unique, of course, was the seemingly authenticated claim that the words in his book had come from the horse's mouth.

The means to attempt the hoax arrived in Ibiza just after Christmas 1970 with the December 21 issue of *Newsweek* magazine, which contained a small photographic reproduction of one page of the "Dear Chester and Bill" letter which Hughes had written to confirm Maheu's termination. It was little enough for a novice forger to go on, but Irving brought to his new trade considerable confidence. As it happened, his last book, entitled *Fake!*, had been an account of the activities of an art forger, Elmyr de Hory, who had produced countless pictures, supposedly by Renoir and Chagall among others, which had fooled most of the art world. De Hory had told Irving that bold forgery often deceived more successfully than meticulous attention to detail, and with that in mind, Irving sat down to write himself a letter—from Howard Hughes.

Irving pretended that he had sent a copy of *Fake!* to Howard Hughes at the Desert Inn and that, in return, he had received a brief handwritten thank-you note which contained this intriguing passage: "I would hate to think what other biographers might have done to him (de Hory) but it seems to me that you have portrayed your man with great consideration and sympathy, when it would have been tempting to do otherwise. For reasons you may readily understand, this has impressed me. . . ."

On January 3, 1971, Irving wrote to his American publishers, McGraw-Hill, telling them of Hughes' note of "thanks and praise." Four weeks later he wrote to

McGraw-Hill again, saying that he had received two more letters from Hughes. Irving explained that in view of the thank-you note which *Fake!* had produced he had written to Hughes suggesting, albeit with faint hope, that The Man might like to consider a biography of himself. In return, he said, he had received first an acknowledgment and then a letter, dated January 20, which seemed to offer Irving the literary coup of the century. It said, in part:

> I am not entirely insensitive to what journalists have written about me and for that reason I have the deepest respect for your treatment of Hory, however much I might disapprove of his morals. . . .
> It would not suit me to die without having certain misconceptions cleared up and without having stated the truth about my life. . . . I would be grateful if you would let me know when and how you would wish to undertake the writing of the biography you proposed.

Answering an excited summons from McGraw-Hill, Irving flew to New York in early February, taking the three "Hughes" letters with him. They were desperately amateurish forgeries, but there was no one at McGraw-Hill who could say from personal experience what Howard Hughes' handwriting looked like. (By the time experts were called in, Irving—using as a model a full-scale and full-color reproduction of the "Dear Chester and Bill" letter published by *Life* magazine— had been able to perfect his new talent sufficiently to deceive handwriting analysts of the stature of Osborn, Osborn and Osborn of New York.)

McGraw-Hill did entertain some doubts about the proposed biography, but they were not based on any suspicion that Irving was a crook. Rather it was Hughes' credibility that was suspect because of his legendary penchant for second thoughts. Irving was therefore asked to try to secure his (mythical) partner's signature on a watertight agreement, and assignment which, under the circumstances, was not very difficult. Still, to continue the deception upon McGraw-Hill, it was necessary that Irving put on something of a show and his first "meetings with Hughes" were conducted with appropriate style and mystery.

After three supposed meetings with Hughes—two in Mexico and one in Puerto Rico—Irving returned to New York at the beginning of March 1970, bringing with him just the type of agreement that McGraw-Hill had hoped for, bearing the signature "H.R. Hughes." The publishers swallowed the bait whole, and in due course Irving signed a contract which, in return for "an unentitled authorized biography of H. with a preface by H.," promised to make him overnight one of the best-paid writers in the world. The advance against royalties was set at $500,000; later, at Hughes' supposed insistence, the figure escalated to $750,000 when Irving's manuscript turned out to be rich enough in Hughes' words to be termed an "autobiography."

McGraw-Hill and *Life,* which was to serialize the book, were sworn to secrecy while Irving spent the next few months supposedly conducting one hundred hours of tape-recorded conversations with Hughes "in various motel rooms and parked cars throughout the Western Hemisphere." The transcription of the tapes, suitably edited by Irving, would provide the bulk of the 230,000 words (more than twice the length of this book) which he had promised. Secrecy was absolutely essential, Irving explained, because Hughes did not even want advisers as close as Chester Davis and Bill Gay to know what he was up to.

For the sake of appearance, Irving did indeed follow an exhausting schedule around much of the Western Hemisphere. But the only secret meetings he conducted in those rented rooms were with women other than his wife, chiefly Baroness Nina Van Pallandt, better known as the Danish folk singer Nina. Meanwhile Hughes remained in seclusion at the Britannia Beach Hotel—oblivious to the fraud that was being perpetrated in his name.

Insofar as Irving's book was to have had any connection with reality, he planned to rely for background material on newspaper and magazine clippings, plus three Hughes biographies—*Bashful Billionaire* by Albert Gerber and *Howard Hughes in Las Vegas* by Omar Garrison, both published by Lyle Stuart, and

the immeasurably superior *Howard Hughes* by John
Keats, published in 1966 by Random House—which
had been published despite spirited attempts by Chester
Davis to suppress them. However, even when modified
and expanded by Irving's fertile imagination, the material plagiarized from these sources would hardly
have been sufficient, in either quality or quantity, for
the kind of epic that McGraw-Hill was awaiting. But
Irving also had a secret source of just the kind of exclusive, unpublished material that his book would
need. Eventually, the blame for providing the missing
ingredient fell on Bob Maheu; actually, the unwitting
culprit was Hughes' much older enemy, Noah Dietrich.

In 1969, ten years after resigning from the empire,
Dietrich had decided that he was going to write a
book about Hughes. As a collaborator he chose James
Phelan, a veteran investigative reporter who had dedicated a good part of his career to "watching Hughes"
in much the same way that some journalists watch
China. Phelan tape-recorded one hundred conversations with Dietrich (curiously, the same number of
sessions that Irving later claimed to have had with
Hughes) and then sat down to turn those reminiscences
into a book. The two men did not have a publisher
at this stage, but they did have a "referral agent" in
Los Angeles named Stanley Meyer who received each
chapter of the book as it was completed. His ambiguous
job was to "refer" the manuscript to another agent in
New York, who, in turn, was supposed to drum up
interest among publishers. In 1971, however, Meyer
"referred" Dietrich's memoirs to a couple of other very
unlikely places.

First, Meyer secretly delivered a copy of the manuscript to Hughes' Hollywood lawyer, Greg Bautzer,
which was just about the best way of sabotaging its
publication. (As a matter of policy Hughes attempted to
suppress any and every book about him, but Dietrich's
was in particular jeopardy. In 1959, as part of his
severance deal, Dietrich had signed an agreement—
drawn up by Bautzer—in which he promised not to
market his recollections about Hughes in any form.
Ten years later, Dietrich came to regard that agreement as an infringement on his First Amendment right

of free speech, but Hughes' lawyers could hardly be expected to see it that way—nor did they.)

And then, on June 12, 1971, Meyer renewed his acquaintance with an old friend—Clifford Irving. He did not know, he says, what Irving was up to* but in any event Meyer gave him to read both a copy of the manuscript and a transcript of the one-hundred taping sessions between Phelan and Dietrich. It was solid gold. From a publisher's point of view the Phelan manuscript might have suffered the drawback that it contained too much about Dietrich and not enough about Hughes. Clifford Irving knew exactly how to redress the balance.

Back in Ibiza, with a photocopy of the tape transcript, Irving set to work with his collaborator, Richard Suskind, a competent writer of potted history books. For eight weeks they conducted daily tape-recording sessions, taking it in turns at pretending to be Howard Hughes while the other played the role of interviewer. There was no need to imitate Hughes' voice because Irving had already warned McGraw-Hill that, at Hughes' supposed insistence, the tapes would be destroyed after they had been transcribed.

Relying on their research material, the Dietrich transcript, and their own imaginations, Irving and Suskind ad-libbed their way through Hughes' life. The resulting transcripts, filled with previously unpublished, colorful anecdotes—many of them fictional, of course —exceeded even McGraw-Hill's expectations. And, as a final touch, Irving provided the promised preface "by" Howard R. Hughes:

I believe that more lies have been told and printed about me than about any living man—therefore it was my purpose to write a book which would set the record straight and restore the balance. . . .

On December 7, 1971, McGraw-Hill announced its coup and its intention to publish the autobiography in

* The best account of this bizarre affair is given in *Hoax: The Inside Story of the Howard Hughes–Clifford Irving Affair* by Stephen Fay, Lewis Chester, and Magnus Linklater published in the United States by Viking. Dietrich's memoirs were eventually published by Fawcett under the title *Howard: The Amazing Mr. Hughes.*

three months time. The story was immediately denied by Hughes' public relations men and by spokesmen for the Tool Company—but they were not believed. As McGraw-Hill pointed out, Hughes had told Irving from the start that he wanted no one in his empire to know about the autobiography; the denials of the spokesmen were only confirmation that they had been kept truly in the dark.

Even when, four weeks later, Hughes broke his fourteen-year silence to publicly denounce the autobiography as a fraud, he did not succeed immediately in killing the lie. Indeed, to many observers, the denial only served to *confirm* the book's authenticity. It was, they said, a classic example of Hughes changing his mind—of his backing out of a deal for intractable reasons.

For its part, McGraw-Hill remained insistent that the autobiography was genuine and offered to share the evidence on which that conviction was based. Most of the $750,000 advance McGraw-Hill had paid had been intended, naturally, for Hughes. The money had actually been given to Irving for delivery, but demonstrating its astuteness, McGraw-Hill had made out most of the checks to H.R. Hughes. Those checks had been paid into a Swiss bank account, belonging to H.R. Hughes. And now, as solid proof of Hughes' participation, McGraw-Hill produced the canceled checks, which carried, for all the world to see, Hughes' unmistakable countersignature.

Of course, the signature was a forgery, and as the world soon found out, the H.R. Hughes who had cashed McGraw-Hill's checks was not *the* H.R. Hughes.

But Irving almost got away with it. Swiss banking-secrecy laws being what they are, it might have been impossible to establish that there were two H.R. Hugheses but for one thing: The bank account had been opened by Irving's wife, using the name Helga Hughes. As Robert Peloquin of Intertel (which made that crucial discovery) said: "If they could have found a man to go instead of a woman, it wouldn't have mattered even if he'd been a dwarf." People had been willing to believe almost anything about Howard Hughes, but not that he had changed his sex.

Up until the moment when it began work on the Irving case in December 1971, Intertel had for more than a year concentrated its considerable investigative resources on Robert Maheu. Perhaps that explains why Intertel and Chester Davis were convinced that Maheu, and not Irving, was really the mastermind of the fraud. After a year of digging into every aspect of Maheu's life (including, Maheu says, his household garbage), they just could not get him out of their minds.

Certainly Maheu had sufficient motive. Days after being evicted from Little Caesar's Palace he had filed suit against Hughes alleging wrongful dismissal and claiming $50 million in damages. The claim was ambitious not only in the amount of money it sought but because there had been no written contract to cement Maheu's relationship with Hughes. His $10,-000-a-week retainer from the Tool Company was based on a fragile arrangement that could be terminated at will, and there was only Maheu's word that Hughes had promised "we would be together for the rest of our natural lives." To stand any real chance of succeeding in his lawsuit, Maheu needed, therefore, to somehow persuade Hughes to come out into the open —to go onto a witness stand and answer questions under oath about his promises.

The prospects of Hughes returning to Las Vegas voluntarily to submit to that type of interrogation were nonexistent—unless, perhaps, his failure to do so caused another threat, far greater than the one posed by Maheu, which might force him to return to Nevada. As Intertel well knew, the autobiography did seem for a while to pose just such a threat because of Irving's claim that he had met with Hughes almost a hundred times "throughout the Western Hemisphere." Soon after Hughes had left Las Vegas, Nevada had acquired a new governor—Mike O'Callaghan—who, together with the chairman of the state gaming board, was not very sympathetic towards Hughes' obsessive reclusiveness. They saw no reason why Hughes should continue to hold gaming licenses when he had not fulfilled any of the normal requirements—such as a personal appearance before the gaming board. As O'Callaghan said, "What's so traumatic about seeing someone?"

Chester Davis had spent a considerable amount of time during 1971 persuading O'Callaghan and his officials that any face-to-face meeting with "strangers" (a category that included Chester Davis) would truly inflict intolerable trauma on Hughes. Nevada's officials had just accepted that story, very reluctantly, when the news broke that Hughes had not, apparently, been traumatized by his meetings—"throughout the Western Hemisphere"—with an unknown hack writer. Nevada lost no time in making it clear to Chester Davis that if the Irving story turned out to be true, Hughes' gaming licenses would be in considerable jeopardy.

But although Maheu had a motive, and although he may well have possessed the necessary deviousness to construct such a plot, neither Intertel nor anybody else produced a scintilla of evidence to suggest that he had any connection with Irving's hoax. Maheu was called before a New York federal grand jury which investigated the hoax, but he denied any knowledge of the affair and the eventual indictments—against Irving, his wife, and Richard Suskind *—did not even mention Maheu's name.

Still, in January 1972, when the threat to Hughes' gaming licenses forced him to stage the telephonic press conference to denounce the autobiography, it was Maheu, not Irving, who was the real target. "Note everything he has done," said Hughes, "everything short of murder as a result of being discharged. I don't suppose any disgruntled employee who was discharged has ever come close to Mr. Maheu's conduct."

If he had been around, Maheu could have told him: "Howard, you ain't seen nothin' yet."

* The Irvings both confessed to mail fraud and forgery. In June 1972 Irving was sentenced to two and a half years in prison and fined $10,000. His wife got an equal fine but was sentenced to a two-year prison term, which the judge immediately lessened to two months. The two sentences were to be served at different times so that the Irvings' children could receive proper parental care.

Until the press conference Maheu had never been totally convinced, he says, that "the intent of Mr. Hughes" had been to fire him. Disregarding all the evidence, he had clung to his suspicion that Hughes—and, consequently, he—were the victims of a kidnap plot. Or perhaps, he said, Howard had been brainwashed.

Hughes' bitter allegations brought him back to earth. The more controversial aspects of the press conference were cut from the version broadcast on national television, but Dial Torgerson, a reporter for the Los Angeles *Times,* provided Maheu with an unedited tape recording.

"I was flabbergasted and simultaneously I was furious," Maheu said. "I recognized the voice of a person who was terribly peeved and many things, frankly, came to my recollection. I remembered over the years how many times this same man had told me that he could either buy anyone or destroy him."

Maheu says he immediately realized that Hughes' charges would make it impossible for him to earn a living, and "I had deep concern about my family, about my grandchildren who bore my name, about my mother."

He also realized that Hughes had provided him with much better grounds for a lawsuit than "wrongful dismissal." A month after the press conference, the $50 million claim in the Las Vegas courts was abandoned in favor of a suit, filed in federal court in Los Angeles, which alleged that "the man who, by telephone, identified himself as Howard R. Hughes" had uttered slander and libel. (The allegation of libel—written defamation, usually considered by juries to be more serious than slander because of its comparative permanence—was possible because Hughes' PR firm, Carl Byoir Associates, had distributed written transcripts of the press conference. The transcripts contained a curious error. The most offensive line, "Maheu stole me blind," was changed to read, "Maheu stole my lines." There was, however, no doubt as to what Hughes had actually said.)

Those who are accused of libel in the United States can normally choose from a number of defenses. One can, for example, claim that the allegedly defamatory words were never written (or, in the case of slander, spoken). Alternatively, one can claim that the words have been wrongly interpreted and that no harm was meant. Even if the offending words were undoubtedly libelous, in that they turned out to be totally untrue, one can still mount a defense by showing that the error was a genuine mistake and that no malice or ill will was intended. Finally, for the grave, there is the defense of "truth"—the offending words were honest, uttering them was justifiable, and one is prepared to go before a jury and prove it.

Of course, with Hughes as the defendant, the major point of speculation was not which line of defense he would choose, but whether he would defend the suit at all. Would Hughes finally come out of hiding and face his now archenemy across what would have been a very crowded courtroom?

As it turned out, Chester Davis was unable to provide quite such a spectacular denouement, but he did come up with an impressive substitute. Hughes' Summa Corporation * announced that it was fully prepared to accept legal responsibility for its sole stockholder's actions and would, therefore, become the defendant in the libel trial.

In the event that Maheu prevailed, Summa said, it would, with assets exceeding $335 million, be able to pay any amount of damages a jury might reasonably award. Summa also said that it would defend the action vigorously, relying on the justification of truth: Maheu, it said in its counterclaims, had stolen hundreds of thousands of dollars from Hughes.

It promised to be a remarkable trial.

It is a strange paradox of libel trials that those who go to court to vindicate their reputations frequently find themselves in the dock—at least figuratively.

So it was that when *Robert A. Maheu* v. *Summa et*

* The old Hughes Tool Company was renamed Summa Corporation on December 6, 1972. The oil tool division of the old company then became the new, publicly owned Hughes Tool Company.

al. went to trial before the U.S. district court in Los Angeles in February 1974 it was Maheu, the plaintiff, who was required to defend his honesty while Summa, the defendant, took on "the burden of proof." Neither side displayed any lack of willingness.

Appropriately enough in such an epic contest, both sides' were represented by lawyers who possessed not only great legal skills but finely tuned gladiatorial instincts.

For the defense—and therefore, paradoxically, the prosecutor—there was Norbert Schlei, a graduate of Yale Law School who had earned the distinction of editing its prestigious law journal. Before joining a Los Angeles law firm—Hughes (no relation to the client), Hubbard and Reed—he had served as a law clerk to U.S. Supreme Court Justice John Harlan and as Assistant U.S. Attorney General in both the Kennedy and Johnson administrations.

For the plaintiff there was Morton Galane. He was an electrical engineer turned lawyer with a practice in Las Vegas whose most celebrated case before the Maheu trial concerned a French review performed by topless (female) artists. Galane had represented the originator of that act, which had been pirated by a Las Vegas club; he took the case all the way to the U.S. Supreme Court and finally won for his client damages amounting to almost one million dollars.

On paper, it may have seemed that in terms of credentials Schlei had something of an edge over his opponent, but Maheu could not possibly have found a more dedicated and committed advocate than Morton Galane, who saw the contest as a battle "on behalf of all individuals who have faced what appears to be overwhelming power."

Maheu had originally hired Galane as his lawyer on December 4, 1970, when Chester Davis had issued his "sundown" ultimatum. Since that time, Galane had devoted hundreds if not thousands of hours to Maheu's cause—much of it without payment because Maheu was broke and deeply in debt.

To Galane the libel trial was a rematch of David versus Goliath: an honorable, affable man up against a sinister corporation, possessing almost infinite re-

236

sources and controlled by a man who considered himself to be above the law.

Norbert Schlei saw it quite differently. He argued to the jury that Maheu was a crook—or as he put it, "a con man"—whose retribution was long overdue.

Not surprisingly, then, the trial which began on February 26, 1974, and which unfolded over the next ten months was at times incredibly bitter. Day after day Judge Harry Pregerson was obliged to referee the verbal brawls that broke out between counsel. Galane in particular found it difficult to control his emotion—perhaps *anger* is a better word—and he was continually rebuked by the judge: "Mr. Galane, quit acting like a child" . . . "Quit shouting at the witness. You are harassing this gentleman, Mr. Galane." Tempers became so heated at one stage that Judge Pregerson suggested to Galane that he might "lock you up overnight" in order to "give you something to think about."

Schlei was, generally speaking, a cooler customer, but he too sometimes lost control of his temper. In the process of questioning Maheu about Hughes' political contributions, for example, Schlei was not in the least amused by Maheu's pointed—but irrelevant—reminder that Schlei had been among the beneficiaries. (In 1966 Schlei had run, unsuccessfully, for the office of California secretary of state. In the course of that campaign he accepted, perfectly properly, a donation from Hughes of $200. For the record, the money was paid by Maheu Associates by check on October 20, 1966.)

Thanks mainly to Judge Pregerson's sense of humor, there were a few moments of levity. For instance, in midtrial it was reported that Maheu had been seen in conversation with a spectator, "a man with a blue shirt," who, it was feared, might be related in some way to juror number six. Maheu had claimed that the conversation concerned the merits of vitamin C. The judge said that was all right—"Just so long as they weren't talking about vitamin E."

But for the most part the trial was a deadly serious affair. Summarizing the charges against Maheu, Schlei said that there was abundant evidence he had "acted dishonestly in connection with his employment."

According to the picture that Schlei painted for the jury, Maheu had wormed himself into the Hughes organization by trickery and by consistently taking upon himself more authority than it has even been intended he should have. The stories about his early work for Hughes—between 1959 and 1966—were gross exaggerations of the truth: In reality, during that period he had been nothing more than an occasional consultant. After Hughes had moved to Las Vegas, without anyone realizing what was happening, Maheu had promoted himself to the nonexistent position of chief executive officer of the Hughes-Nevada Operations. Then, with the help of old and new friends, Maheu had devised a plot to "steal Hughes blind." The conspirators led by Maheu had first "conned" Hughes into buying hotels such as the Desert Inn at inflated prices and had then taken "kickbacks" from the sellers, which they had shared.

Maheu's retainer of $520,000 a year had been arrived at "by a fraudulent procedure in which he lied and misrepresented the facts" to the Tool Company.

Not satisfied with that, Maheu had stolen money which he was supposed to donate to various political campaigns. For examples, there was the $50,000 in cash which he failed to give to Hubert Humphrey and another $50,000 in cash which had disappeared from the Sands Hotel. That $100,000 was "up in the air and we will have to think about who got it," said Schlei, leaving no doubt as to his conclusion.

Then there was the $300,000 withdrawn from the Silver Slipper which Maheu's buddy, Jack Hooper, had refused to account for, and the discrepancy of at least $60,000 between the amount Tom Bell claimed to have given to various politicians and the amount they had admitted receiving. Where had that money gone? asked Schlei. Again, he personally seemed to have little doubt that Maheu and his coconspirators had stolen it all.

The jury was given many more examples of Maheu's alleged perfidy, but there was, of course, another and very different side to each story. The total conflict in testimony can perhaps best be demonstrated by one of those examples.

In 1967 Hank Greenspun, the publisher of the Las Vegas *Sun*, had received from Hughes a loan of $4 million on which he was required to pay the very modest interest rate of three percent. According to Summa's version of events, Maheu had arranged the loan and then, a day later, taken a "kickback" from Greenspun of $150,000.

The alternative version presented to the jury was very different. It was Hughes, not Maheu, who had instigated the loan, and he did not want to charge Greenspun any interest at all. The only role Maheu had played was to suggest to Hughes that the interest rate should be a realistic (in those days) six percent. Greenspun had told Maheu to mind his own business, and after that the details of the loan were settled by Greenspun and a lawyer from the Tool Company.

It was not denied that Greenspun had given Maheu a check for $150,000, but they both told the jury that there was nothing sinister in that. Despite the size of his retainer, Maheu was (indisputably) always short of money because of the need to live up to the image he felt Las Vegas expected of a man in his position. Just after Greenspun had received his $4 million loan he learned—from lawyer Ed Morgan—that Maheu was in desperate need of cash to pay yet another tax bill. Greenspun, who, to his wife's annoyance, was in the habit of making loans to almost anyone, agreed to lend Maheu $150,000 on the promise that it would be repaid in a few weeks. So there could be no doubt about the nature of the transaction, he had written the word "loan" across one corner of the check.

Called to the witness stand, Greenspun agreed that despite frequent requests Maheu had not honored his promise to repay the loan—by then almost seven years old—and had not even paid any interest on it. Greenspun said he was very unhappy about that, but what could he do?

Summa's lawyers treated this explanation with the deepest cynicism. But in maintaining that nothing improper had occurred, Maheu offered one more bit of testimony that Schlei and his colleagues could not easily counter: Hughes had been fully aware of the

Greenspun loan to Maheu and he had "acquiesced in it."

Time and time again Maheu presented that same impenetrable defense: Almost every transaction that, painted by Summa's brush, now seemed so dubious had been carried out, Maheu said, with Hughes' full knowledge and consent.

Morton Galane missed no opportunity to drive the point home. Hughes was the one man who could challenge Maheu's testimony, who could with any credibility say, "That is a lie," but he had chosen not to testify. The five male secretaries, who must have been privy to some of the events now in dispute, might have been able to provide some proof, but they too were conspicuous by their absence.

Having made his accusations against Maheu in the most dramatic manner possible, Galane said, Hughes was now hiding, a fugitive from United States justice, refusing to provide substantiation.

Even Schlei, with his impressive credentials, found this a difficult line of reasoning to resist. Nor could he properly explain why Summa had failed to produce more than just one of the hundreds of memos which Maheu had written to Hughes, and which might have thrown some light on the true nature of their relationship.

Not surprisingly under the circumstances, on Monday, July 1, 1974, the jury returned a unanimous verdict "in favor of the plaintiff, Robert A. Maheu."

Having decided that Maheu had been libeled, the same jury was asked—after a respite of almost four months—to decide how much money in damages he should receive.

Maheu testified, during this second part of the trial, that the injuries he had suffered were both financial and emotional. To begin with, he was broke. Soon after he was fired, in December 1970, the First National Bank of Nevada had seized such funds as he then had to satisfy debts he owed the bank. But those debts had represented only a fraction of his obligations, the rest of which, almost four years later, he was still unable to meet.

Maheu said that any chance he may have had of getting back on his feet was blown away by Hughes' press conference. "All the potential clients that I may have had available would not touch me after that with a ten-foot pole." He did act as a consultant to a Las Vegas company, which, among other things, owned a small gambling establishment named, ironically, Little Caesar's Casino, but it was apparently not much of a job, and after the press conference his fee had been cut because his boss thought the damage to Maheu's integrity had damaged his usefulness.

Evidently, the emotional impact had been no less severe. Maheu's wife, Yvette, told the jury: "It was difficult for him to really get any rest. He would awaken at night and just think and wonder which way to turn, what to do and where to go. . . . I guess maybe the hurt is still there. He didn't want to see people socially, and he was not himself. In talking to me only, he would talk about the past years—the years he had given up for Mr. Hughes. This was such a shock. He was thinking about his invalid mother, his children, his family name. On a few occasions he actually sobbed."

And Maheu said: "Although I knew that the statements were wrong, I still felt ashamed. I was morose. I was depressed . . . . I can't hide it when I'm happy, and I can't hide it when I'm sad. All I can say is that they were not very pleasant days."

Intertel's investigation of Maheu, aimed at producing evidence of his supposed dishonesty, had not helped matters any. Maheu said that the investigation had continued for four years and that no avenue, no matter how personal, had been left unexplored. The records of the Maheu family's bank accounts going back twenty years had been subpoenaed, "including my little teenaged boy's bank account reflecting his [earnings] from his paper route."

These revelations obviously made some impression on the jury, for on December 4, 1974, it awarded Maheu as compensation for the defamation $2,823,333 —and 30 cents.

Set against that was an award of $644,000, which, it was ruled, Maheu owed Hughes. (Summa had filed counterclaims against Maheu for $4.4 million, which it claimed was the amount he owed Hughes on, among other things, unpaid promissory notes. Maheu admitted the outstanding loans and the fact that he had —accidentally, he said—overcharged Hughes for some of his assignments. He also agreed that, again accidentally, Maheu Associates had kept $87,000 which Nadine Henley had sent to Las Vegas for the payment of political contributions. Judge Pregerson ruled that these sums of money should be repaid, but the rest of Summa's counterclaims were dismissed—leaving Maheu with a net award of a little under $2,200,000.)

Neither side was happy with the result. Maheu believed that the calumny was so gross, and so tinged with malice, that he was entitled to punitive damages far in excess of the compensatory damages the jury gave him. Summa, for its part, believed that the evidence at the trial overwhelmingly demonstrated Maheu's dishonesty. Both sides appealed, and at the time of writing the case is awaiting the consideration of the Ninth Circuit Court of Appeals in San Francisco.

The libel trial, surely one of the most bizarre cases ever to come before the American courts, produced some insight into the unbelievable world of Howard Hughes, but it did not go far in solving the mystery of what Judge Pregerson described as "the extraordinary relationship that existed between Mr. Maheu and Mr. Hughes."

Quite early in the trial the judge posed the key question: What was it about Maheu that allowed him to become for a while the alter ego of one of the richest men in the world?

In the absence of Hughes, there could be no satisfactory answer, and now that he is dead it is unlikely that one will ever be provided.

Maheu remains an enigma. As Judge Pregerson said, "On one hand he can be described as affable, intelligent, imaginative, articulate. . . . He is a friendly man, with important friends in high places. He has enormous energy and drive, and the ability to get things done. . . . Looked at from another angle, Mr. Maheu appears to be talkative, somewhat naive, artless, careless, imprecise—an overly trusting man whose personal affairs were in a state of disarray."

One of the witnesses at the trial, Maheu's tax lawyer, had described his client as "a walking calamity." The judge thought differently: "I would describe him as a walking paradox."

12: AN ORDINARY DEATH

No action, whether foul or fair,
Is ever done, but it leaves somewhere
A record, written by fingers ghostly,
As a blessing or a curse. . . .
—Henry Wadsworth Longfellow

Despite his wealth, despite the influence in high places he had bought and paid for, despite the expertise of his high-priced lawyers, Howard Hughes spent his last years on the run—a fugitive from adversity largely of his own making. An ever-increasing number of lawsuits, both civil and criminal, kept him out of the United States, but also pursued him to wherever he sought sanctuary: the Bahamas, Nicaragua, Canada, Nicaragua again, England, the Bahamas again, and finally Mexico. He dared not return to his own country until the very end, and then he did not quite make it. He died, on April 5, 1976, in a chartered jet somewhere over south Texas.

It seems safe to assume that those final years were for the most part deeply unhappy ones for Hughes. Back in January 1972 during his brief—and, as it turned out, final—excursion into the limelight, he had talked about his plans for the future. He did not really know why he had lived the life of a recluse, he said at the press conference, but "I will tell you one thing. I am rapidly planning to come out of it." He was going to start flying again—he had "planned it definitely", because "it's good for me in every way." He wanted to make more movies: "I have always thought that in the later years of my life I would like very, very much to make motion pictures that would be worthwhile." He was going to have his photograph taken and distributed to the press because "somebody ought to know what I look like." He was also going to have a face-to-face interview with a group of reporters as soon as "[Chester] Davis and some of my associates tell me I can do these things—I'm ready and willing." And he was going to have his biography written: "I would like to see an accurate story of my life printed because I think I have had experiences that could be helpful to others."

Perhaps those assertions were just more castles in the sky, based on no more solid a foundation than wishful thinking, but the impression left behind by the press conference was of a man who, having been forced to talk to real people again, had actually found the experience enjoyable. Nobody, however, could possibly have enjoyed the consequences and the aftermath, of which Maheu's libel suit was just the beginning.

Five weeks or so after the press conference, on the afternoon of February 14, Bahamian immigration officials turned up at the Britannia Beach Hotel demanding to inspect the work permits of the Americans on Hughes' staff. This sudden display of bureaucratic zealousness was a little overdue, for Hughes and his men had been living in the Bahamas without regard to immigration formalities for fifteen months. As they were about to find out, though, the climate had changed.

Because of Irving's hoax and because of the press conference, Hughes had once again begun to dominate the headlines to the point where, in some newspapers, even President Nixon's historic visit to China had some difficulty in making the front page. The inevitable result was an outbreak of Hughes mania: Noah Dietrich's book came out with suitable fanfare; Hughes T-shirts were (until Chester Davis—claming copyright—intervened) on sale everywhere; and, in New York, a pornographic movie called *Helga and Howard* (about which even Chester Davis could do nothing) played to full houses. All of which made Paradise Island, and the Bahamas in general, the focus of international attention.

In some quarters the publicity was not entirely welcome. At the Nassau parliament, members of the opposition party, the Free National, began asking pertinent questions of the government about Hughes' legal status. It might not have mattered if Hughes had troubled to inject just a fraction of his wealth into the Bahamian economy during his illicit fifteen-month stay, but contrary to all expectations, he had not invested a dime. Prime Minister Pindling decided it was time to exert a little black power.

On February 14 the immigration officials had failed to penetrate Hughes' fortress on the ninth floor of the Britannia Beach, but they returned two days later in a more determined mood. This time, equipped with suitable warrants, and receiving no reply to their demands for access, they broke down the doors. They were too late for any real action, for early that same day Hughes had fled. But a handful of his aides were still around and they were, as the subsequent government press release said, "escorted out of the Commonwealth by immigration officials," which made the point adequately.

Meanwhile, a converted Coast Guard cutter called the *Cygnus* took Hughes to Miami, where a chartered Boeing 727 waited to take him to his next sanctuary, the Nicaraguan capital, Managua.

Nicaragua, the largest but also the most sparsely populated republic in Central America, is not an attractive country in almost any sense. But for Hughes, fresh from his unpleasant experience in the Bahamas, Nicaragua had the overwhelming appeal that parliamentary politics there was of very little relevance. The country was—and is—run by Anastasio Somoza Debayle (the job of president has been in the Somoza family since 1934), who made it very clear that Hughes would be a welcome guest in his country at any time. Accordingly, Hughes moved into the seventeen-room penthouse of the pyramid-shaped Intercontinental Hotel in Managua. This was to be only a temporary rest stop, but before moving on, Hughes went to what were for him extraordinary lengths to cement his newfound friendship with President Somoza*: He met him.

The event was arranged through Turner Shelton, U.S. Ambassador to Nicaragua, who on the night of March 13, 1972, went with Somoza to the Managua airport, where Hughes had already boarded an executive jet. Once again Hughes found the novelty of talking to real people enjoyable, and what was to have been a brief chat went on for almost an hour and a half. "Don't rush off," said Hughes. "This plane isn't going anywhere until I tell it to." According to a report Ambassador Shelton sent to the State Department, Hughes was "about six feet, three inches tall, very thin, weighing from 140–150 pounds, graying hair and neatly trimmed Van Dyke type beard." His handshake was firm and he was articulate, but, Shelton reported, he had considerable difficulty in hearing, and complained that over the years he had tried forty to fifty different types of hearing aids but had found "none to be completely satisfactory." During the conversation Hughes wore a pair of slippers and an old robe, both of which, Shelton said, "would have gone at a bargain basement for about 80 cents."

For the most part Hughes talked to his guests about his flying experiences, but he did try to explain why he had become a recluse: "Years ago when he had been actively engaged in designing and inventing, Hughes had gotten sick and tired of all the time he lost every

* Somoza ceased to be president two months later, in May 1972, when, under the terms of Nicaragua's constitution, he was obliged to retire. However, no one was allowed to replace him, Congress was suspended, and he remained commander in chi . of the army while the constitution was rewritten to allow him to return to office. He was formally reelected in September 1974.

day taking telephone calls and meeting all the people who wanted to see him. He just decided to make himself inaccessible. . . ." Shelton said that Hughes had come to feel that his retreat from the world "was a mistake," but he enjoyed the freedom from interruption so much that "he found it extremely difficult to change."

When the meeting finally ended, Hughes told Somoza that his business affairs demanded that he go to Canada for a while, but, he said, he would be returning to Nicaragua—to begin making some investments.

Sure enough, Hughes did return. After a fairly uneventful sojourn at the Bayshore Inn in Vancouver, British Columbia, he left Canada before the authorities could impose any tax demands on him, and in August 1972 he reoccupied the penthouse of the Intercontinental Hotel. There was no immediate sign of the promised investments, but that may have been due to the fact that Hughes was still short of ready cash. Nicaragua remained hopeful, however, because Hughes seemed to be taking steps to remedy that deficiency.

The backbone of the Hughes empire and, of course, the source of its original wealth was the Tool Company. Even when it had been contributing as much as $30 million a year to his personal bank account, Hughes had displayed disinterest and even antipathy toward the Houston operation, perhaps because he had played no part in its creation and little part in its success. Now, in 1972, with the Tool Company's patents expiring and with its profits ($3.68 million in 1971) down to a fraction of what they had been, Hughes decided it was time to get out of the oil-drilling business.

Inevitably, surrendering control of what was the last great American industrial concern still in the hands of one man was no simple affair. Firstly, The Man's myriad enterprises were gathered together under a new umbrella, the Summa Corporation. In the process of that reorganization, Summa—which was wholly owned by Hughes—acquired all of the five million shares of the Hughes Tool Company, which it then offered to sell to the public along with the legendary name.

In early December 1972 the Tool Company's stock went on sale, and at an asking price of thirty dollars a share, it was eagerly snapped up by investors.* After paying some bills, Hughes was left with $130 million in cash, but before he could inject very much of it into the Nicaraguan economy—if, indeed, that is what he had intended to do—Hughes and Nicaragua received, literally, a very nasty shock.

On December 23, the day before Hughes' sixty-seventh birthday, Nicaragua was pulverized by the third and worst earthquake in its history. In Managua, between seventy and ninety percent of the buildings collapsed, leaving well over 6,000 dead, 20,000 injured, 300,000 homeless, and 60,000 jobless.

The Intercontinental Hotel was of a far more sturdy construction than most other buildings in Managua and it did not collapse, but it was badly damaged. Hughes and his aides escaped from the penthouse via the emergency staircase and spent the night in a rented car parked in a nearby field while the city was largely consumed by fire and panic.

According to Howard Eckersley, when the earthquake first struck Hughes had been "cool." But, after the rigors of a night in a parked car, he had lost that composure when General Somoza saw him early the next morning. "He was fairly disturbed," the general said. "He is used to living in places where they do not have earthquakes."

Just as soon as the structural integrity of the Managua airport's runway could be confirmed, the ever-present Hughes executive jet took off, with The Man and his aides on board, leaving Nicaragua to its fate.

By this time Hughes had been absent from the United States for more than two years, but official American

---

* The stock has turned out to be a considerable bargain. Most of the Tool Company's senior executives, including Raymond Holliday and Calvin Collier, kept their jobs in the new publicly owned company, and, freed from whimsical restraint, they have brought about a resurrection of its fortunes. By the end of 1975 it had achieved a fourfold increase in sales, and the profit that year was more than $43 million. In August 1975 shareholders benefited from a two-for-one stock split, and the per-share price has been as high as fifty-two dollars.

interest in his affairs had not slackened. Indeed, during 1972 Internal Revenue Service agents had devoted a good deal of time to studying the financial machinations of the empire, and Bob Maheu and Richard Danner, among others, had been interviewed. But far too many pieces were still missing from the jigsaw and, the IRS agents came to believe, the only person who might be able to supply those was Hughes. A subpoena demanding information from Hughes about his political contributions was issued, although, of course, the chances of serving it were extremely remote. Just on the off chance that Hughes might show up, however, the IRS informed both Customs and Immigration that Howard Robard Hughes was wanted for questioning.

On December 24, a customs officer at Miami International Airport who was checking a list of incoming flights noticed that a flight plan had been filed for a privately owned Lear jet, inbound from Nicaragua. He also noticed that the unnamed passengers from the Lear jet would not be "entering" the U.S. but would immediately transfer to a longer-range JetStar, owned by the Summa Corporation, for a flight to London, England. Putting two and two together, the customs man tipped off the IRS that its wanted man was, most probably, about to make a brief appearance.

As it happened, the Lear jet landed at Fort Lauderdale, Florida, not Miami, but the IRS agents were able to learn about the change of plan in time to send a welcoming committee. As soon as the Lear jet had parked, in a remote hangar, the agents sent word that they would like to speak to Hughes. The reply that came back was "Call Chester Davis."

Reached in New York, Davis asked for a brief delay in action while he made some telephone calls. The agents agreed to wait thirty minutes. They did not have to, because in less than ten Davis called back to announce, with some relish, that the agents' assignment had been canceled: Senior IRS officials in Washington had issued new orders that the subpoena was not to be served.

Leaving aside the fact that it was Chester Davis, an eminent but still a private attorney, who secured and then delivered the new orders, it was an astonishing

249

decision. The IRS had good information that Hughes was party to a tax fraud in that he had apparently given President Nixon $100,000 which had not been used in any political campaign—and which had not been declared as income by Nixon or anybody else.*

It is difficult to imagine a more material witness than Hughes was in this case, but the opportunity to question him was blatantly disregarded. Predictably, he did not give the IRS a second chance. (This curious episode was eventually revealed in March 1976 by the columnist Jack Anderson, who was unable to get any explanation from IRS officials. They denied that the decision to let Hughes escape was a result of pressure from Chester Davis, but beyond that they refused to discuss the case.)

Understandably, the agents who had gone to Fort Lauderdale were not pleased by the sudden and mystifying turn of events. They were also unwilling to totally disregard this unique opportunity to establish once and for all if Howard Hughes actually existed. In retrospect, that may seem absurd, but at the time there was a body of opinion which believed that Hughes was dead, or, at the least, that he was a vegetable no longer capable of controlling his empire.

The IRS men could not very well defy their new orders from Washington, but there was no such restraint on the customs officers at Fort Lauderdale, and eventually one of them boarded Hughes' jet.

According to Jack Anderson's account of the affair, the customs officer found Hughes—or rather, a man with a black hat pulled down over his ears—concealed behind a blanket that had been draped across the aisle. His face was extremely thin and he had a full beard. Asked if he was Howard Hughes, the man answered, "Yes," at which point the officer began reading out loud a written message from the IRS which said, in effect, that Hughes was wanted for questioning. The man in the black hat interrupted, saying that he was hard of hearing, so the officer gave him the written

---

* At this stage Bebe Rebozo had not yet revealed to the IRS that the $100,000 was lying "untouched" in one of his safe deposit boxes.

message to read. Asked if he understood the message, the man in the black hat replied that he did.

And that was the last the U.S. government saw of Howard Hughes.

With good cause, in view of its size and population, Britain imposes some of the world's most rigid immigration rules, but they can, on occasions, be bent. When Hughes' JetStar landed at Gatwick Airport in Surrey, about thirty miles from London, it taxied to a quiet part of the tarmac, where it was surrounded by official cars which were there to deter intrusion. Hughes had no passport and neither would he allow immigration officials to see him, yet he was given a visitor's visa. Within a few minutes, he was safely ensconced inside a curtained Rolls-Royce and on his way to London.

Those remarkable courtesies had been arranged with officials of the Home Office by the merchant bankers Rothschilds, which, doubtless, pointed out that Hughes had some $130 million to invest. Under those circumstances, of course, the lack of a passport was a mere triviality. Rothschilds had also made the arrangements for Hughes to occupy, as his new sanctuary, part of the ninth floor of the Inn on the Park, which is not an inn but a discreetly luxurious hotel overlooking Hyde Park.

At the beginning of his stay in London, Hughes adopted much the same lifestyle as before, spending most of his time alone in one room while his aides took turns standing by round-the-clock, ready to provide whatever was needed. (It seems that there were six male secretaries in London, four longtime members of the "inner circle"—Howard Eckersley, John Holmes, Levar Myler and George Francom—plus two new recruits, Clarence Waldron and Jim Ricard. Roy Crawford, who had been the fifth male secretary in Las Vegas, ceased to be a member of the "inner circle" sometime in 1971, but he remained a member of the Summa organization, working for Bill Gay.)

According to the few details given by Levar Myler and John Holmes, each aide would be on duty at the Inn on the Park for two weeks at a stretch, working "as long as necessary" but "hopefully" no more then eight to ten hours a day. Usually after such a stint they would return to their homes and families in the U.S.— John Holmes lived in Los Angeles, "Beebe" Myler in Salt Lake City—for a few days before returning to London. While at the Inn on the Park, their duties included keeping in constant touch, via telephone and telex machines, with the various parts of the Summa empire, and passing along Hughes' instructions. Both Holmes and Myler said they were paid a salary of $65,000 a year plus, during their time in England, a $10,000 bonus.

At first, Hughes' presence attracted predictable attention from British reporters and from a whole army of photographers who had been recruited by the rumor that an American magazine was willing to pay $50,000 for the first authenticated picture of the recluse. A great deal of ingenuity was expended in attempts to reach the ninth floor, but the hotel's security proved to be a match for every trick. (For example, the windows of Hughes' sanctuary were covered with black masking tape to keep out prying eyes—and telephoto lenses.) Eventually the professional voyeurs moved on to other assignments, leaving Hughes in comparative peace.

Indeed, it became so peaceful that, reportedly, Hughes was able to leave the hotel unrecognized on several occasions for sight-seeing tours around the British isles. On these trips he was accompanied by Jack Real, the former Lockheed Aircraft vice-president who had joined the empire in 1970, and it is said that, among other places, they visited the Channel Islands, near the coast of northern France, for brief holidays. Apparently, the outings only ceased when, Hughes fell and broke his hip.

The sojourn in London was also remarkable in that Hughes gave personal audiences to some old friends and servants, including Nadine Henley and Bill Gay (now returned to favor) and to a new one, Chester Davis.

And in March 1973 he finally agreed to resolve the lingering doubts the Nevada authorities had had since Hughes' abrupt departure from Las Vegas. On March 16, after flying to London, Nevada Governor Mike

252

O'Callaghan and the chairman of the Nevada Gaming Control Board, Philip Hannifin, met with Hughes in his sanctuary to discover that there was no longer cause for concern: "He had a firm handshake, his eyes were bright, his questions intelligent and relevant."

It might have seemed for a while that Hughes was genuinely preparing to come out of his shell, but as he must have known, back home in the U.S. some very ominous clouds were gathering. Besides the separate hazards posed by Maheu's libel action, which was nearing trial, and the IRS investigation, which was continuing, there was the threat of trouble from two further investigations—one by the Securities and Exchange Commission and one by the Justice Department—into the manner of Hughes' acquisition of Air West. Perhaps, then, Hughes regarded his stay in London not as a foretaste of a new lifestyle, but as a last fling, an Indian summer before a winter of adversity.

In any event, in mid-December 1973 news reached London that a federal grand jury in Las Vegas which had been investigating the Air West deal was expected to hand down *criminal* indictments against Hughes by the end of the month. There was speculation that those indictments would be serious enough to justify a request to the British authorities that Hughes be arrested by the police and held for extradition.

Four days later, on December 19, just short of a year after arriving in London, Hughes and his entourage decamped and returned to their original sanctuary —the Bahamas.

In view of the unpleasantness which had surrounded the end of Hughes' previous visit to the islands, it was, on the face of it, a little surprising that he should seek refuge there once again. However, the Bahamas held what was now for Hughes the considerable attraction that its courts did not always see eye to eye with other legal jurisdictions as to what constituted a crime.

In 1973, for example, an attempt by the U.S. to extradite financier Robert Vesco from the Bahamas on charges of fraud had foundered on the rock that no crime similar to the one he was accused of in America existed under Bahamian law. (The charges against

Vesco, like those to come against Hughes, arose from alleged violations of the laws governing the stockmarket. The Bahamas, of course, does not have a stockmarket.) And while Vesco had been obliged to appear in court in Nassau to resist extradition, it seemed highly unlikely that Hughes would be subjected to even that inconvenience. During his absence from the Bahamas, somebody in his empire had been judiciously mending fences.

The style of Hughes' return to the islands on December 20 demonstrated just how much the climate had improved. Although it was four A.M. when his plane landed at Freeport, on the island of Grand Bahama, there was a distinguished welcoming committee, led by Mrs. Barbara Pierre, head of the immigration service—and, incidentally, a sister of the deputy prime minister.

Mrs. Pierre had held the same job back in 1972 when Hughes had been chased off Paradise Island for flouting the immigration law; now she was on hand to personally greet the former illegal immigrant and issue him and his men all the resident and work permits they could possibly require.

In those circumstances Hughes could confidently take out a long-term reservation on the top two floors of the Xanadu Princess Hotel on Grand Bahama. (He later saved himself the rent of around $2,000 a day by buying the hotel.) And just in case there remained any doubts about Hughes' status, Prime Minister Lynden Pindling explained his government's new position: The Bahamas, he said, welcomed rich men who lived within the law. Bahamian law, of course.

The Securities and Exchange Commission had first reopened its files on Air West when stockholders began complaining that the eight dollars or so a share which Hughes had paid was far less than they had expected to receive. The job of investigating the background of the deal was assigned to William Turner, a bearded twenty-nine-year-old attorney in the SEC's Enforcement Division who may have lacked experience, but not enthusiasm. He began work on the case in September 1972 and spent the better part of a year interviewing those witnesses who were within the reach of his subpoenas. Because of the bitterness inspired by Hughes' public accusation against Maheu, some of those witnesses were a good deal more willing to talk than they might otherwise have been. The answers he got convinced Turner that Air West's dramatic slump in value before the takeover had not been entirely accidental.

The SEC does not have a mandate to pursue criminal prosecutions, but Turner was not alone in his conviction that Hughes had acquired Air West through criminal conspiracy. The U.S. attorney for Nevada, DeVoe Heaton, was of a similar mind, and in November 1973 he empaneled a federal grand jury to hear the evidence. On December 27, in line with confident predictions, the grand jury handed down indictments charging Hughes and four others* with stock manipulation and conspiracy to defraud.

A grand jury indictment is no more than an assertion that there is a *prima facie* case to be answered, but it does have one unpleasant—for Hughes, unthinkable—consequence in that those indicted must appear *personally* before a court for arraignment. Failure to appear for arraignment usually results in the court's issuing an arrest warrant.

A warrant against Hughes would have been difficult to serve and—unless Bahamian hospitality cooled—impossible to enforce. But Hughes would then have become, officially, a fugitive, which would have been enough to place almost every part of the Summa empire in awful jeopardy. His gambling licenses in Nevada and the federal license to run the Las Vegas TV station all depended upon the owner being a person of "good moral character," which fugitives, by definition, are not; the licenses of Hughes Airwest would have been similarly threatened; and Hughes

---

* They were Robert Maheu, Chester Davis, David Charnay, head of Four Star International and an alleged participant in the dumping of Air West stock, and James Nall, who had worked for the Hughes-Nevada Operations. The indictments against Nall were later dropped. Named by the grand jury as coconspirators but *not* indicted were Hank Greenspun and George Crockett.

Aircraft and Hughes Helicopters could scarcely have expected to continue receiving government contracts while their owner was on the run from that government.

Not surprisingly, then, Summa mounted an epic campaign to prevent an arrest warrant being issued against Hughes. It won the first round by a knockout.

On January 30, 1974, at Summa's behest, the federal district court in Reno, Nevada, summarily dismissed the indictments on the grounds that they had been faultily drawn. In order to beat Nevada's statute of limitations, which was fast running out and which could have provided Hughes and his codefendants with immunity against some of the charges, the U.S. attorney's office had been obliged to compose the wording of the indictments hastily. The result was, according to Federal Judge Bruce Thompson, "the worst criminal pleading" he had ever seen. But that by no means ended the matter, for Judge Thompson gave U.S. Attorney Heaton six months to seek fresh indictments.

Heaton said he was confident that he could do the job in time. He might not have been so assured if he could have foreseen the quality of the resistance he was going to be up against—chiefly from his own superiors in Washington, D.C.

Secret influence, the kind that is exerted behind closed doors, was coming to be regarded as a dubious commodity in the Washington of spring 1974. Former Attorney General John Mitchell was under indictment for allegedly lying to a grand jury about a $200,000 campaign gift from Robert Vesco (he was later acquitted); former Attorney General Richard Kleindienst was charged with lying to the U.S. Senate about the persuasive influence of ITT (he was later convicted); and Howard Hughes' $100,000 payment to Bebe Rebozo had been revealed and the Watergate prosecutor was seeking the nature of the *quid pro quo*.

Nevertheless, Attorney Heaton was summoned to Washington by his superiors at the Justice Department and placed under colossal but secret pressure to abandon his charges against Hughes. It was not suggested that he drop the case altogether. Indeed, Heaton was told to actively seek the reindictment of Maheu, Davis, and David Charnay; Hughes, however, should be left in peace.

The chief advocates of this curious cause were, apparently, John C. Kenney, deputy assistant attorney general, and Thomas McTierman, head of the fraud section of the Justice Department. Both men had been closely associated with Robert Peloquin, head of Intertel, during his days at the Justice Department. According to the Las Vegas *Sun* Peloquin met with Kenney and McTiernan in Washington. And while we do not suggest that Peloquin acted improperly, he was probably active in trying to persuade his former colleagues to change their minds about Hughes' indictability.

Attorney Heaton refused to give way. He argued that if there had been a conspiracy—as his colleagues appeared to believe because they wanted to press ahead with the charges against the other defendants—then Hughes must have been among the conspirators because he was the *only* substantial beneficiary of the Air West deal. There was not a scintilla of evidence to show that Maheu or Davis had benefited by as much as one cent from their roles in the alleged plot. Hughes, on the other hand, had benefited to the tune of some $48 million.

Accordingly, Heaton refused to have anything to do with a plea for reindictment that did not include charges against Hughes. He could not be fired—only the President can remove a U.S. attorney—but he could be removed from the case. And he was.

When the first indictments had been thrown out by the federal court on technicalities, the deadline for any reindictment had been set at July 30, 1974. The day before that deadline was due to expire, Attorney Heaton's deputy Dean Vernon was instructed by the Justice Department to reconvene the grand jury and seek new indictments against Maheu, Davis, and Charnay —but not against Hughes.

It was a shallow endeavor, and it failed because the grand jury, refusing to indict anybody unless Hughes was a defendant, returned a "no true bill." But the fact that it was even attempted suggested irresistibly that influence in high places was still currency in some parts of Washington.

The next day, his reasoning vindicated, Attorney Heaton returned to the case. He explained that there had been a "professional difference of opinion" within the Justice Department over a "complex and complicated case" which had "been resolved." Then, with only hours left before the deadline expired, the grand jury was reconvened yet again.

The jurors began to assemble in the Federal building in Las Vegas at about three P.M. Sixteen members were required for a quorum, but by four P.M. the necessary number had not shown up. The local FBI office was asked to find some of the tardy ones. Finally, at four thirty-five P.M., the sixteenth juror arrived. According to reporters who were waiting outside the jury room, he was greeted with applause.

Less than twenty minutes later, the grand jury returned new indictments against Maheu, Davis, Charnay—and Howard Hughes. The substance of the charges was the same as before.

In Washington, the Justice Department announced straight-faced that it would "actively" seek Hughes' extradition from the Bahamas unless he appeared, voluntarily, for arraignment.

There were to be a few more twists and turns in the drama.

On September 5, 1974, in response to a telegram signed by Secretary of State Henry Kissinger, no less, a U.S. consular officer in the Bahamas effected service of a summons on Hughes, demanding his appearance before the federal district court in Reno. (According to a telegram sent by the U.S. embassy in Nassau to the Department of State, serving the summons was no easy task: "As all personnel at the Xanadu Hotel refuse to acknowledge the whereabouts or the existence of Howard Hughes, the Consular Officer was unable to serve the summons on Hughes personally," the telegram said. "The Consular Officer attempted to leave the summons in the possession of Mr. William Mulder, manager, Xanadu Hotel, who irately refused to accept it saying Howard Hughes was not registered at the hotel and he (Mulder) knew nothing of Hughes' whereabouts or how he might be reached. Mulder returned the summons to the Consular Officer by throwing it through the open window of the Consular Officer's car. Consular Officer then contacted Freeport postmaster who stated that one Vance Tynes is serving as a messenger of Hughes' interests in Freeport. . . . Consular Officer then returned to Xanadu Hotel and waited at hotel gate until a man whom the gate attendant identified as Mr. Tynes returned from lunch. . . . Consular Officer placed an envelope containing summons into Mr. Tynes' hands stating it was an important message to be delivered to Howard Hughes. Mr. Tynes proceeded to the hotel with the envelope and the Consular Officer departed the hotel premises.")

A week later Robert Peloquin turned up at the U.S. embassy in Nassau, protesting the attempted service of the summons, saying that the federal court had not yet had the opportunity to rule on the validity of the new indictments.

Peloquin seemed to have a point, because on November 13, 1974, Federal Judge Bruce Thompson again threw out the grand jury indictments, saying this time that the alleged conspiracy may have been "an abuse of great wealth" but that there was no evidence of criminal acts. The Justice Department lodged an appeal.

Meanwhile, Bill Turner of the SEC was collecting evidence to begin civil proceedings against Hughes. On March 27, 1975, the SEC filed a civil complaint in the federal district court in San Francisco, alleging fraud and stock manipulation on the part of Howard Hughes, the Summa Corporation, Hughes Airwest, Robert Maheu, Chester Davis, David Charnay, Hank Greenspun, George Crockett, Jimmy "the Greek" Snyder, and Patrick J. Hillings.* The SEC asked the court for an order, enjoining the defendants from

---

* It was Hillings who arranged the original meeting between Maheu and Nick Bez. The SEC complaint alleged that Hillings, a former Republican congressman, secretly received more than $50,000 from Hughes while he was still a director of Air West, in return for his support of the takeover.

"further violations" of federal securities laws—and requiring them to surrender $48 million of allegedly illicit "profits" resulting from the takeover deal.

To add to Hughes' troubles, a group of Air West stockholders also filed suit in San Francisco against the same ten defendants, alleging the same perfidy and asking for unspecified but exemplary damages.

Finally, the criminal charges were resurrected. In May 1976 the Ninth Circuit Court of Appeals ruled that Judge Thompson had been in error and that a *prima facie* case of conspiracy to defraud had been made out against Hughes and Maheu, Davis and Charnay. The appeals court ordered the indictments reinstated.

It was too late to matter. The Man was already dead.

Late in the evening of Sunday, April 4, 1976, two young pilots who ran a flying ambulance service out of Fort Lauderdale, Florida, received a special charter from a local doctor to fly to Acapulco, Mexico. Roger Sutton and Jeff Abrams were told that an unnamed patient required transportation to Houston, Texas, where he would receive urgently needed medical attention. They took off in their jet ambulance at five the next morning and got to Acapulco four hours later, where they were kept waiting without explanation for about five hours.

Meanwhile, at the Princess Hotel in Acapulco (where Hughes had occupied the top floor since mid-February when, fearing perhaps that the climate had changed yet again, he had fled the Bahamas), staff and guests were told to move away from the doors leading to a service elevator. From a distance a small, curious crowd watched seven men and a four-wheel stretcher emerge from the elevator. An old man lay on the stretcher, covered to his chin by a sheet. He appeared to be unconscious.

Outside the hotel a yellow and white ambulance, hired from the Manzanares Funeral Parlor, had been waiting three hours. The stretcher and its burden were loaded on board and the ambulance driver, Jaime Quevedo, headed for the airport as fast as he dared.

To pilots Sutton and Abrams their passenger, when

he arrived, looked wasted "like tired worn-out old person." He may then have been conscious because, according to Sutton, "he moved his lips a little when they put him on the plane but I couldn't hear if he said anything." After the stretcher had been loaded, two doctors boarded the plane. They did not volunteer the identity of their patient.

The jet ambulance took two hours to fly from Acapulco to Houston, landing at one-fifty P.M. local time. By that time the patient had been dead twenty-three minutes.

His body, covered with a blanket, was taken to Houston Methodist Hospital for an autopsy. It weighed ninety pounds and was "extremely shriveled" and "emaciated." The frame was now only six feet two inches long,* but FBI agents took fingerprints and "positively identified" the body as belonging to Howard Robard Hughes.

The cause of death was established by Dr. Henry MacIntosh, chief of the Department of Internal Medicine at the Methodist Hospital, as chronic renal failure. "Renal means kidney, two of them. Chronic means a long time. And failure means that they don't work so well," the doctor said. "The kidneys have the responsibility of getting rid of the waste products the body makes and they come out in the urine. The kidneys are marvelous organs and when they don't function very well the waste products accumulate. And unless something is done about it, the patient will die. And this is what I think has happened."

The county medical examiner agreed with Dr. MacIntosh that it was an ordinary death, nothing to get excited or suspicious about: "It's an extraordinary individual involved, perhaps, but his death was just like any other death."

That might make a suitable epitaph.

* In 1972 Hughes had said he was a fraction under six feet four inches tall.

EPILOGUE: WATERGATE AND THE CIA

It seems to us, and we have tried to so demonstrate, that the relationship between Howard Hughes and Robert Maheu ended disastrously for both men. The intriguing question that remains is whether there was a third victim of their mutual belligerency—President Richard Milhous Nixon.

Of course, Hughes and Maheu were not the direct cause of the events that led to Nixon's downfall, but there is tempting evidence to suggest that the breakup of their relationship may have acted as a catalyst. Specifically, it now seems at least possible that the Watergate break-in happened because the Nixon White House was terrified of the possible consequences of the feud between Hughes and Maheu.

The primary target of the Watergate burglary, which occurred during the early hours of June 17, 1972, was Lawrence O'Brien, then chairman of the Democratic National Committee, and formerly Hughes' PR man in Washington, D.C. The burglars, financed by CREEP (Committee for the Re-Election of the President) were caught red-handed as they attempted to install an electronic listening device in the ceiling of O'Brien's office. A month earlier, the burglars had made an unsuccessful attempt to bug O'Brien's telephone. Why?

O'Brien's contractual relationship with Hughes ended shortly after Maheu had lost his battle for control of the Las Vegas empire. Contrary to widely held belief, O'Brien was not fired; indeed, by both men's account, Chester Davis asked O'Brien to continue as Hughes' Washington consultant. But O'Brien realized that he was regarded by the Nixon White House as a dangerous adversary who, in the forthcoming 1972 Presidential election, would naturally be fighting for the Democratic cause. In that climate, O'Brien found it impossible to establish any rapport between the White House and the Hughes empire—which is what Hughes wanted—and, after some discussion, he and Davis agreed to call it a day. O'Brien's contract was ended on very amicable terms.

At first, the White House regarded the event with great excitement. The man who replaced O'Brien as Hughes' Washington consultant was Robert Foster Bennett,* the son of a Republican senator who was regarded by Nixon's men as a "trusted loyalist and good friend." Charles Colson, special counsel to the White House, wrote an internal memorandum that said, in part: "I'm sure I need not explain the political implications of having Hughes' affairs handled here in Washington by a close friend. . . . This move could signal quite a shift in terms of the politics and money that Hughes represents."

It even occurred to Colson that their "close friend" might be able to provide the White House with information about assignments O'Brien had carried out for the Hughes empire: should any "embarrassing" facts emerge, they could be leaked in the hope of damaging O'Brien and consequently the Democratic Party, of which he was now national chairman.

However, it gradually dawned in the corridors of power that any critical examination of the O'Brien-Hughes relationship might well rebound on Nixon's administration. Bebe Rebozo, the President's personal friend, sounded the first warning by asking the White House to tread very carefully in any matter relating to Hughes. As another White House internal memo said, ". . . forced embarrassment of O'Brien in this matter might well shake loose Republican skeletons from the closet."

What skeletons? Two obvious ones come to mind.

First, by 1971 Rebozo had received at least $100,-000 of Hughes' money and it had *not* been used to advance the Republican cause in either the 1968

---

* Like so many others who worked for Hughes, Bennett was a Mormon—indeed, he was a member of the bishopric of the Church of Jesus Christ of Latter-day Saints.

Presidential or the 1970 Congressional elections. At best, that money was sitting in Rebozo's safe-deposit box awaiting some future but unspecified rainy day; at worst, parts of it had already been spent for Nixon's *personal* benefit. Either way, public disclosure of Hughes' generosity toward the incumbent President would have been embarrassing.

Second, both Rebozo and the White House would have been anxious to keep firmly closeted the continuing link between Hughes' empire and the President's brother, Donald Nixon. It was, remember, Hughes' generous loan in the mid-1950s to Donald, which, in Rebozo's opinion, cost Nixon the 1960 race for President. Eleven years later, just as another Presidential race was about to begin, Donald reckoned that Hughes owed him another favor. He believed he had been instrumental in bringing Air West to Hughes' attention and, as a "finder's fee," he wanted a contract to supply the airline with in-flight meals. Donald did not get the contract, but in the course of what might be called the negotiations he met constantly with John Meier, Hughes' "scientific adviser"—to the considerable embarrassment of the White House.

Because of O'Brien's political affiliations, it seems unlikely that he would have been made aware of these particular "skeletons" at the time he worked for Hughes. But, by 1972, when the Watergate break-in took place, he almost certainly did know, through either Bob Maheu or Hank Greenspun: Maheu, furious about the allegation that he had "stolen Hughes blind," was revealing secrets of the empire all over the place; Greenspun, also no longer kindly disposed toward Hughes, had publicly said that he held in his safe copies of eighty or so memos written by The Man that might reveal goodness knows what.

It is, therefore, entirely plausible that the Watergate burglary was designed to discover what O'Brien knew about Hughes' $100,000 and his links with Donald Nixon and, more to the point, what if anything he was going to do with the information. Further support for the theory comes from the fact that O'Brien was not the only victim of attempted larceny during the summer of 1972: in August, Hank Greenspun's office in

Las Vegas was broken into and a determined, if unsuccessful, attempt was made to open his safe.

But potentially embarrassing though those two skeletons may have been, were they really sufficient cause to inspire the Watergate conspiracy? There are people who believe that the answer to that question is no and that the secret the conspirators were out to protect was of an unholy alliance among three of the most powerful institutions in the U.S.—Hughes, the Nixon White House, and the CIA.

If any such alliance existed, its exact nature and purpose are as yet unclear. But there is considerable evidence that Hughes' empire did establish links with the CIA. By Bob Maheu's account, the genesis of the idea occurred during the campaign to take over Air West.

In late 1968 or early 1969 Maheu reported to Hughes by telephone that the "initial inputs" he had received from Washington, D.C. regarding the proposed takeover were "not very favorable." It seems that Hughes' ownership of TWA and, later, Northeast Airlines had left "very bad tastes" in the mouths of some powerful people. Maheu suggested, he says, that they mount a publicity campaign to emphasize Hughes' accomplishments in the aviation field. But, according to Maheu, The Man had other ideas:

"During the telephone conversation Mr. Hughes suggested that I try to work out some kind of arrangement with the CIA whereby either he or the Hughes Tool Company become a front for this intelligence agency. I told Mr. Hughes that I could not understand why he would have such a desire and he pointed out to me that if he ever became involved in any problem with the government, either with a regulatory body or with an investigative arm of the government, that he thought it would be very beneficial to him [if he were] a front of some sort through one of his businesses for the CIA. I told him I could not believe what he was telling me and that under no circumstances would I participate in assisting him in an endeavor of that nature."

Maheu's piousness is a little hard to take: after all, Robert A. Maheu Associates had in its time acted as

265

a kind of front for the CIA and Maheu himself was heavily involved in the CIA's apparent attempt to murder Fidel Castro. In any event, and whether or not Maheu helped to make the arrangements, Hughes' empire did fall into collaboration with the agency.

To begin with, there was the connection provided by Robert Bennett, who replaced Larry O'Brien as the Washington consultant. In September 1971, after he had accepted the Hughes assignment, Bennett was persuaded by a Nixon aide to purchase a Washington public relations firm called Mullen & Company. It has since emerged that, from at least 1962 on, Mullen & Company acted as a CIA front, providing cover for agents. For example, Mullen's office in Stockholm was exclusively staffed by two CIA men, James Everett and Jack Kindischi, who pretended to be working on a study for General Foods when in fact they were debriefing Russian and Chinese defectors. Eventually the Stockholm office had to be closed after Everett and Kindischi had secured the defection of an important official of the Soviet KGB. The two agents subsequently used Mullen & Company as cover while working in Mexico City and Amsterdam. Another CIA agent, Arthur Hochberg, ran what was supposed to be Mullen's office in Singapore.

Whether Mullen & Company continued its patriotic role after Bennett's takeover and after it began working for Hughes is a matter of conjecture. But there is no doubt that it continued to employ some very dubious characters. In 1972 those on its payroll included Howard Hunt, Jr., a former CIA agent—and the "brains" (if that is not the wrong word) behind the Watergate burglary.

Then, too, there is the very direct link that Hughes' Summa Corporation established with the CIA. In 1972 Summa built a deep-sea salvage ship called the *Glomar Explorer,* under the pretext that it would be used to retrieve valuable cargo, such as that contained in sunken galleons, from the seabed. Actually, as the world now knows, the *Glomar Explorer* was constructed and operated by Summa on behalf of the CIA, and its quarry was a Soviet nuclear submarine that had foundered and sunk to the floor of the Pacific Ocean.

The CIA was hoping that the wreckage of the submarine might yield secrets about missiles and radio codes. Unfortunately, only part of the submarine was recovered, and all it contained was the badly decomposed bodies of some Russian sailors. Further attempts at recovery were sabotaged by public revelation, initially by the columnist Jack Anderson, of what was going on.

So, Hughes undoubtedly did become, through his businesses, a CIA front, just as he told Maheu he wanted to be. The tantalizing question that remains is what else did he do for the CIA—and what if anything did he extract from the Nixon Administration in return?

The only safe bet is that we have not yet heard the last of it.

ABOUT THE AUTHORS

Elaine Davenport is a freelance journalist who has worked in the U.S., South America, and Europe, primarily for U.S. media. Paul Eddy is a member of the Insight Team of *The Sunday Times* of London and was coauthor of *Destination Disaster,* an investigation of the world's worst air crash, published in 1976 by Quadrangle/The New York Times Book Company. Mark Hurwitz, who conceived the idea for this book, is a California attorney, well known as a staunch advocate of freedom of the press.

These books? Fiction.
Keep telling yourself that as you read.